LITERATURE, LANGUAGE, AND THE RISE OF THE INTELLECTUAL DISCIPLINES IN BRITAIN, 1680–1820

The current divide between the sciences and the humanities, which often seem to speak entirely different languages, has its roots in the way intellectual disciplines developed in the long eighteenth century. As various fields of study became defined and to some degree professionalized, their ways of communicating evolved into an increasingly specialist vocabulary. Chemists, physicists, philosophers, and poets argued about whether their discourses should become more and more specialized, or whether they should aim to remain intelligible to the layperson. In this interdisciplinary study, Robin Valenza shows how Isaac Newton, Samuel Johnson, David Hume, Adam Smith, Samuel Taylor Coleridge, and William Wordsworth invented new intellectual languages. By offering a much-needed new account of the rise of the modern disciplines, Robin Valenza shows why the sciences and humanities diverged so strongly, and argues that literature has a special role in navigating between the languages of different areas of thought.

ROBIN VALENZA is Assistant Professor of English at the University of Chicago.

LITERATURE, LANGUAGE, AND THE RISE OF THE INTELLECTUAL DISCIPLINES IN BRITAIN, 1680–1820

ROBIN VALENZA

CAMBRIDGE
UNIVERSITY PRESS

CAMBRIDGE UNIVERSITY PRESS
Cambridge, New York, Melbourne, Madrid, Cape Town, Singapore,
São Paulo, Delhi, Dubai, Tokyo

Cambridge University Press
The Edinburgh Building, Cambridge CB2 8RU, UK

Published in the United States of America by Cambridge University Press, New York

www.cambridge.org
Information on this title: www.cambridge.org/9780521767026

First published 2009

Printed in the United Kingdom at the University Press, Cambridge

A catalogue record for this publication is available from the British Library

Library of Congress Cataloguing in Publication data
Valenza, Robin.
Literature, language, and the rise of the intellectual disciplines
in Britain, 1680–1820 / Robin Valenza.
p.   cm.
Includes bibliographical references and index.
ISBN 978-0-521-76702-6 (hardback)   1. English poetry–
18th century–History and criticism.   2. Literature and science–Great Britain–
History–18th century.   3. Language and culture–Great Britain–History–
18th century.   4. Science and the humanities–Great Britain–History–18th century.
5. Great Britain–Intellectual life–18th century.   I. Title.
PR555.S33V36 2009
820.9′005–dc22   2009026029

ISBN 978-0-521-76702-6 Hardback

Contents

List of Figures	*page* vii	
Acknowledgments	viii	
1	The Economies of Knowledge	1
2	The Learned and Conversable Worlds	37
3	Physics and its Audiences	54
4	Philosophy's Place Between Science and Literature	92
5	Poetry Among the Intellectual Disciplines	139
	Coda: Common Sense and Common Language	173
	Notes	178
	Works Cited	222
	Index	236

Figures

1 An anatomy of the kinds of books reviewed in the *Literary Magazine, or, the History of the Works of the Learned* *page* 101
2 A "Systematical View of Human Knowledge," from Croker's *Dictionary* 140

Acknowledgments

I owe immeasurable debts of gratitude to many people. Without John Bender's guidance as expert and friend this book would not have been possible. His willingness to read endless drafts and to offer wise and kind advice has been nothing short of superhuman. Terry Castle's brilliant imagination and wit have inspired me from the instant we met. Her eighteenth century is a marvelous one, and I thank her for helping me to find my way in it. Meeting Franco Moretti was an unexpected gift and an extraordinary blessing. Our conversations have deepened my understanding of so many things, that I cannot begin to number them here. John, Terry, and Franco have all shown me what interdisciplinary scholarship can be, for which I can only say, "thank you."

Among the many wonderful teachers I have had, I would especially like to thank Shirley Brice Heath for being a wonderful mentor, Seth Lerer for extending his boundless intellectual generosity, and Denise Gigante for teaching me about madness and sensibility. I am also grateful to Andrea Lunsford, Jennifer Thorn, George Gopen, and Cynthia Herrup, who continue to foster my growth as a teacher and a scholar.

Jesse Molesworth, Jenn Fishman, and Adam Casdin read my work at its most vulnerable stages. This project has benefited enormously from their wisdom. I am also immensely appreciative of Joann Kleinneiur's eleventh-hour assistance with Stanford Special Collections.

My time in Chicago has sharpened my work in ways that only the University of Chicago can. Jim Chandler has been an extraordinary interlocutor, without whom the finished book would have been unthinkable. Beth Helsinger, Bill Brown, Tom Mitchell, and Josh Scodel have given me invaluable responses to my work. Working on the same corridor with Lauren Berlant, Bradin Cormack, Sandra Macpherson, and Eric Slauter has led to serendipitous and fruitful discussions, for which I am truly grateful. I also thank Jay Schleusener, Elaine Hadley, Richard Strier, and Christina von Nolcken for their careful reading of my work. A full list of my colleagues who have made their mark on this book would need to include Lorraine Daston, Adrian Johns, Leela Gandhi, Alison Winter, Dipesh Chakrabarty, Larry Rothfield, Bob von Hallberg, Chicu Reddy, Ken Warren, Clark Gilpin, Jackie Goldsby, Raúl Coronado, and Arnold Davidson, but even this list is sadly incomplete.

The Eighteenth- and Nineteenth-Century Cultures workshop has been a godsend. I am indebted to our graduate student and faculty participants. Special thanks go to Criscillia Benford, Andrea Haslanger, John Barrell, Jenny Davidson, Samantha Fenno, Penny Fielding, Kate Gaudet, Sarah Kareem, Emily Ponder, Heather Keenleyside, Jonathan Kramnick, Jon Mee, Mary Poovey, Eli Thorkelson, Cynthia Wall, and Abigail Zitin.

Early versions of Chapters 3, 4, and 5 were presented as talks at the University of British Columbia, the University of Chicago, and Dartmouth College. I thank the faculties at these universities, in addition to the faculty at the University of Illinois, for their thoughtful responses to my work.

The writing of this book was funded by grants from the Mellon Foundation, Stanford Humanities Center, and the Stanford English department; all three organizations have nourished this project in ways that would not have been possible without their aid. Linda Bree and Maartje Scheltens at Cambridge University Press have made publishing my first book an exhilarating experience. They deserve universal applause. I am also beholden to the two anonymous readers whose careful, detailed comments guided my revisions to the manuscript.

My family has sustained me through this strange and overwhelming adventure. Patricia Valenza has given me a lifetime of love and support. Tim Yu has stood by me in sickness and in health, in laughter and in tears. Each has read every page of this book a dozen times over without a word of complaint. This book is dedicated to them, and to the memory of my father, James Valenza.

CHAPTER I

The Economies of Knowledge

A contradiction lurks at the core of ideals of enlightenment. The resolution to generate new knowledge is often incompatible with a simultaneous desire to share this knowledge with an ever-expanding pool of readers.[1] While eighteenth- and nineteenth-century writers took up Francis Bacon's seventeenth-century rallying cry to advance learning across fields of study, the commitment to this Baconian project often ran at cross-purposes with the Addisonian wish, articulated on the pages of the early eighteenth-century *Spectator* papers, to illuminate the minds of the widest possible readership. Francis Bacon himself encouraged limiting the publication of and access to knowledge.[2] The discordance between these two goals was only rarely voiced straightforwardly in the eighteenth century, but nonetheless their dissonance came to define the development of the republic of letters.

In one of the few trenchant treatments of enlightenment's dilemma, physician, playwright, poet, and novelist Oliver Goldsmith explains,

We now therefore begin to see the reason why learning assumes an appearance so very different from what it wore some years ago, and that instead of penetrating more deeply into new disquisitions, it only becomes a comment on the past; the effort is now made to please the multitude, since they may be properly considered as the dispensers of rewards. More pains [are] taken to bring science down to their capacities, than to raise it beyond its present standard, and his talents are now more useful to society and himself, who can communicate what he knows, than his who endeavours to know more than he can communicate.[3]

These lines argue that efforts to pursue individual topics more deeply keep knowledge out of the broad grasp of the "multitude." In Goldsmith's estimate, the author who recognizes that this multitude is the wellspring of fame and financial gain would eschew the pursuit of new knowledge in favor of appealing to a wider audience. Goldsmith allies this profit motive with social benefit – the more readers who reap the benefits of learning, the more useful the learning is to society. In a bit of Mandevillian sleight of hand, Goldsmith proposes that a writer with a self-interested eye to

I

fame and fortune is also looking out for the public good because authorial decisions based on a desire to secure the widest audience guaranteed
that knowledge is made available simultaneously to as many readers as
possible.[4]

Popularizations, Goldsmith writes, "may justly give a scholar dis-
gust, yet they serve to illuminate the nation." Some modern historians
of Great Britain have followed suit in adopting the values of writers such
as Goldsmith, lauding a country and a century of writers who were not
"ivory-towered academics but men (and women) of letters who made
their pitch in the metropolitan market place and courted the public."[5] The
anachronism of the ivory tower metaphor notwithstanding, such constructions tend to gloss over the scourging difficulties that writers across
the intellectual disciplines had in bringing or refusing to bring the written expression of scholarly researches into concord with these communicative goals. When, alternatively, intellectual historians have rejected the
essayists' values, they have often also thrown out most of the intellectual
production of eighteenth-century Britain. It is a mistake to believe that
most essayists, or popularizers, espoused a complete sacrifice of learned
discourse. It is equally misguided to believe that specialized study did
not make tremendous leaps and bounds forward during this century. To
complicate matters, not everyone agreed with the project of making the
scholarly and sociable worlds linguistically coextensive. Disciplinary fields
often benefited from having expert languages that were inaccessible to
practitioners of other disciplines and to the reading public at large.

In other words, our critical perspective has made too simple a densely
tangled phenomenon. While Elizabeth Eisenstein's "print culture" and
Benedict Anderson's "imagined communities" remain useful ways to con-
ceptualize an era, their critical paradigms are often taken out of context
by scholars wishing to celebrate the unlimited potential of print to share
information with the widest of audiences.[6] Abuses of these analyses have
had the unfortunate side effect of cementing in the literary-critical mind
a conception of a public literary realm with a consistent and idealized
notion of audience and an equally shared system of objectives, even when
the authors they cite gave attention to fragmentation and discord.

Along the same lines, when Jürgen Habermas and Reinhart Koselleck
gave their respective accounts of the European Enlightenment, each confronted the weakness of public access to the political process in 1950s
Germany, and both looked to the eighteenth and nineteenth centuries for
the origins of and alternatives to the present condition. For their purposes,
finding a unified, Weberian ideal type of what constituted "society" or a

"public sphere" in opposition to a "state" before the nineteenth century in Europe was an effective and necessary measure.[7] But taking Habermas's public sphere or Anderson's national community as givens and asking how those social formations were realized in the eighteenth century often twists these paradigms to the breaking point.

Another problem emerges from uncritical appropriations of these models. Because science does not figure centrally in either Habermas's or Anderson's portrayal of the eighteenth and nineteenth centuries, latter-day Habermasians or Andersonians tend to assume that by default science followed a fundamentally different, and separate, course from the humanities.[8] Modern academic tunnel vision thus comes with a high price: a scholar who focuses on the origins of his or her particular field of study avoids exploring in any depth what the disciplines had in common with one another both before and during the centuries-long process of differentiation. Literary scholars in particular treat their field as a special case in the emergence of the disciplines because, they argue, literary criticism had a peculiar responsibility to create a national community by explaining and creating a shared literary heritage, and therefore the field had much more difficulty in specifying both its potentially universal audience and its potentially limitless object of study than other disciplines.[9]

But while it is safe to say that no two disciplines followed identical courses, I argue that practitioners across all disciplines – both those that are now known as humanities and those currently classed as sciences – found the process of defining and describing their fields of study to non-experts both wrenching and difficult. And most struggled to negotiate how print could help them reach targeted audiences of fellow experts at the same time that it could help them gain wider public support for their work.[10] Recent academic writers who propose reuniting several academic disciplines under the common heading "science," may wish to consider this early history of modern disciplinary differentiation.[11]

Although the growing distance between the expert and the reader may have been overlooked by later historians, it was a signal preoccupation of the eighteenth century. The public perception of intellectual specialization created a crisis of relevance. Critics of specialization pointed out that if disciplines became narrower in their focus, it would no longer be clear how their research pertained to the daily lives of individuals, or to the political life of the state. This was exactly the problem the long eighteenth century had identified as the fault of the medieval scholar: his researches bore not at all on the world outside his study. Now eighteenth-century thinkers faced the same difficulty in a new form: they ran into roadblocks in arguing for the importance of what they did when it had no obvious or immediate bearing on individual lives.

From the eighteenth century into the present day, the real-world applications of scholarly research have been held up as the standard for measuring its importance. Indeed, it was those who worked in specialized fields who most vociferously propagated this standard. In examining attempts to link theory and practice, I argue that the connection between scholarly work and life was often manufactured precisely to gain public attention for a discipline. Popularizers and promoters of Newtonian physics, for instance, made broad claims for the applicability of the new physics to problems in engineering and navigation, although the solutions to these problems had little to do with Newton's own contributions to science. Such an emphasis on practical results and public benefits was often the means by which specialized fields both announced and defended their own expertise even while closing it off from general access.[12]

When managed well, popularization and specialization could thus be complementary phenomena, two sides of the same coin. By the late eighteenth century, many writers believed that the ability to bring specialization and popularization into productive tension was necessary because specialization had already become so pervasive as to prevent turning back. Individuals had already come to be limited intellectually by their occupations so that even known intellectuals required occasional assistance from a popularizer or teacher.

Efforts to create a *lingua communis* to describe a common knowledge, or to appeal to a common sense – so often seen as characteristic of the eighteenth century – had their origins in the need to build bridges between the difficulty of learned writing and the abilities of an often ill-educated body of readers. It is perhaps all too common a practice to mistake Addison's familiar claim in *Spectator* No. 10 to bring "Philosophy out of Closets and Libraries, Schools and Colleges, to dwell in Clubs and Assemblies, at Tea-Tables and in Coffee Houses" for a more republican statement than it is. Marshaled alongside a few key lines from the preface to Locke's *Essay Concerning Human Understanding*, this sentence has often been used to argue that the reaction against monastic scholasticism in the long eighteenth century entailed widespread participation in philosophical conversations that came to shape the course of British letters.[13] But such readings downplay the early century essayists' explicit claims to expertise in contradistinction to the abilities of their audience.

Even within the confines of *Spectator* No. 10, Addison describes his readership as a vacant, occupationless body of persons – "Blanks of Society" – who must wait for an infusion of thought and opinion from those more intellectually focused than themselves. He imagines not a participatory readership but an absorptive one. And Richard Steele's *Tatler* is built on the premise of *reporting* news from the learned world to the sociable one. He does not undertake the task of making his readers as learned as he.[14] The career of the popularizer depended on having something to bring to a popular audience, or at least on making that audience believe he could do so.

This attitude toward the abilities of the average reader raises its head again in the mid-century essays of David Hume, who suggests that most readers are shallow thinkers only capable of the superficial cogitation requisite for "coffee-house conversation." In his account, these mental lightweights depend on a separate class of abstruse philosophers to provide them with new information. Addison, Steele, and Hume depict the reading public as participating in learned discourse only at a remove, consuming it secondhand as fed to them by those capable of digesting learned discourse and regurgitating it for a broad audience. In their portrayals, knowledge chiefly moves only in one direction, downslope from the learned to the unlearned.[15]

This book aims to confront the double-edged sword of enlightenment by telling a story of the intellectual disciplines' emergence in their modern form. Perhaps surprisingly, it is a story that has yet to be told. No single, general description of how intellectual disciplines form, evolve, or die has – to date – been written. My account assembles a band of strange bedfellows. It puts Adam Smith and his compatriots of the Scottish enlightenment alongside twentieth-century sociologist Talcott Parsons, Immanuel Kant next to Benedict Anderson and John Guillory, Karl Marx with Richard Feynman, Mary Poovey in the company of Emile Durkheim, and Lorraine Daston beside all ten members of the Gulbenkian Commission on the Restructuring of the Social Sciences. An account born of these forced couplings may remain somewhat Frankensteinian, connecting, perhaps crudely, pieces from economic, sociological, historical, political, philosophical, biological, and literary-critical writings. But I nonetheless put forward my effort at forming such a creature, this intellectual monstrosity, to draw attention to where disciplines come from, how they function, and why they sometimes slip away.

I propose here a working definition of "discipline." A discipline is a field of study that has a recognized community of researchers who have in common most of the following: an agreed-upon name, a loosely identified object of knowledge, shared research goals, a finite set of methods of inquiry, a generally accepted intellectual tradition, a group of institutions that persist and remain stable over time (such as university departments and academic journals), a system for perpetuating the discipline by training new practitioners, a group of working concepts and rules for adding new rules and concepts, and an established manner for communicating their findings.[16]

While much of the existing work on academic disciplines has been based on an analysis of natural and social sciences, part of this book's motivation lies in determining how concepts of disciplines change when the histories of the humanities and the arts enter into the disciplinary conversation. I have borrowed from Parsons's classic sociological definition of a discipline, which requires the following three characteristics: "formal technical training accompanied by some institutionalized mode of validating both the adequacy of the training and the competence of trained individuals"; "mastery of a generalized cultural tradition ... in a manner giving prominence to an *intellectual* component – that is, it must give primacy to the valuation of cognitive rationality"; and "institutional means of making sure that such competence will be put to socially responsible uses."[17] This definition is both broader and narrower than my own; I aim to be more precise about what practitioners of a discipline do in their working hours and give a bit less emphasis to their training. I also try throughout to heed Foucault's cautions in *The Archaeology of Knowledge* about the difficulty of identifying stable "objects of knowledge," and the equally trenchant advice of Ellen Messner-Davidow, David Shumway, and David Sylvan to "refuse to equate disciplinary knowledge with 'truth.'"[18] I treat each discipline's proposed object of knowledge in combination with an aggregate of properties, methods, and means of expression.

My definition of a discipline can be roughly construed as a Weberian ideal type, but, more precisely, it is what biological taxonomists now call a *species* – "an entity composed of [individuals] which maintains its identity from other such entities through time and over space, and which has its own ... evolutionary fate and historical tendencies," or, as the organizational systematists have put it, "a form of organization that exists through generations of individual[s] ... which are members of the species."[19] Turning to a biological definition of species as a model for "discipline" has the additional advantage of providing an account of speciation, or specialization, the tendency for a species to come to occupy a particular niche in an environment by "performing a few activities well" instead of "many activities poorly."[20] The modern systematist's descriptions of species or types are polythetic; that is, they do not require that every member possess a single, defining characteristic that can distinguish a member of one species from members of all others. Although such singular qualifications were demanded by earlier, Aristotelian systems of classification, modern taxonomic systems define groups by using a network of properties, each of which will be possessed by many, but generally not all, members of the species. For my study, this means that not every disciplinary species will fall into exactly the same mold, meet the same set of specifications, or possess a single quality that separates it from all other disciplines. Rather, each discipline and its members will have many, if not most, of the qualities enumerated above in common, which unite their practitioners over time and over geographical distances.[21] Though most practitioners of a discipline, living and dead, will never have met one another, their connections, their "invisible colleges" as Robert Boyle famously called them, remain closer than one of Benedict Anderson's "imagined communities" because those working in a discipline are few enough in number to know the research of many of their colleagues, thanks to the implicit requirement that research be circulated in at least a limited manner.

Changes in manners and methods of publication were key to the rise of new structures of disciplinary organization that began to coalesce in the eighteenth century. My study of the intellectual disciplines, their literary productions, and their relationship to public culture begins in the late seventeenth century and follows the development of three disciplines – physics, philosophy, and poetry – through the early nineteenth century.

My study thus focuses on three particular cases, cases which bear the considerable burden of standing in both for other examples within the disciplines represented here and for disciplines that are not represented here at all. My justification follows one that Auerbach gives in his work on literary language: "It is patently impossible to establish a synthesis by assembling all the particulars. Perhaps, however, we shall be able to do so by selecting characteristic particulars and following up their implications."[22] In other words, I have chosen here to cover an immodest topic in modest form in the hope that it will be suggestive, not comprehensive.

These three disciplines are the necessary first nodes of analysis for the long eighteenth century in Britain, and, I argue, can stand in for the rise of the intellectual disciplines in their modern form more generally. (I return later to the significance of each of these particular fields.) This book could but does not contain chapters on biology, chemistry, painting, musicology, history, and rhetoric, among other disciplines. Material for (and in a few cases drafts of) these potential chapters occupies much of my filing cabinet and could easily have swelled (or bloated) this book to enormous proportions. Those other disciplines have been left out in part for the sake of keenness of focus and because they have failed at least one of two tests: either their modern disciplinary center of gravity is not the British Isles, or their signal move into modernity arrived later than the early nineteenth century. A book that concentrated more centrally on the European Continent or reached further into the nineteenth century might, as Michel Foucault's *The Order of Things* has done, name "life, language, and labor" as the three flashpoints of disciplinary change.

Biology does not have a chapter in this book because it fails both tests. The eighteenth-century developments in the sciences of life resided primarily in Scandinavia with Linnaeus and in France with Buffon and Lamarck. And all of this work was turned on its metaphorical head in Britain and elsewhere by the Darwinian revolution of the later nineteenth century.

Like biology, chemistry also saw two major shifts between 1700 and 1900. Although some of chemistry's key players (Boyle, Priestley, Kirwan, Davy) worked in the English-speaking world, the story about the establishment of chemistry as a discipline that distinguished itself from alchemical research comes to its climax in pre-Revolutionary France, with the formal transformation of chemical nomenclature and the definitive rejection of the phlogiston theory. The complete story of chemistry's disciplinary modernization, including the erosion of the Vitalism hypothesis, would need to include the quiet rise of organic chemistry, where no single, revolutionary shot was fired. Rather, the history of organic chemistry is diffuse – both temporally and geographically: it emerges from a gradual accumulation of knowledge across western Europe over the nineteenth century.

All this is to say that the first wave of disciplinary modernization in Britain was felt more palpably in some disciplines than in others. In much the same way, the eighteenth-century writing of history in Britain saw major works produced by Hume, Smollett, Robertson, and Gibbon, among others, but the emergence of the modern academic historian was a creation of later years that moved outwards to the rest of the globe from its center in the German university among Leopold von Ranke and his students.

To the list of chapters that did not make it into this book, I must add one on linguistics: the modern discipline of linguistics arrived in Britain much later than the other disciplines discussed in this book. The discipline that has the strongest claim to demand its own chapter is political economy, Foucault's "labor." As a discipline, it is often visible through-out this book, but as one of the tools of disciplinary analysis rather than an object of it. The eighteenth century saw the mere glimmering of what political economy would become in future centuries.

Medicine, law, and theology are not candidates largely because they are professions as much as or more so than disciplines, and in most respects their key attributes were already well established before 1650. I should pause to note that although one can reasonably speak of the profession-alization of a discipline if one is referring to increasing levels of organi-zation and internal cohesion in a disciplinary field, a distinct difference persists between a discipline and a profession. Disciplines are committed to research and to the advancement of knowledge. Some professionals attached to universities may also serve this function; when they do, we say that their research and teaching belong to the discipline of law, medicine, or theology. But by and large the professions of law, medicine, and the clergy are primarily committed to providing a public service, rather than pursuing research. Similarly, the teaching of law, medicine, and religion is first and foremost designed to shape those who will perform the services of lawyer, doctor, priest, rabbi, minister, or imam. Most professionals will never do first and foremost research in their field and will not consider teaching future professionals to be a primary function of their profes-sional activity. This division between the intellectual disciplines and the professions was already very much alive in the eighteenth century. Kant's *Conflict of the Faculties* finds the separation of professions from disciplines salubrious for scholarly research. In Kant's reckoning, the "lower faculty" – the professoriate committed to scientific and humanistic research – do not directly answer to public needs. But the higher faculty – which edu-cates future doctors, lawyers, and clergymen – and their students are ulti-mately beholden to the populations that they serve and as such are subject to governmental regulation to a much greater degree than the practition-ers of the intellectual disciplines.[23] This study pertains almost exclusively to the development of the intellectual disciplines, and not the professions, because the courses of their respective developments do not always run parallel, especially with respect to financial compensation and training.

Though the western university has actively resisted being conquered by economic forces since well before the seventeenth century, the mod-ern articulation of disciplinary forces and the simultaneous change in the structures of knowledge are coeval with eighteenth-century theories of market capitalism and with modern notions of labor. It is also not coin-cidental that the terms in current use to describe biological species bear a strong resemblance to those that describe economic specialization: the term "ecology" was coined in the nineteenth century by analogy with "economy." The evolutionary pressures that lead towards biological specialization (or away from it) seem to operate by mechanisms similar to the market pressures that produce specialists in different fields of human labor. Scottish academic philosophers of the long eighteenth century were well aware of market forces at work in their field at the same time that they were theorizing this market. Writers of this period across disciplines represented scientific and humanistic researches as intellectual *labor* supported by investments of financial capital. Isaac Newton's work, for example, was characterized by early historians of science as being composed of "many vast and laborious trains of research" that were "confirmed, illustrated, and completed, by the labours of succeeding philosophers." And such investment of human labor likewise demanded "an expenditure of private and public resource" – both financial and intellectual.[24] Similarly, in arguing for chemistry's status as a full-fledged science on a par with mathematical physics, early nineteenth-century chemists and historians of chemistry emphasized "the months of incessant labour" required for even the smallest of chemical discoveries followed by "months in detailing" the experimental results for publication, all supported by the budgets of newly formed research institutes and private fortunes. The intellectual exertion and monetary expense demanded by the project of scientific enlightenment were frequently defined against the perceived cerebral laxity of previous generations of scholars who had only produced "dark speculations," unfounded in systematic, mental and experimental toils.

This emphasis on cerebral labor is notably absent from discussions of fields that failed to gain university disciplinary status, such as the writing of poetry. While poetry had, over the preceding centuries, competed with history as the most important means of representing knowledge for a general readership, nineteenth-century British poets opposed the idea that "labor and study" could produce better poetry.[25] While the inspired genius of a philosopher also entailed an attendant amount of difficult cranial work, the poet's inspired genius was portrayed as existing in a realm that took no account of the value of labor, mental and otherwise. However, the poets did have in common with the natural and moral philosophers the observation that over the course of the eighteenth century individuals had increasingly adopted narrow intellectual frameworks in which they pursued their vocations. Poetry was thus deaccessioned, undisciplined.

Writing in the 1770s, Adam Smith urged his audience to take note of the relationship between an individual's occupation, the limitations on his or her time and training, and the consequent limits on the intellectual contributions he or she could make to the advancement of learning. In an early draft of his great economic treatise, *The Wealth of Nations*, he writes,

In opulent and commercial societies, besides, to think or to reason comes to be, like every other employment, a particular business, which is carried on by a few people, who furnish the public with all the thought and reason possessed by the vast multitudes that labour. Let any ordinary person make a fair review of all the knowledge which he possesses concerning any subject that does not fall within the limits of his particular occupation, and he will find that almost every thing he knows has been acquired at second hand, from books, from the literary instructions which he may have received in his youth, or from the occasional conversations which he may have had with men of learning. A very small part of it only, he will find, has been the produce of his own observations or reflections.

All the rest has been purchased, in the same manner as his shoes or his stockings, from those whose business it is to make up and prepare for the market that particular species of goods.[26]

Knowledge acquired in the classroom, through private reading, or, less frequently, from direct contact with "men of learning" is knowledge purchased "second hand." Obtaining information in this manner is no different, Smith suggests, from the buying of any other product. As with the trade of material goods, there are individuals whose particular task it is to create knowledge and prepare it for market. It has long been recognized that the chief innovation of Smithian economics is its insistence that the division of labor is the driving factor behind modern social and economic systems. What is less often remarked, however, is that Smith extends his theory of the division of labor into the republic of letters itself. Adam Smith offers us the earliest statement about the division of *intellectual* labor, identifying it as endemic to the advancement of learning, the progress of societies, and the accumulation of wealth.

Smith's characterization departs from earlier descriptions of the divisions of knowledge because he argues not only that knowledge is divided among different fields of study but also that individual human beings have themselves become specialized, each eventually committing to advance a single field of knowledge. Before Smith, for example, in Bacon's *Advancement of Learning* or in the tree of knowledge at the front of Diderot's *Encyclopédie*, disparate fields of knowledge were distinguished by the different mental faculties used in pursuing each of them; however, the tacit assumption was that because every person possessed all faculties, he could thus readily participate in the range of disciplines. Chambers's *Cyclopedia* recognizes the longstanding "Distribution of the Land of Science" into "a number of Provinces, under distinct Names." But Dugald Stewart, professor of moral philosophy at the University of Edinburgh from 1785 to 1820, explained that all evidence derived from the previous century of experience points to the mistakes in Bacon's or the *Encyclopédie*'s system of knowledge based on mental faculties. "[I]t seems to follow," Stewart writes, "not only that the attempt of Bacon and of D'Alembert to classify the sciences and arts according to a logical division of our faculties, is altogether unsatisfactory, but that every future attempt of the same kind may be expected to be liable to similar objections."[27]

What Smith adds to this sort of theoretical articulation is a recognition of the growing need for scholars to associate themselves with smaller and smaller pieces of intellectual territory, a process that had already rapidly begun to accelerate towards the moment at which a scholar who wanted to increase the store of human knowledge would need to confine his research to only one discipline. Increasingly, the Baconian model began to be replaced by Smith's,[28] as the "field of knowledge" was less often described according to the seemingly arbitrary hierarchies derived from Aristotle and more in terms of disciplinary divisions deemed necessary for advanced research.[29]

Both Smith and Stewart treat intellectual specialization as a natural consequence of the division of labor, arising from no intentional human wisdom, but rather from propensities inborn in the species itself. This innate tendency towards division and exchange does not stop at the production of foodstuffs, cloth, ships, or machine parts, but permeates all aspects of life because modernity and progress hinge on the adoption of a commercial attitude, acknowledged or not, towards every element of human existence.[30] Unlike writers of later generations who take on a tone of lament, Smith is matter-of-fact about the connection between an individual's occupation and the limits of his or her knowledge.

Samuel Johnson had much the same to say in a posthumously published fragment on the character and duty of an academic. He writes that although in "places thinly inhabited ... necessity compels every man to exercise more arts than he can learn," the great mark of civil society is the "distribution ... of employment" so each person becomes an expert in a particular practice or study.[31] In this distribution, the "task assigned" to the academic is "diligence of inquiry and liberality of communication": study, teaching, and writing. This set of duties stands in contradistinction to that of men "whose active employments allow them little time for cultivating the mind, and whose narrow education leave[s] them unable to judge of abstruse questions." In the best of circumstances, these narrowly educated men rely on their academic teachers for finding out and certifying truth: indeed, they "may repose upon their instructors, and believe many important truths upon the bare authority of those from whom they received them." This discussion revisits *Rambler* 121 (1751), in which Johnson argues for the inevitability of intellectual specialization: "Even those to whom Providence hath allotted greater strength of understanding, can expect only to improve a single science. In every other part of learning, they must be content to follow opinions, which they are not able to examine." Bare authority may have been shunted from the eighteenth-century political stage, but it played a leading role in the public realm.

One need not wholeheartedly embrace the eighteenth-century perspective to notice that the economic model of knowledge generation and transmission still has a useful descriptive function.[32] The "balance of trade" paradigm for the disciplines describes a world in which, by marking off individual areas of specialization, more knowledge is contributed to the intellectual marketplaces. And we can likewise see that certain protectionist measures – requirements for greater levels of training, mastery of expert languages, and the like – gradually prevented lay men and women from participating in the production of knowledge and sealed their role as consumers, rather than producers, of information.

In proposing that the realms of learning were also subject to economic pressures, Smith was not making a novel argument. The relations between the advancement of knowledge and economic transaction had been examined often in the eighteenth century. In the thinking of the period, the intellectual disciplines could only advance when supported by a full and thriving commercial economy predicated on the division of labor. David Hume wrote in his 1752 essay "Of Refinement in the Arts" that "*industry, knowledge*" and civilized notions of "*humanity*" were "linked together by an indissoluble chain." "We cannot reasonably expect," he asserts, "that a piece of woolen cloth will be wrought to perfection in a nation, which is ignorant of astronomy, or where ethics are neglected."[33] Hume's succinct formulation captures perfectly the complex interdependence of the divided fields of labor, while at the same time confirming that their division is what makes progress possible. Only by establishing a class of individuals and an industry to make woolen cloth, a separate group to study astronomy, and a third to pursue ethical theory, could the arts and sciences – and therefore humanity itself – drive towards social and economic advancement. This, according to Hume, is what distinguished England from barbarous nations that were uncivilized precisely because they had not instituted separate fields of activity managed by distinct (intellectual) classes of individuals who had committed themselves to progress in each field.

Fellow economist and philosopher Adam Ferguson stressed that not just science or industry, but civil society itself, benefited from the division. In his treatment of the "Separation of the Arts and Professions" (his term for the division of intellectual labor), Ferguson argues that "a people can make no great progress in cultivating the arts of life, until they have separated, and committed to different persons, the several tasks, which require a peculiar skill and attention."[34] Ferguson notes that some of this specialization is inevitable, if at times regrettable. And Hume looks back with some nostalgia at ancient Greece and Rome, when, for example, "The study of the laws was not then a laborious occupation, requiring the drudgery of a whole life to finish it, and incompatible with every other study or profession."[35] Like Hume, Ferguson expresses some reservation about the writing of *belles lettres* becoming a trade and requiring "all the application and study which are bestowed on any other calling."[36] But both men also celebrate the benefits that fall from the intensification of professional or vocational focus.

Hume goes so far as to predicate conversability or sociability – arguably the most central quality in British self-representation from Locke through Coleridge – on this division. The more the "refined arts advance," Hume argues, "the more sociable men become." As Great Britain becomes "enriched with science," its inhabitants are simultaneously awarded a "fund of conversation" that forces them among their fellow Britons for the purposes of intellectual exchange. This is what separates them from "barbarous nations."[37] If the pre-condition for specialization in the economic realm is a mechanism for exchange, the same holds true for intellectual specialization. A specialist needs to bring his knowledge to the marketplace. But where does one find such a marketplace?

Smith also implies that the division of intellectual labor depends on a mechanism for sharing disciplinary knowledge – "second-hand" – with those for whom the production of such information is not their primary responsibility. That is, a thriving press is an essential part of large-scale intellectual specialization. Smith underscores the consumerist attitude that most take towards learning. During the leisure time available to those of the middling and upper ranks, they buy and partake of knowledge in much the same way they do tea or chocolate. Knowledge for many constituted a species of entertainment, and was often represented as such.

Throughout the eighteenth and nineteenth centuries, acquiring a modicum of erudition through self-directed reading was portrayed as a method of self-improvement, but the moral or social elevation it entailed came not through participation in the generation of knowledge but rather from the ability to display that knowledge. The desire for this sort of mental acquisition bolstered and was bolstered by the printed book, a medium whose production increased rapidly after the 1709/1710 alteration in English copyright law, and by the popularizer or educator, whose task it was to "prepare for the market that particular species of goods [i.e. books]."[38]

Implicit in Smith's and Hume's arguments is that the division of labor has multiple layers. One divide cuts between manual and mental labor; another between experts and lay persons; and a third among experts themselves who specialize in different fields. In his *Lectures on Jurisprudence*, Smith clarifies that all three layers of this divide further the advancement of the intellectual disciplines:

Philosophy itself becomes a separate trade and in time like all others subdivided into various provinces: we have a mechanical, a chemical, an astronomical, a metaphysical, a theological, and an ethical philosopher. This division improves it as well as all other trades. The philosophers, having each their peculiar business, do ... more work upon the whole and in each branch than formerly.[39]

Stewart bolsters this argument, by proposing that focusing attention on a small piece of intellectual territory furthers science and philosophy even more than it contributes to the streamlining of the pin-making industry. He writes that "with those who have in view the investigation of truth, and the acquisition of scientific knowledge ... much more intellectual work ... will be performed, and much more successfully, in a given time" by allowing a single person to follow through a scholarly task, rather than demanding he or she be master of all subjects at all times.[40] We can recognize in Stewart's remarks a distinct step away from the Renaissance model of the man, still reflected in Francis Bacon's writings of the 1610s, in which, during the course of a day, an individual moved from one discipline to the next in an effort to have a fully rounded mind. "Indeed," Stewart adds, "it would not be difficult to shew that the observation [that dividing labor induces progress] applies far more forcibly to intellectual exertion than to mechanical labour."[41] Both Smith and Stewart underscore the increasing intellectual and methodological distance between practitioners of various academic disciplines.

In 1793, Stewart dubbed Smith's description of the divided world of the reasoning disciplines "the division of intellectual labor." This is the first occurrence of that phrase that I have identified in English letters, although it reappears often in European literature of the late nineteenth and early twentieth centuries. Commenting on Smith's *Wealth of Nations* in his own lectures on political economy, Stewart explains that the diversity of intellectual abilities among individuals serves the human species well because it "gives rise ... to a limitation of attention and study; and lays the foundation of all the advantages which society derives from the division and subdivision of intellectual labour."[42] Living in a world irreversibly altered by Marxian economic theory, we hear distinct undertones in "the division of intellectual labor," signaling the ultimate disjunction between manual and mental labor.[43] The gap between intellectual and physical labor cannot be ignored in Stewart's own use of the term, and he acknowledges that freedom from repetitive, less desirable forms of labor that the public of the middling to upper ranks enjoyed, just as both Gramsci and Durkheim later do. But this mental/manual separation only describes a portion of the significance of the division of intellectual labor.

As previously mentioned, the concept of "division of intellectual labor" has historically adumbrated three separate divides. The first divide is the one to which I have already alluded – between labor that is primarily mental and that which is broadly construed as manual.[44] Mental includes the intellectual disciplines, as well as the professions of law, medicine, and the like. Under "manual," Smith and later writers have included work directed towards manufacturing, agriculture, or trading. It is this split between intellectuals and workers that Marx and his early followers believed had progressed too far in nineteenth-century Europe, a distinction to which Marx and Engels advert in *The German Ideology*, where they briefly note that the "division of labour only becomes truly such when a division of material from mental appears ... Division of labour means that intellectual and material ... devolve on different individuals, and the only possibility of their not coming into contradiction is the negation of that division of labour." The "Adam Smith problem" frequently referred to in economic literature rests on Smith's seemingly simultaneous endorsement of and regret about this division of manual from mental. Both Smith and, later, Antonio Gramsci note that while most individuals possess the innate capacity to become philosophers, "not all men have in society the function of intellectuals."[45]

Founder of the Analytical Society Charles Babbage also pursued this idea in the *Encyclopaedia Metropolitana* (1829), in a passage which was later republished under the slightly better known title *On the Economy of Machinery and Manufactures* (1832). Babbage's work adheres closely to Smith's explanation of the division of labor in manufacture as it expounds on reasons why modular organizational methods increase productivity through an increase in concentration and dexterity and a decrease in wasted time and materials, and therefore in prices. Babbage also takes up Stewart's point about intellectual labor: "It has been shown, that the division of labour is no less applicable to mental productions than to those in which material bodies are concerned." Babbage takes this a step further than Stewart had, producing what might be deemed an early account not only of intellectual specialization but also of so-called "big science," in which a single research project is divided up among many individual practitioners.[46] Babbage describes the construction of mathematical tables for the metric system in post-Revolutionary France, in which different research groups were asked to use one another's findings without verifying them – or even knowing how to verify them – in conducting their own portion of the work.[47] This is perhaps the ultimate form of the division of labor in the intellectual world; it is the closest equivalent to Smith's division of labor in manufacturing.

Over a century later, it is Hannah Arendt who explicitly connects the modern interest in defining intellectual activity as work – as opposed to imagining what the intellectual does as apart from the busy world of work – with the modern age's turn to "usefulness" as the standard by which it measures its members. She remarks that "it was only natural that intellectuals, too, should desire to be counted among the working population."[48] Arendt begins to suggest that the most apt term might be the division of "intellectual work" (a phrase that Stewart had also used) in that the term "work" refers not to the activity of thinking itself, but the research product made when thinking is converted into material form – the book, the article, the patent, and the like. (This distinction might be rendered in Adam Smith's terms as the difference between productive and unproductive labor, that is, the difference between labor that produces a material product and labor that does not.[49]) After all, Arendt notes, "thinking and working are two different activities which never quite coincide; the thinker who wants the world to know the 'content' of his thoughts must first of all stop thinking and remember his thoughts. Remembrance in this, as in all other cases, prepares the intangible and the futile for the eventual materialization."[50] Arendt's own work in dividing up human activity between work and labor begs comparison with Smith's in making the division of labor: in many ways, the philosopher-critic's activity in the division of labor remains the same.

The division of labor's to-and-fro movement among various inter-locking spheres of study and action should not blind us to the com-plex relationships between intellectual and social divisions. This intellectual/material labor split is treated more recently in John Barrell's examination of *The Wealth of Nations,* which emphasizes the difference that eighteenth-century political theory describes between those who *do* and those who only *think.*[51] The class markers of this division were clear at all levels of eighteenth-century society; adver-tisements for courses on science and philosophy promoted their abil-ity to improve the intellectual standing of their students, regardless of rank, while stressing that their audiences could become – if they were not already – ladies and gentlemen.[52] This division constitutes the most crucial one in developing a theory of labor that explains how power differentials function in emerging capitalist economies. If we regard this division in isolation, we may mistakenly find both a strong coherence within the intellectual classes and a straightforward association between those who produced knowledge and those who held the most financial power. But neither of these qualities accu-rately describes the Britain of the eighteenth and early nineteenth centuries.

For the purposes of understanding the emergence of the modern intellectual disciplines on their own terms, the idea of division needs to be further pursued and heed paid to the dynamics of two more lev-els of division that have affected the generation and representation of knowledge since the late seventeenth century. The second division of intellectual labor divides the philosophers, scientists, and other authors who perform intellectual labor from those who buy, read, or otherwise consume their products.[53] Eighteenth-century writers characterized this split as one between the "learned" and the "conversable" (or "sociable," or "fashionable") worlds. This division sifts apart two intellectual strata: those who primarily spent their time producing knowledge and those who primarily consumed it. Of course, this division was less clear-cut than the mental/manual distinction: those who wrote were also read-ers, and those who read sometimes became writers. Nonetheless, the categories "learned" and "conversable" do roughly plot out a separation between the authors of scholarly works and the reading population at large. While to modern ears the terms "learned" and "conversable" do not smack of economic significance, their polite veneer only thinly cov-ers over the complex economy of exchange that they describe, as the next chapter discusses.

The third division of significance appears within the learned world itself. This last break marks the division that separates, for example, the study of chemistry from the pursuit of moral philosophy; it divides the physicist's work from the poet's. We might call this third division "intellectual specialization" or "discipline formation."[54] This disciplinary division replaces an older one in western Europe, which can be traced back to the dissension between the sophists and the philosophers in ancient Greece, a dynamic based primarily on intellectual parties.[55] The new division is instead grounded in distinctions among disparate disciplines, although, of course, academic parties never fully disappear. This third, disciplinary partition is now seen most clearly in the modern university system, in which university departments bear the indelible mark of disciplinary specialization enforced by intra- and inter-institutional boundaries. Such concentration on an individual discipline or object of study did not reach its modern proportions in England until much later in the nineteenth century, but the recognition that an individual field of study increasingly consumed more of one person's mental time and energy emerges much earlier.

This study attends primarily to the second and third of the divisions outlined above; it gives attention first to the varying distances that intervened between learned experts and lay readers and then to the specialization of the intellectual disciplines themselves. Though these two levels have distinct properties, the final two divisions are rarely so easily teased apart from each other.[56] Working in tandem, these processes of stratification accelerated the division of the intellectual classes from the laboring ones because they ratcheted up the training and information required to understand, let alone to participate in, the advancement of learned knowledge.[57] They also underscore the movement from the Renaissance ideal of a disciplinary system in which a single person participated in many fields of knowledge to the modern one in which an individual primarily belongs to a single discipline.

Indeed, even when they disagree with Smith's specific thesis that the wealth of nations is primarily produced by the division of labor, modern economists argue that dividing tasks into modular parts is the fundamental human method of problem-solving and that the sciences produced by human artifice must operate through the method of division.[58] Whether this is the essential human behavior or an artifact of western disciplinarity matters not to the present argument because in either case, the "division of labor" figures as the central activity in doing scholarly work and in thinking about such work.

This discussion of the division of intellectual labor hints at a bit of leg-erdemain in the early pages of this book, in which I lament the absence of a general, theoretical account of how disciplines form, grow, and sometimes fade away. This lamentation may be misleading: it is not that there is a complete vacuum where literature addressing disciplinarity should be. The literature that discusses "disciplinarity" in some form or another is, in fact, legion. However, such accounts usually concentrate on a specific discipline or set of related disciplines, and much, though not all, of this writing has been done in the service of an at least mildly polemical argument for or against a particular discipline or approach to the discipline. Arguments that outline the current state of a field commonly appear at the beginning of academic books. If one wants to know the state of the art in a given field or subfield, one can now – as one could in the eighteenth century – read the introductory chapter to almost any scholarly book in that field.

Perhaps the best account of the historical significance of disciplinarity more generally may be read between the lines of Michel Foucault's extensive *oeuvre*. The historical association between the multiple meanings of "discipline" points up the sense that a disciplinary field can feel like a mental straightjacket of sorts, limiting the range of one's intellectual movement.[59] One might take these lines of Foucault's as the consumate description of the social and internal processes that lead to the specialization of individuals in the academic arena:

> The chief function of the disciplinary power is to "train," rather than to select and to levy; or, no doubt, to train in order to levy and select all the more. It does not link forces together in order to reduce them; it seeks to bind them together in such a way as to multiply and use them. Instead of bending all its subjects into a single uniform mass, it separates, analyses, differentiates, carries its procedures of decomposition to the point of necessary and sufficient single units. It "trains" the moving, confused, useless multitudes of bodies and forces into a multiplicity of individual elements – small, separate cells, organic autonomies, genetic identities and continuities, combinatory segments. Discipline ... is not a triumphant power ... it is a modest, suspicious power, which functions as a calculated, but permanent economy.

It is perhaps no accident that, in Britain, the internalization of academic disciplinary boundaries seems to begin in the eighteenth century at the same time that the institutions of modern discipline, in Foucault's sense, came into being.

The particular goal of this book is to do some of the work in connecting particular conceptions of departments and disciplines into a study that asks how different disciplines are and are not alike. It uses disciplinary language as a common ground for comparing fields that now look as if they are far apart on the intellectual spectrum. Perhaps the closest projects to this one in terms of motivation if not means are Tony Becher's *Academic Tribes and Territories: Intellectual Enquiry and the Cultures of Disciplines*; Thomas Kuhn's "Second Thoughts on Paradigms," his reflections on the reception of *The Structure of Scientific Revolutions*; and Steve Fuller's "Disciplinary Boundaries: A Critical Synthesis."

Becher follows the sociological paradigm of conducting surveys of practitioners of academic disciplines and subsequently analyzing the responses. His research points in many suggestive ways, not least of which is its recognition that the amount of data on the many intellectual units that go by the name "discipline" is small but what can already be seen is that there is a remarkable amount of consistency among them that "transcend[s] the institutional boundaries within any given system."[60] Much work remains to be done in this direction; I hope that my own book does some of the historical groundwork that provides a foundation for future efforts at such data collection and consolidation.

My study suggests that some of the specific arguments that Kuhn has made about the difference between the sciences and other kinds of intellectual pursuits seem misguided, in part because Kuhn – and he is certainly not alone in this – takes the fine arts as a stand-in for all that is not science and measures the distance between "art" and "science" accordingly. But what I do take from Kuhn is his move towards recentering the concept of "paradigm" by referring to it as part of a "disciplinary matrix" that embraces "symbolic generalizations." In other words, while he does not discard his trademark idea of "normal science" (the slow accumulation of scientific detail in accordance with a widely held paradigm that characterizes the everyday work of scientists), he expands the terrain of the ordinary practice of scientists to include the language or notation in which they express their agreement. Following on Kuhn's work, Steve Fuller offers this definition of how a discipline works,

Once a discipline's domain of inquiry has been "staked out," its practitioners must define and maintain the "normal" state of objects in the domain. This involves experimental and textual techniques for foregrounding the problematic claims under study against a background of claims that are stipulated to be unproblematic ... [W]hat probably separates practitioners of the "sciences" most from those of the "arts" is the scientist's sense that the time and effort spent in interpreting his precursors is time and effort taken away from contributing to the growth of knowledge.[61]

The "arts" here again seems to refer more to the practice of poets than, say, historians or academic philosophers, but Fuller nonetheless makes a crucial gesture here. I take from Fuller the sense that the "sciences" generally take a quite different attitude from other fields towards "writing up" their findings; they imagine a detachment between the work itself and the printed representation of it. In contrast, many practitioners of the humanities do not believe that there *are* findings before they are written; much of the work itself is felt to be done in the writing of it. A key reason for my undertaking this historical study is to trace how this separation between doing and writing comes into being for certain fields and not for others.

Adam Smith hitches the growth of the wealth of nations to the division of labor. His pivotal example is the pin factory, in which making a single pin is "divided into about eighteen distinct operations" distributed among as many different workers. This example requires – of course – an enormous need for pins. In other words, it is a commonplace of classical economics that specialization has limits, limits that are pegged to market size. A larger market can afford and therefore reward greater specialization with decreasing costs and rising profits. However, the other part of Smith's economic system, the invisible hand, creates a problem for the narrative that connects increased specialization to the constant multiplication of rewards. The invisible hand regulates markets through competition, and competition creates *diminishing* (not increasing) returns and rising (not falling) costs as more players enter the market.[62]

The appeal of Smith's brand of economics is that the total wealth of nations will continue to grow. In classical economics' terms, this view entails the assumption that *market size* will continue to increase. Otherwise, subdividing labor into smaller tasks would no longer provide increasing returns. Not all of Smith's successors retained his optimism about increasing returns; it proves hard to sustain both ideologically and mathematically. In the second half of the twentieth century, economists effactually revived a version of Dugald Stewart's idea that the increasing specialization of knowledge fosters the growth of knowledge, and they have added to this idea proposal that growth in technological knowledge is the true force that propels markets constantly skywards. Entailed in this model is the belief that technological growth is effectively limitless, although market turns may temporarily retard market growth.

The relatively new subdiscipline that has adopted the name "the economics of knowledge" seeks to explain how the discovery, acquisition, and deployment of knowledge drives financial markets while also attempting to discern how the properties of knowledge differ from those of labor and capital, the conventional inputs of classical economics. While nodding to a few political economists from Smith to Marx, the field traces its modern origins to a seminal essay, "The Use of Knowledge in Society" (1945), by Austrian economist Friedrich Hayek; a cluster of essays by Kenneth Arrow in the 1960s; and the extraordinary volumes by Fritz Malchup published over two decades beginning in 1962.[63] In recent years, alongside a handful of influential articles and conference proceedings, there has been an international explosion of monographs that address this subfield.[64]

Among the key attributes of knowledge identified by these studies is that most knowledge is tacit and "sticky." That is, knowledge tends to adhere to the knower and is difficult to transfer from one person to another. Most knowledge is produced locally and stays that way without efforts for it to be otherwise. Thus, knowledge tends to be uneven, scattered, and fragmented, which also means that wisdom is always being lost. This is as true now as it was in previous centuries when the loss of ancient learning, such as the destruction of the fabled Ptolemaic library of Alexandria, was more often and more loudly lamented. Perhaps such intellectual bereavements are now felt less keenly because reproducing mere data becomes ever easier (duplicating a digital file or running a photocopier), and this is confused with the always expensive and comparatively inefficient process of education – necessary for the passing on of knowledge – the ability to understand, organize, and use information.

Knowledge becomes visible to a larger world, and thus runs less risk of being lost, when it is codified, "so articulated and clarified that it can be expressed in a particular language and recorded on a particular medium."[65] One of the characteristics of a research community, as opposed to a lay one, is that it has established mechanisms of publication designed to communicate knowledge and to educate newcomers in this knowledge. Of course, even without publication, knowledge can always get away from its producer. This is a mixed blessing, depending on one's point of view. Unlike capital or labor, knowledge is a nonrival good: knowledge may be possessed and used by any number of people at the same time without loss to any of the users. (In contrast, a rival good's use by one consumer prevents its use by others. Most consumables, like food, clothing, or cars, are rival goods.) In practice, of course, knowledge is often acquired or accessed or packaged in the form of a rival good.[66] An idea, for instance, may be contained within the pages of a book of which a limited number of copies exist, or a computer program may be distributed under a licensing agreement that limits its use to a set number of users.

The field of economics of knowledge borrows from intellectual property law, including its concerns with patents, trademarks, and copyrights, where many of the qualities of knowledge have been most thoroughly debated, although legal writers note that their field has been at least ten years behind the technologies in actual use at least since the invention of the photocopier, perhaps since the development of moveable type. In theory, a patent protects an original application of knowledge in the industrial realm; a copyright, a literary or artistic work. (I leave aside "trademark" for the moment.) A patent requires a novel *idea*; copyright, a distinctive *form*. This way of explaining the difference between patent and copyright suggests that the dominant feature of the literary, at least in a legal context, is its particular form or arrangement of words, as distinct from whatever ideas are held therein, whose originality is not expressly evaluated and is not afforded legal protection. This implies that copyrighted ideas can be *used* in many ways without legal penalty. Indeed, in an academic context, copyrighted publication *makes it possible* for other persons to use one's research.

This book engages the burgeoning field of the economics of knowledge by addressing an earlier moment of its relevance. While not equating the twenty-first century with the eighteenth, the book does draw parallels between these two information ages, between the emergence of one knowledge economy and another. The emphasis throughout the book is historical and is further focused on how language and disciplinarity mutually shape each other.

A question may nonetheless remain for the present reader: to which discipline does this book, *Literature, Language, and the Rise of Intellectual Disciplines in Britain, 1680–1820*, belong? The short answer is "English Language and Literature," because that is the primary field in which I am trained and to which I currently belong, and current classificatory habits favor the author's stated aims over other factors. (For example, the Dewey Decimal system's instructions for classifiers begin, "A key element in determining the subject is the author's intent." The document later warns, "Do not ... disregard the author's intent and emphasis.") In so asserting this book's intellectual allegiances, I refer less to the techniques of literary reading that emphasize contingency and ambiguity and more to the ecumenical nature of the discipline of English, which takes in many methodologies that are flexibly held together by the language itself.

By describing the book as such, I nonetheless try to resist making imperial claims about my home discipline – or any other – of the sort that drew sparks in the friction between Habermas and Derrida. Habermas's particular frustration with Derrida was this: Derrida "level[s] the genre

distinction" between philosophy and literature.⁶⁷ In, other words, Derrida
upends the disciplinary spectrum by refusing to recognize it as such, by
proposing that all writing can be treated as if it were literature. Further,
Habermas argues, Derrida flattens distinctions between literature and literary criticism, between the art object and the study of it. This is a problem
for Habermas because he regards the disciplines not so much as a spectrum but as a hierarchy. Habermas's essay on Derrida ultimately erupts
into the explicit complaint that Derrida elevates literary criticism to the
status of literature and lowers philosophy to the level of literary criticism.
Specialization protects this hierarchy, in which criticism is "a discourse
specialized for questions of taste," an expert discourse that derives its man-
date from the increasing "autonomy" of "linguistic works of art."

In the historical narrative embedded in Habermas's argument, literary
criticism is produced by literature and has domain over it and it alone.
The major function of the expert culture of literary critics is to mediate
between its judgments of literature and the everyday world, primarily for
evaluative purposes. Philosophy, by contrast, has a much loftier aim and
larger reach, "[I]t directs its interest to the foundations of science, morality, and law and attaches theoretical claims to its statements. Characterized
by universality problematics and strong theoretical strategies, it maintains
an intimate relationship with the sciences." Moreover, the one outstand-
ing virtue that Habermas allows literary criticism, its "*bridging function*"
between the academy and a broader audience, is also claimed by philosophy, "[P]hilosophy is not simply an esoteric component of an expert culture. It maintains just as intimate a relationship with the totality of the
lifeworld and with sound common sense, even if in a subversive way it
relentlessly shores up the certainties of everyday practice." This response to
Derrida reasserts philosophy's primacy as the *scientia scientarum*, the science of sciences, allowing philosophy to be the discipline that simultaneously underpins all others and oversees all of them.

Perhaps needless to say, Habermas's complaint also reinstates the ancient
distinction between philosophy and rhetoric, one that is always invoked
to establish the superiority of the former over the latter. Throughout
this book, I am certainly guilty of the opposite fault, of giving language
extraordinary emphasis. However, I do not make the claim that literary
criticism is the *scientia summa*. Rather, I want to call attention to the way
in which one discipline's practices can illuminate those of another.

If I were to be more specific, I would say that this book is literary history in the Baconian sense. In his 1605 *Advancement of Learning*, Francis
Bacon laments that "literary history" is deficient because "no man hath

propounded to himself the general state of learning to be described and represented from age to age, as many have done the works of nature and the state civil and ecclesiastical." While there are some particular histories written by particular groups,

a just story of learning, containing the antiquities and originals of knowledges, and their sects; their inventions, their traditions; their diverse administrations and managings, their flourishings, their oppositions, decays, depressions, oblivions, removes; with the causes and occasions of them, and all other events concerning learning, throughout the ages of the world; I may truly affirm to be wanting.

Four hundred years later, the general thrust of this statement still seems true. Some truly brilliant histories of particular fields have emerged in the interim, and I depend on them throughout this work. However, this global project largely remains undone.

The present book – in form and content – aims to be a step in the direction of a Baconian literary history that encompasses "literature" in the sense of general learning and moves towards the moment in which "literature" can no longer fill this semantic role because it refers to a special quality of some kinds of writing that can be read literarily as opposed to informationally. In this process of differentiation, learning becomes a question of information, where the matter – the core bits of information that one can take away from what one reads – prescribes that the manner – the way in which that information is represented – become as transparent as possible.

Broadly speaking, this ideal of a transparent manner – or style – of writing has been interpreted in two significantly divergent ways. The first way has predominated in the hard sciences; it holds that the most transparent writing is that which is the most technical and mathematics-like because the descriptive notation is so precise that it disallows the kind of ambiguity found in ordinary uses of language. Transparency in this model is transparency between specialists who share an understanding of this technical language. This leads to an inverse relationship between transparency to those within a discipline and transparency to those outside it; the more information (and the less noise) the language communicates among specialists, the harder it becomes for an outsider to understand the language.

The second ideal has largely held sway in the humanities, at least in the Anglo-American tradition. This version insists that the standard for transparency is comprehensibility to any moderately educated user of that language, say, someone who can and does read the *Guardian* or the *New York Times*, or, in the eighteenth century, the *Spectator*. Indeed, the eighteenth-century figure of the "impartial spectator" – a coinage that first appears on the first page of the first collected edition of the *Spectator* and ultimately becomes the popular and philosophical standard for calibrating oneself by the anticipated responses of other people – is a useful representation of the standard for and the judge of written intelligibility. In this case, transparency is transparency to everyone: there is no inverse relationship between insiders and outsiders. If there were, the inversion would indicate that there was an insufficient degree of clarity or universality.

At moments, historians of all three individual disciplines that I treat – physics, philosophy, and poetry – may find frustration in this book's continued insistence on matters of linguistic style. This close attention to what happens on the pages of a particular book does not tell us, one might argue, what really happened in Newtonian physics, and, in any case, these happenings are already well known. But this book argues that this very insistence that the real science lies outside stylistic dimensions reveals how much the literary aspect of writing has been excluded from other domains of study, including history. My work investigates why style was – and still is – integral to historical substance, and why disciplinary blinkers make this a difficult problem to see, especially in the most familiar cases in which we feel confident that we already know what happened.

In the years that this study covers, disciplines marked their territory in large part by their debates over the correct languages to use in the new physical and human sciences. Words were believed to be intimately if arbitrarily connected to ideas; therefore, those writing about different kinds of things might need different kinds of language. Each field of knowledge and the disciplines that it adumbrated worked to discover a language that would reflect its knowledge. Ephraim Chambers, the great eighteenth-century English encyclopedist, argued that no science, no systematic study, was possible without language – humanity's "sixth sense," which enabled and shaped perception.[68] The eighteenth century witnessed many searches for an ideal scientific language (and not only in fields now considered to be sciences) that married logic to signification, meaning to method. Whether such a language would be constructed out of the language of common life or from the emergence of new technical vocabularies was and still is a matter of unceasing debate.

Writers of popular science and those who wrote humanistic treatises for lay readers found their particular niche lay in acting as ambassadors from the "Dominions of Learning to those of Conversation."[69] The conflict between disciplinary jargon and the "language of common life" was, then, both a cause and the most obvious sign of a larger process of intellectual stratification. However, the matter of whether a "republic of letters," or a public culture, should or even could do away with this stratification, and what the consequences would be for the advancement of learning, remained an open question.

While such extreme nominalism or erstwhile positivism in theories of language may now seem naïve, the connection between disciplinary language and disciplinary identity nonetheless dies hard in the present-day academy, although it is often well disguised. Now, as in the eighteenth century, the relationship between scholarly writings and the general reader is hotly contested. Evaluations of disciplinary languages still lie at the heart of arguments over academic knowledge and prove often to be obstacles to interdisciplinarity.

Disciplinary languages in the fields now called the sciences and those in the ones currently identified as the humanities have developed and have been received along very different lines during the past four centuries. My study of the disciplines originally emerged from my attempts to answer the question "What distinguishes the literatures of the sciences from those of the humanities?" More precisely, how do the disciplines we call "sciences" describe, represent, and explain their work differently from the ones we now classify as "humanities"?

Versions of these questions appear frequently in academic and popular publications. For example, when the learned journal *Philosophy and Literature* began presenting the "Bad Writing Award" to scholarly writers, the world outside the academy took notice. The dubious prize, given in 1999 to Berkeley professor Judith Butler, earned wry mention in the *New York Times*, which seized the occasion to inflame the controversy over the unintelligibility of technical academic writing in the humanities to the workaday world of "plain English."[70] The expectation that specialized humanistic studies always be communicated in a vocabulary easily understood by a broad readership outside the profession contrasts sharply with the popular attitude towards the technical writing of scientists. Even the science pages of newspapers and popular science magazines assume that scientists need a separate, technical idiom to communicate their work to fellow specialists, an idiom by definition unavailable to the lay reader because, as noted science writer James Gleick remarked in the London *Independent*, "much of science has grown distant from our common-sense understanding."[71] Nonscientists are expected only to have access to expert writing at a remove, through metaphors and analogies meant to represent science to the untrained. The public is not expected to understand scientific writing itself, only popularizations of it.

The genealogy of the academic disciplines and their relationship to public culture reveals that the rift in popular perceptions of the languages of the sciences and those of the humanities was not always so wide. Through the flurry of editorials and letters that followed *The Times* article about Judith Butler, readers were reliving a debate that had played itself out many times before – in the eighteenth- and nineteenth-century periodical press. However, during these earlier centuries, not only humanistic but also scientific researches were embroiled in this controversy.

In these earlier debates, writers across fields of study disputed whether specialized pursuits demanded specialized languages to describe them. Novelists, essayists, physicists, chemists, and poets argued over the necessity of professional argots to the development of their respective disciplines. I turn the pages of this debate back several centuries because the simultaneous rise of our modern disciplines and the critical press in the eighteenth century engendered many of the categories, assumptions, and values that undergird the debates about public and disciplinary languages and cultures that remain with us.

A word remains to be said on what, in practice, the difference is between a disciplinary or technical language and an ordinary or public one. It first behooves us to notice that both labels carry immense psychic and moral baggage. They are as often used to derogate a writer's style as they are used as accurate descriptors of actual writing; they operate on both conscious and unconscious levels. The following chapter discusses eighteenth-century approaches to the technical/ordinary split, but before embarking on that history, a bit more needs to be said about the definitions of disciplinary and ordinary languages that have been in circulation since the eighteenth century.

Following in Ludwig Wittgenstein's enormous footsteps, the cluster of philosophers sometimes known as the "ordinary language" school approached exactly this theme in the 1950s and 1960s, and most of their conclusions seem still to represent conventional wisdom on the subject. Their consensus is that an ordinary language is

everyday language rather than simply any (part of) language which a group of people shares. Ordinary language in this sense is the language which defines the boundaries of linguistic communities, the boundaries within which people speak the same language or at least the same dialect. It is the language that makes possible their daily dealings with each other. It will be a large part of what a physicist or a carpenter uses in talking or writing to his colleagues, a still larger part of what they use in talking to their wives, and perhaps all they do or could use in talking to each other, or to children, shopkeepers, and policemen.[72]

Ordinary language is thus "what anyone can count on in talking to anyone else in his linguistic community."[73] Gilbert Ryle has pointed out that when we refer to "ordinary" language, we mean "'common,' 'current,' 'colloquial,' 'vernacular,' 'natural,' 'prosaic,' 'non-notational,' 'on the tongue of Everyman,'" a description which would have served as well in the eighteenth century as now. The opposite of ordinary language in this sense is "'out-of-the-way', 'esoteric,' 'technical,' 'poetical,' 'notational' or, sometimes 'archaic.'"[74] Whether or not this brief list describes synonymous or partly synonymous terms is a matter for debate, and indeed is discussed throughout this book.

To focus for the moment on "technical" language alone, technical language is, in contrast to ordinary language, the "other part of … language [that] physicists [can only use] with other physicists or people who happen to know some physics, farmers with other farmers or people who know something about farming." As such, they are "a part of some language like English or French and a part defined only by reference to some particular discipline or occupation or activity among the practitioners of which it is current."[75] In the ordinary-language-school sense, technical language "is always an *adjunct* of ordinary language" because it must "be acquired against the background of ordinary language."

I accept the general premise of the above definition (minus the dated gender messages) but contest the sense that a technical language is only an adjunct of ordinary language, since it often transcends national boundaries in a way that ordinary languages do not. After Latin had by and large declined as the international language of scholarship, the technical terminologies of individual disciplines, especially in the sciences but occasionally also arts and letters, were designed specifically to transgress national boundaries and become simultaneously a part of several different languages, particularly in written form. This is one of the peculiar attractions of technical language – in its ideal form, it does not need to be translated, and is often difficult to translate into a vernacular, because its meaning is held to be constant across many languages. Of course, the success of attempts to form scientific languages that carry across national or even university boundaries varies tremendously by discipline.

I hasten to mention that I do not linger over the writings of so-called ordinary language philosophers out of bibliographic or disciplinary naïveté: I am under no illusions that philosophy of language, even of ordinary language, either began or ended with a particular cohort of twentieth-century writers. Rather, I think that the group of writings that goes under the banner of "ordinary language philosophy" confronts and crystallizes questions about technical language in ways that make especially perceptible the stresses and strains entailed in the act of representing scholarship to readers. Many of the moments that I find significant in the writings of these philosophy professors seem by-products of the work that these writers did, perhaps even side-effects of the felicitous naming of the movement. In other words, the passages of interest for this study turn up when these writers try to ward off misunderstandings of what the role of "ordinary language" is in "ordinary language philosophy": is "ordinary language" simultaneously the object of study, the tool or method of study, and the means of representing that study?

In "The Meaning of a Word," J.L. Austin hints at the sense shared by many modern-day scientists that a technical language can have a much stricter logic embedded in it than ordinary language and thus functions at least slightly differently. Austin writes that "[o]rdinary language breaks down in extraordinary cases," but when doing physics, "our language is tightened up in order precisely to describe complicated and unusual cases concisely."[76] Empirical evidence suggests that the closer a technical language is to mathematics, the more it is "*not* just another language" or part of a language. As Richard Feynman has put it, "Mathematics is a language plus reasoning; it is like a language plus logic." Feynman also points out the psychological value of technical formulations and the advantages gained by developing a range of different technical formulations possible for a given phenomenon or object. He writes that "all the alternative ways of looking at a thing" give "clues" about the many different ways of solving or describing individual problems.[77] If this is true for mathematical physics, surely it may also be true for disciplines with less rigid forms of description, in which an even wider range of technical and everyday descriptions is possible.

But even while many scholars and members of the public agree on the basic need for certain technical languages, they often disapprove of their function in the humanistic disciplines in a way that they do not in the sciences. In his essay on "Ordinary Language," Gilbert Ryle offers a long, careful defense of why philosophy should not be enslaved to general usage in what it studies or in how it uses terminology, and concludes by noting that

[t]he vogue of the phrase "the use of ordinary language" seems to suggest to some people the idea that there exists a philosophical doctrine according to which (a) all philosophical enquiries are concerned with the vernacular, as opposed to

more or less technical, academic or esoteric terms; and (b) in consequence, all philosophical discussions ought themselves to be couched entirely in vernacular dictions. The inference is fallacious.[78]

But after defending his theoretical commitment to this position, he then immediately drops his technical, philosophical analysis and begins voicing his opinion about the "bad literary manners" of writers who use such "technical expedients" overmuch:

> Most philosophers have in fact employed a good number of the technical terms of past or contemporary logical theory. We may sometimes wish that they had taken a few more pinches of salt, but we do not reproach them for availing themselves of these technical expedients; we should have deplored their long-windedness if they had tried to do without them.
>
> But enslavement to jargon, whether inherited or invented, is, certainly, a bad quality in any writer, whether he be a philosopher or not. It curtails the number of people who can understand and criticise his writings; so it tends to make his own thinking run in a private groove. The use of avoidable jargons is bad literary manners and bad pedagogic policy, as well as being detrimental to the thinker's own wits.
>
> But this is not peculiar to philosophy. Bureaucrats, judges, theologians, literary critics, bankers and, perhaps above all, psychologists and sociologists would all be well advised to try very hard to write in plain and blunt words.[79]

Ryle hereby falls back on two opinions widely held at least since the eighteenth century: first, that the prison-house of language restricts thought, and technical language only further closes in the mental cell; and second, that if technical argots restrict access to a scholar's writings, then the writer has probably been intellectually naughty. I mention these not to berate Ryle but rather to suggest that such viewpoints have come to be so deeply felt that a writer can hardly forebear announcing them, even while acknowledging that they are not central to (and often run antithetical to) a research program. The intertwining of this sort of feeling with a range of political and intellectual programs inevitably colors the history of disciplines' relationships to their language. Ryle finds that in any technical language in which the words do not correspond to "special materials or objects of their specialism" but rather describe concepts, the technical language may and should be "jettison[ed] *in toto*" at regular intervals because such terms may always be misused. The closet positivism implied by this statement also suggests the general sense that scientists deal with real things and humanists with fictional mental constructions. But modern physicists' forces and particles are as metaphoric as those of philosophers; hence, Ryle's grounds may not be the strongest ones for challenging terms of art in philosophy, as even fully fabricated entities can be highly serviceable fictions, in science or in letters.

These arguments run much deeper than their surface quibbling about literary manners allows. They are largely arguments about which disciplines can claim the power to describe the mental and physical world accurately and who deserves access to these descriptions. As Feynman writes, "To those who do not know mathematics it is difficult to get across a real feeling as to the beauty, the deepest beauty, of nature. C.P. Snow talked about two cultures. I really think that those two cultures separate people who have and people who have not had this experience of understanding mathematics well enough to appreciate nature once." Feynman makes the perhaps startling claim that physics, and its brand of mathematics, not only best describes the natural world but also is the only true aesthetic representation of the beauty of that world. While his lectures provide some access to these concepts, he notes that listeners or readers will inevitably be barred full entry into the realm of beauty and truth if they lack the ability to understand the technical representations of physicists. These are fighting words, and Snow's or Feynman's version of the science/humanities divide begs reevaluation.

To put my point schematically for a moment: the linguistic spectrum of the disciplines, as it was conceived in the eighteenth century and often is now, ranges from the literary to the mathematical. Mathematical and literary abilities are each given particular emphasis because they stand at the respective ends of the array of knowledge, or at least of this representation of knowledge. Both certainly received and now receive educational emphasis. In the eighteenth century, the polarization began to suggest that literary and mathematical abilities might not only be different ways of organizing thought but might also belong to different persons. In other words, not only could a discipline be more or less literary or mathematical, but so could a person. By the twentieth century and probably earlier, this distinction is a given, not even worth remarking upon. But before the later seventeenth century, this was not a standard belief, not a part of the way that humans and their knowledge were imagined. My book argues that developments surrounding Newtonian mathematical physics and subsequent developments in other disciplines are key to understanding this change in our background assumptions about the world and its inhabitants.

The subsequent chapters of this book begin from the premise that, from the mid-seventeenth century until our own time, debates over disciplinary languages have been only the most visible symptom of the struggle to create, strengthen, and defend expert cultures that move beyond ordinary understandings of the world. This linguistic discord holds particular interest because it arises at the same moment in history as attempts to forge a *lingua communis* and a common reading public through the medium of print. These two aims seem contradictory, but their simultaneity is no accident. The desire to form a "republic of letters," or a "commonwealth of learning," came in response to the intellectual and disciplinary stratification of the print sphere. Essayists, lecturers, and other popularizers arrogated to themselves responsibility for interceding between expert cultures and a body of readers. The desire for a settled, vernacular *lingua communis* arose in answer to the fragmentation of the intellectual disciplines. Popularizers' self-appointed task of translating learned discourse for broader readerships *depended* on the perceived difficulty of disciplinary knowledge and language.

Chapter 2 addresses the core problem of the ideal of intellectual enlightenment as theory and as practice as it becomes visible when examining the problem of disciplinary languages. The claim that enlightenment meant broadly educating as many people as possible ran at cross purposes with the assertion that enlightenment entailed researching specialized topics as deeply as possible. When Goldsmith writes that "the meanest mechanic has raised his mind to a desire for knowledge; and the scholar condescends to become his instructor," he indicates that the spread of print entails a positive democratization of knowledge but that this egalitarian vision could come with an intellectual price. When writers focus their efforts on lucidity for a broad audience, they often sacrifice depth of inquiry, which hamper the progress of the intellectual disciplines. The second chapter thus challenges the now-canonical Habermasian view of the eighteenth century as one in which rational discourse holds sway and a common debating public comes to the fore. The limitations of twentieth- or eighteenth-century articulations of the public sphere lie in their desire to see as singular a phenomenon that has never been so and grows ever more fragmented over time. There was no consistent literary public sphere in England in the eighteenth century – even within the pages of Addison and Steele's famously popular *Spectator* periodical – because in 1710, writers were already confronting a fractured communicative landscape. In fact, the role of the popularizer – the individual who transferred knowledge from the learned to the sociable or domestic realms – originated in the eighteenth century precisely because the communicative landscape was so riddled with black holes of mutual incomprehension that it demanded expert translators.

Chapter 3 is about the first coffee-table book: Isaac Newton's *Principia*. It was *the* book everyone wanted to own (and be known to own) but that no one had read. In writing the *Principia*, the text that brought science into the modern era, Newton used mathematical language to sift apart those who could *do* physics from those who could be taught to *appreciate* its unique precision in describing the physical world. The many popular-izations of the *Principia* reinforced the divide that Newtonian physicists had instituted between experts and lay readers.

Attempting to imitate physics' extraordinary success, eighteenth- and nineteenth-century moral philosophers aimed to "introduce the experi-mental method of reasoning into moral subjects." However, unlike the physicists, moral philosophers fostered the belief that a popular and a scholarly work could be coextensive, that a single book could advance a discipline and still be readable by a broad audience. The fourth chapter focuses on the writings of John Locke, David Hume, Thomas Reid, and Dugald Stewart, arguing that British moral philosophers' refusal to put in place an insulating divide between experts and general readers affected both the tenor and the content of philosophy in England for the succeed-ing centuries, forcing a divergence in popular perception of the humanities and the sciences with respect to how each field contributed to a grander scheme of knowledge.

Chapter 5 turns to the domain where the literary came to reside almost exclusively. Instead of becoming a discipline along the lines of phys-ics or philosophy, poetry became a specialized field whose paradoxical task was to defend common life against the advance of specialization. Responding to what he saw as increasing intellectual territoriality, William Wordsworth asked, if we know what the "Man of science, the Chemist and Mathematician" do, "What then does the Poet?" By examining evolv-ing conceptions of the disciplinary hierarchy from Francis Bacon to J.S. Mill alongside poetry and prose by William Wordsworth and Samuel Taylor Coleridge, the final chapter argues that many of the still-familiar writings of the romantic poets arose in response to the need to provide evidence for poetry's claim to remain among the intellectual disciplines, even as that claim was gradually eroded by a refusal or inability to adopt the new disciplinary structures emerging in both the humanities and the sciences.

The concluding pages consider how the kind of knowledge that goes by the name "common sense," a mixture of natural predilections and educational biases, often runs counter to what researchers find in their intellectual labors. As Adam Smith so succinctly put it, habits of the imagination "suffer the greatest violence when obliged to pursue" new ways of looking at the world. Unsettling, revolutionary knowledge first spreads itself within a field of knowledge among "disciples," who trained in the methods that led to the discovery and who subsequently develop the apparatus for convincing a wider range of scholars. Only then can the lay public's "natural prejudices of the imagination" be "overturned." The book thus ends with a call for academic practitioners in the humanities and social sciences to find a public voice for articulating what it is that they do.

CHAPTER 2

The Learned and Conversable Worlds

They that content themselves with general ideas may rest in general terms; but those whose studies or employments force ... closer inspection must have names for particular parts, and words by which they may express various modes of combination, such as none but themselves have occasion to consider.

– Samuel Johnson, *Idler* 70 (1759)

"Every author does not write for every reader," Samuel Johnson noted in his 1759 essay on "hard words." Johnson's pronouncement has the air of a commonplace, presenting the obvious as self-evidently true. But its settled tone belies how polemical a statement this was. Johnson's essay stakes out his position in the eighteenth-century debate about the politics of writing in the English language. The controversy revolved around the much dis-puted question of whether or not there should be a single, shared English language, accessible to all readers and fixed in its vocabulary and usage.

There were those who endorsed the view that any writing should be intelligible to all broadly educated readers of English, regardless of the topic addressed. This eminently democratic position was often advocated by early eighteenth-century essayists, such as Richard Steele, who enjoined youthful literati to heed Aristotle's advice: "Think with the wise, but talk with the vulgar."[1] Johnson disagreed with Steele and his early-century compatriots, arguing instead that even the most cursory glance at the communicative requirements of a particular science or a trade reveals the necessity of its maintaining its "peculiar language" in contradistinction to the corrupted and capricious vocabulary of common life.[2] For Johnson, forms of expression *had* to be modified to fit the occasion of their use. The kind of expression a writer needed would delimit the audience that could have access to his or her writing.

Johnson garnered few unwavering allies in this debate. Indeed, his own position was not always consistent. Only a smattering of authors lined up decisively on one side or the other. Even those, such as Joseph Addison and Richard Steele, who vaunted an ideal of a pure, enlightened prose that allowed the public to grasp philosophical discourse often found that this ideal remained illusory. Periodical essayists, popular press reviewers, and authors of scholarly works struggled in trying to define the relationship between their language and their audience. The possibilities of print seemed endless, but the rules of the print sphere were less clear.

And while the authors of the burgeoning periodical media promoted a new *lingua communis*, a common language forged through the medium of print, authors writing on scholarly or otherwise technical subjects were likewise confronted with novel concerns, concerns related to Latin's decline as the language of learned communication.[3]

For a time in western Europe, as the Roman Empire spread, the Latin language had provided a partial solution to the problem of Babel. Even after the fall of the Roman Empire, among the educated, Latin continued to function as an international lingua franca, even though, with few exceptions, from the sixth century onwards Latin was a foreign language to all of its users. That is, no one learned it from the cradle; it was taught by tutors and in schools. This gave the language certain advantages: because Latin was learned from ancient texts and common textbooks, and because its uses belonged primarily to particular vocational and communicative contexts, it was relatively a conservative language such that during the period after the fall of the Roman Empire when the vernaculars of western Europe became increasingly distinct from one another, developing into the modern Romance languages, Latin resisted many of the changes that affected these languages.

In other words, within and across Latinate communities such as universities, monasteries, and courts of law, the Babel problem could be minimized. However, increasingly over the course of centuries, different Latins for different purposes emerged such that liturgical Latin and university Latin were not identical in the Middle Ages. Nor was the church Latin in Ireland the same as that of France. In other words, in medieval Europe, Latin could be described as a *set of technical languages*. As early as the eighth century, readers, writers, and speakers of Latin recognized that international cooperation was necessary to keep the language alive and to maintain its transparency among its dispersed readership. In 735, for example, Charlemagne brought the English monk Alcuin to the Continent to teach a restored pronunciation of Latin because Latin had begun to be spoken differently among users of different Romance languages. Local pronunciations tended to preside and these pronunciations affected spelling as well. Alcuin's mission was to standardize the use of Latin in the church. And, of course, centuries later, the rise of humanism and the various Renaissances across Europe again tried to restore Latin (and eventually Greek) to their ancient standards, a process that emphasized how different Latin had become from its classical self.

While Latin's prominence in learned, legal, liturgical, and literary contexts held advantages for the communities that used it, its dominance in these contexts was also a handicap both for other languages and for persons without access to a Latin education. Latin learners were always in the linguistic minority: most men and women were not educated in Latin. As late as the sixteenth century, the vocabularies and linguistic styles of vernacular European languages were widely considered inferior to those of Latin, largely because the vernaculars had not been cultivated for literary and professional purposes. Doctors, lawyers, priests, and scholars used Latin. Schools taught the reading and writing of Latin poetry. The growth of Protestantism in the sixteenth and seventeenth centuries contributed to a burgeoning sense that vernacular languages and literacy needed attention in order to make the Bible and biblical interpretations available to more people. The rise and spread of the printing press played a role as well: the technology carried the potential to make more books available more inexpensively to more readers, books that were often accompanied by commentary on the many virtues of vernacular publishing, chief among which was making knowledge available to persons who could not read Latin. Indeed, books often extolled the benefits of what they took to be the relative impoverishment of vernacular languages: the absence of a literary or vocational vocabulary meant that they communicated plain knowledge in plain language.[4]

This sense that "vernacular" and "plain" were synonymous held particular sway in sixteenth- and seventeenth-century England. The first recorded uses of "English" as a verb meaning "to translate into English" were simultaneous with the first, fourteenth-century translations of the Bible into English. By the end of the sixteenth century, "to English" had taken on the additional meaning of rendering into *plain* English. Thus, the act of translation into the vernacular was represented as simultaneous with the act of stripping the text of its rhetorical flourishes and technical terminology and making it available in its purest, simplest form to the widest possible audience. Seventeenth-century writers devoted much ink to explaining why English could – or could not – compete with the eloquence of Latin or French, but nearly all took it as given that the core meaning of texts could be unwrapped and represented in English.

Twentieth- and twenty-first-century linguists have established the close connection between the prestige of a language and the number and kind of domains in which it is used.[5] Early modern proponents of English literacy thought much the same. As R.F. Jones puts it, "The idea that the worth of a language is in direct proportion to the amount of knowledge to which it furnishes the key finds frequent expression, both as a motive for, and an argument in behalf of, translations and original works, for the more works published in English, the more valuable it becomes."[6] The cash-poor but intellectually rich Scottish universities proved their modernity by lecturing in English rather than Latin in the early eighteenth century, and, shortly thereafter, by teaching English alongside Latin literature. (By comparison, it was not until the later nineteenth century that Oxford and Cambridge made a comparable move.)

The growing practice of using vernacular languages for presenting scholarly research raised questions: Did learned writers have the same responsibility or desire as those writing for more popular publications to aspire to a broadly intelligible diction? Could one describe separate strata of readers within a vernacular readership? Could there still be learned publications aimed at a small, or even coterie, audience, or did publishing in English imply a commitment to broad intelligibility? In the absence of other, controlling institutions, such as strict censorship laws, what did the institution of print imply about what should be published and who would read it? In other words, when the learned of Britain began writing almost exclusively in English, the language of scholarship and the language of everyday life suddenly overlapped, leading to questions about whether the idioms of university-trained specialists and the conversational vernacular of a reading public should, in fact, be identical in vocabulary and style and therefore identical in their availability to the common reader.

These questions became caught up in the broader currents that carried the intellectual disciplines towards specialization. Increasingly, writers were forced to ask how they could mediate between the technicality inherent in disciplinary research and the need to enlighten a reading public with their findings. Did the increasing specialization of the intellectual disciplines in turn imply that each would have its own professional language? And, if so, were these languages what defined the disciplines as fields set apart from common comprehension?

I. LEARNED AND CONVERSABLE WORLDS

In a 1742 essay, David Hume characterized the conflict between specialized and public languages as a split between the "learned" and the "conversable" worlds. Hume puts these two categories at opposite poles of the field of private communication about public matters. Each world, or sphere of reference, describes a set of writers and a kind of audience belonging to each. These categories had a particular resonance in the mid-eighteenth century, which sought to define a general reading audience against a learned one and a world of rational social exchange against a world of solitary study.

Just as with Smith's model of the division of intellectual labor, which Hume had in many ways anticipated, one need not accept Hume's representation of readers as incontrovertible fact in order to find it useful as a guide to the relationships among writers and audiences in the eighteenth century. Borrowing Hume's vocabulary although not always his bearings, one might usefully imagine the learned and conversable worlds as separate but interlocking spheres of reference that enveloped both persons and institutions. In advancing this model, I begin with a capsule definition of the "learned" and "conversable" worlds and their related constellation of terms based on the textual traces of eighteenth- and nineteenth-century usage. Hume's usage of these words drew heavily on the literature already to hand, and the categories continued to be invoked in the succeeding decades.[7]

Though not new to the eighteenth century, the category "learned world" enjoyed considerable vogue between its use in the early-century periodical papers and the mid-nineteenth century. In its strictest sense, the "learned world" took in the body of men (and they were almost always men) who had university educations or their equivalent and who were deeply read in and sometimes also wrote about intellectual subjects. Hume defines the realm of the learned as follows: "[T]he Learned are such as have chosen for their Portion the higher and more difficult Operations of the Mind, which require Leisure and Solitude, and cannot be brought to perfection, without long Preparation and severe Labour." Hume's definition of the learned insists upon the same association between learned subjects and mental labor discussed in Chapter 1. Hume's definition of the learned can also be read as a spin on the definition for "scholar." The first edition of the OED uses the "the body of scholars, the learned world" as the definition for "scholarhood," which suggests that to a late Victorian audience "the learned world" had a well-known signification as synonymous with a "body of scholars." Years of philosophical labor and inevitable solitude characterize the denizens of the learned world.

Accordingly, the first definition in Johnson's dictionary for "Learned" is "Versed in science and literature." Literature, for Johnson, spanned the entire reach of the intellectual disciplines, from the systematic study of *belles lettres* to the pursuit of mathematics. But though Johnson shows himself generally sympathetic to the learned world, reading further under the definition of "learned" in his dictionary may give us pause. Half the illustrative examples he offers under the term "learned" lend rather negative or at least satirical connotations to the category. The mixed feelings the long eighteenth century had towards the learned world lay in part in the two meanings of "learned" at the time. While "learned" could and often did mean knowledgeable, it could also refer more specifically to the discredited intellectual predilections of medieval scholastics, who stood for all that Bacon, Locke, and their later followers rejected. These schoolmen were held in contempt because they were believed to have invested all their mental energy in technical, obscure disputes that had no relevance to the world outside their debates. The connotations of the latter meaning of learning ("skilled in scholastick knowledge") seeped into the former ("versed in science and literature") and cast the whole learned body under a cloud of suspicion. That is to say that the association of scholastic obscurity with any form of learnedness contributed to suspicion of the learned world more generally.

In an effort to disassociate himself from the tradition he wanted to discredit, Locke, himself deeply learned, often used "learned" in a pejorative sense. Johnson borrows several such definitions for his dictionary. Locke's success in associating the learned world with the then-disgraced scholasticism figures in Johnson's third definition for learned, "Skilled in scholastick, as distinct from other knowledge," in which he cites Locke's disregard for the "greatly learned" scholastics who are nonetheless "little knowing." While Locke's position is not strictly anti-intellectual, it is one that sets itself up as wary of those who deliberately mark themselves as learned. However, Locke has difficulty maintaining this pose throughout the many pages of his *Essay*, ultimately coming to admit that there need to be special, learned ways of communicating in philosophical contexts, ways that belong to the learned.

As Locke ultimately shows, against his initial leanings, new forms of learning were as likely to be associated with difficulty, obscurity, and lack of practical value as the older ones. Jonathan Swift, a proponent of ancient (although not necessarily scholastic) learning, was among the vanguard of those who argued that the technical languages of the new sciences and philosophies suffered from the same ailments that they diagnosed in earlier forms of learning.[8] Throughout his oeuvre, Swift calls attention to the communicative difficulties and intellectual divisiveness among the learned, making these undesirable qualities of scholarship a particular butt of his satire. In part three of *Gulliver's Travels*, Swift targets the Royal Society for its particular brand of learnedness, marked by self-absorption, muddled thinking, and a lack of practical ability. He suggests that the divided colleges and societies for pursuing each of the several "arts, sciences, languages, and mechanics" both in the British Isles and on the flying island of Laputa will ultimately lead to the wholesale devastation of all common sense and common communication so that the "whole country" will lie "miserably waste." Novelist Tobias Smollett points up a similar conundrum in his ramble novel, *The Adventures of Peregrine Pickle*: learned schemes that project revolutionary benefits are as likely to do harm as good when attempting to improve agriculture, manufacture, or commerce.[9] Although a researcher might emphasize the novelty or practical application of a body of research, this was no guarantee that it would contribute in the slightest to the advancement of either learning or common life.

As the number of societies for the promotion of knowledge multiplied, it became increasingly clear that the learned world was not a coherent body. Oliver Goldsmith pursues this idea in his essay on the so-called republic of letters, arguing that "nothing is more unlike a republic than the society which goes by that name. From this expression one would be apt to imagine, that the learned were united into a single body, joining their interests, and concurring in the same design."[10] Goldsmith tends to view the problem as strife created out of a self-interested lack of cooperation, a portrayal which has persisted to the present day. At the same time, he points us towards a recognition that by the mid-eighteenth century the division of intellectual labor has already taken hold. And whether one believes that divisions arise out of a perverse sense of factionalism or that the division of intellectual labor is fundamentally necessary to progress, Goldsmith suggests that the "jarring constitution" of the republic of letters, which takes in the range of disciplinary writings and their popular representations, "instead of being stiled a republic of letters should be entitled, an anarchy of literature."[11] The "anarchy of literature" serves as a fitting metaphor for the differing languages, subjects, and audiences which writings could and did reach throughout the century.

In other words, the disciplines did not generally come together under a common governance or polite ruling body, and individual scholars were often very isolated in their work. In his 1766 novel *The Vicar of Wakefield*, Oliver Goldsmith depicts the dangers and disappointments of intellectual insularity. When the eponymous Vicar's eldest son returns from his travels abroad, he reports having tried setting himself up as a scholar. The Vicar, having nursed an obsession with his own learned treatise for many years, questions his son about his scholarship:

> "Well said, my boy," cried I ... "[Y]ou published your paradoxes; well, and what did the learned world say to your paradoxes?"
>
> "Sir," replied my son, "the learned world said nothing to my paradoxes; nothing at all, Sir. Every man of them was employed in praising his friends and himself, or condemning his enemies; and unfortunately, as I had neither, I suffered the cruellest mortification, neglect."

Goldsmith points up one of the oft-described faults of the "learned world" – it is difficult to grab this audience's attention if one is not likewise an insider. Or, as Raymond Williams has put it, the "bureaucracy of letters" – the *de facto* solution to what otherwise might seem an anarchy – judges not on substance but on allegiance.[12] And the hopes for an audience outside a scholarly realm for productions that required similar levels of study were perceived as equally slim. "Learned world" still carries some currency in modern British usage as a slightly antiquated and therefore quaint (or hostile, depending on circumstances) designation for an academic realm.

But the learned world also had positive, even enviable qualities. Early eighteenth-century authors had a clear sense that the learned world had a limited membership that did not include everyone who could read, nor did it include every aspect of polite letters. Nevertheless, Addison suggests, being regarded as a member of the learned world was often considered desirable among readers, authors, and those in the bookselling trade who sometimes pretended, by virtue of their association with print, that they had earned immediate entry into this realm. Addison devotes a *Spectator* paper to mocking these assumptions.[13] Similarly, one of Oliver Goldsmith's "Citizen of the World" essays targets the "philosophical beau" who, in possession of only a "gilt library, a set of long nails, a silver standish, or a well-combed whisker," aims to pass for a man of learning.[14]

If the learned world's primary failing is its proclivity for intellectual solipsism, the conversable world's chief fault was its tendency towards vacuous conversation conducted in a state of ignorance about scientific progress. Samuel Johnson's dictionary tells us that conversable means "Qualified for conversation; fit for company; well adapted to the reciprocal communication of thoughts; communicative." The idea that one needs to be "fit for company" or adapted to conversation looms large in eighteenth-century letters, from the philosophies of Locke and Shaftesbury to the novels of Charlotte Smith and Jane Austen. For Shaftesbury, conversability expresses aristocratic breeding, but the essayists and novelists of the eighteenth century transform it into a quality that could be acquired by those who ingested the wisdom of the polite periodical or the dialogue of the novel.[15] The conversable world erases class divisions insofar as those divisions are predicated on hereditary status alone, and instead makes the standard of behavior a standard of middle-class sociability.[16]

The conversable world has no fixed location: Addison and Steele identify it with the breakfast table and the coffee house; novelists find it equally within the household, the ballroom, and the bath house. The conversable world is a realm perhaps now best known from inside the pages of Jane Austen novels. *Emma's* Mr. Knightley withholds judgment of Emma's bosom friends until he discovers whether they have achieved conversability; he is surprised to find the less-than-aristocratic Harriet "more conversable than ... expected," thus proffering the hope that the Austen reader, regardless of her birth, may become the same. Conversability is a disposition of self as well as a set of acquirable skills; the brooding or the withdrawn could disqualify themselves from being classed as conversable. In *Pride and Prejudice*, Wickham explains that Mr. Darcy "can be a conversable companion if he thinks it worth his while ... With the rich, he is liberalminded, just, sincere, rational, honourable, and perhaps agreeable," but when not among those he deems his "equals in consequence," he envelops himself in a foreboding cloud of aristocratic pride, hiding his potential for polite verbal communion and sealing himself off from the conversable world. *Pride and Prejudice's* educational program for Mr. Darcy brings him towards the realization that a communicative disposition need not be restricted to those with unentailed peerages or unembarrassing parents. Austen schools Darcy in the contrast between the conversable Elizabeth Bennet and the financially well-qualified but otherwise socially unpleasant Miss Bingley. In coming to model his own sociability on that of his female interlocutors, Darcy learns that conversability is not born, it is made.

Nancy Streuver has observed that for Austen, "domestic discourse improves on Hume's general conversation as the best provider of ruled liberty; conversation is not simply an idle, leisurely preoccupation but the purposeful construction of life and attitude and value, a project with socially redemptive values."[17] Her point is well taken; however, while not precisely "an idle leisurely preoccupation," the cultivation of a sociable domain in Austen's fiction depends on the occupation of and preoccupation with leisure time. The conversable world stood apart from what Steele had deemed "the busy world" because it was kept free from overt signs of truck, trade, or barter, while at the same time predicated on transfers of wealth and knowledge that could easily be described as forms of truck, trade, and barter. Austen models the conversable world's relationship with the busy one in much the same way Steele does; that is, news occasionally seeps into the novel from foreign parts or from activities treated as necessarily alien to readers. The author briefly comments on these matters and then moves on. This is in part why middle- to upper-class women were the leading citizens of the conversable world; all their time, at least in appearance, could be leisure time.

The relationship between gender and sociability it is not always so straightforward. As Daniel Defoe's *Essay upon Projects* (1697) explains, women's educations hardly prepare them for rational social exchange:

One would wonder indeed how it should happen that women are conversable at all, since they are only beholding to natural parts for all their knowledge. Their youth is spent to teach them to stitch and [sew], or make bawbles; they are taught to read indeed, and perhaps to write their names or so; and that is the heighth of a woman's education.

Girls' boarding schools became a venue in which women could achieve a modicum of conversability, although these institutions were duly and frequently mocked for the narrow learning they imparted in the service of cultivating shallow conversability in their students. In John Galt's 1821 novel *Annals of the Parish*, the Reverend Micah Balwhidder of Dalmailing describes the years during which he sends his daughter Janet to the boarding school in nearby Ayr, where she has "become a conversable lassie, with a competent knowledge, for a woman, of geography and history; so that when her mother was busy with the wearyful booming wheel, she entertained me sometimes with a tune, and sometimes with her tongue, which made the winter nights fly cantily by." A fashionable education makes Janet an entertaining companion for her father and raises her above her mother's intellectual level, but her schooling decidedly and deliberately does not make her learned. More so than the essay, the novel comes to define the kind of writing that stood at the opposite pole of polite letters from learned discourse because it not only affects a conversable style but also attempts to model conversability.

Influenced by eighteenth-century French *salonnières*, David Hume notes that if the strength of the conversable world consists in the mixing of genders, that is also its weakness: for lack of education, women tend "to sacrifice the substance to the shadow" in their reading and their conversation. Addison, too, uses the presence of women in his audience as an excuse to condescend to his readers, specifying how they should think in the absence of their own ability to do so.[18]

To return, then, to Hume's formulation, he imagines that in writing his essays, the separation of learned and conversable worlds is a necessary expedient to the advancement and spread of learning, but that without mutual exchange, the separation could also be destructive. The conversable world offers the learned at least one crucial service: the fashionable realm has the ability to bring scholars out of their respective monastic closets into a social atmosphere of convivial, social commerce. Hume keeps the distinction between these worlds by describing the learned and conversable worlds as two nation-states that cooperate for the sake of mutual exchange. He then styles himself the "Ambassador from the Dominions of Learning to those of Conversation," calling it his "constant Duty to promote a good Correspondence betwixt these two states."

Instead of seeking to erase the difference between these two sovereignties, Hume's essay cements the necessity of the continued existence of a separate, learned world whose function is the "manufacturing" of the "Materials of th[e] Commerce" between learned and conversable.[19] However, the main problem of any projected ambassadorship is the difficulty in translating between the languages of the two realms.

II. LOCAL PERSPICUITY

In their print conversations, eighteenth-century writers made much of the twinned notions of "perspicuity" and "propriety," as well as their antithesis, "pedantry." These terms, inherited from centuries of use, were modified and given increased prominence by the popularization of Lockean theories of language. Samuel Johnson's heavy reliance on John Locke's writings, both in the "Preface" to his dictionary and in the individual dictionary entries, evinces how central the *Essay Concerning Human Understanding's* perspective on words had come to be in the English conception of how language ought to be used. Even as modern readers find them, laden with their Lockean baggage, this cluster of terms merits revival as part of our critical vocabulary about language because they still embody useful theoretical concepts.

In its narrowest sense, following Quintillian, the eighteenth-century sense of "perspicuity" referred to language stripped of ornament. In "Some Thoughts Concerning Reading and Study for a Gentleman," Locke couples the meaning of "perspicuity" with his theory that language ought to be an exact representation of thought, transferable from one mind to the next: "Perspicuity consists in the using of proper terms for the ideas or thoughts, which he would have ... pass from his own mind into that of another[.]"[20] Following Locke, Johnson defines the term as "Clearness to the mind; easiness to be understood; freedom from obscurity or ambiguity." Johnson also ties intelligibility to perspicuity, defining "intelligibleness" as the "possibility to be understood; perspicuity," citing Locke's *Essay*: "It is in our ideas that both the rightness of our knowledge, and the propriety or intelligibleness of our speaking, consists."[21] When Hugh Blair composed his *Lectures on Rhetoric and Belles Lettres*, he took up Locke's cause, urging that philosophical prose ought to be first and foremost perspicuous, which implied that the philosopher must therefore "employ no words of uncertain meaning, no loose nor indeterminate expressions, and should avoid using words which are seemingly synonymous, without carefully attending to the variation which they make upon the idea." In avoiding elegant variation for its own sake, the philosopher runs the risk of precipitating readerly *ennui*, Blair notes, but only in this way would the philosopher not be lost in the poet.[22]

In sum, "perspicuity" embodied a criterion for evaluating prose that emphasized representational precision and therefore clarity over other qualities of written language. For example, a mathematical language could be more perspicuous in representing the motions of the planets than could a description in vernacular English. The eighteenth-century neologism "carbon dioxide" could describe a gas more precisely than the older term, "fixed air." And, later in the nineteenth century, symbolic representations of elements and compounds could achieve an even greater degree of perspicuity. Similarly, the terms of art used by moral philosophers could – within the boundaries of philosophical debates – take on meanings not common in vulgar usage in order that these terms might be used more exactly. In other words, each of these fields developed a system of *local perspicuity*, an exactness of representation within the boundaries of a text or a discourse.

This idea of local perspicuity brings up the notion of "propriety" that dominated eighteenth-century discourse about so many aspects of life, language included. Linguistic propriety indicated an exactness in the use of language; it indicated, as the *Oxford English Dictionary* (OED) notes, a "correctness or purity of diction," fitted exactly both to the writer's meaning and the occasion of use. For writing aimed at a broad audience, two standards were frequently held up as the measure of linguistic propriety: first, the prose works of a handful of seventeenth-century English authors, and second, common use. These two measures tended to become intertwined; Blair notes that the best English writers hold to the purity and the propriety of the English tongue because they choose their words based on native, established usage. Johnson's dictionary cites Locke's *Essay* on linguistic propriety: "Common use, that is the rule of propriety, affords some aid to settle the signification of language." But this is only half of Locke's story; as Johnson warns us in the dictionary's "Preface," his dictionary's abbreviated, deracinated quotations may at times be misleading. In the essay, Locke goes on to identify the limitations of "common use" for defining words used in philosophical contexts:

'Tis true, *common* use, that is, the Rule of Propriety, may be supposed here to afford some aid, to settle the signification of Language ... Common use *regulates the meaning of Words* pretty well for common Conversation; but no body having an Authority to establish the precise signification of Words ... common Use is not sufficient to adjust them to philosophical Discourses; there being scarce any Name of any very complex *Idea,* (to say nothing of others,) which, in common Use, has not a great latitude, and which, keeping within the bounds of Propriety, may not be made the sign of far different *Ideas.* Besides, the rule and measure of Propriety it self being no where established, it is often matter of dispute, whether this or that way of using a word be propriety of Speech or no.[23]

Thus, Locke himself, often held up as the standard-bearer for the accessibility of learned discourse, advocates a narrowed sense of linguistic propriety that departs from common use when it comes to philosophical ways of understanding the world. While he opposes the specific vocabulary of the schoolmen, he wants to replace it with a new notion of "philosophical propriety." Locke distinguishes the *"civil use"* of language in "common Conversation and Commerce" from the *"philosophical use* of Words." The philosophical use is "very distinct" from the civil use insofar as the former aims at a greater precision and thus departs from the meaning of the latter.[24] This becomes the chief question of the intellectual disciplines with regard to their language: Could they describe a propriety apart from common usage, one that would mark out a partially separate sphere of meaning? Or would such attempts always be condemned as efforts to hide or deliberately obscure what the learned were doing from the rest of the world? In the English tradition, the answer seems to have been yes to both questions.[25]

The language used within expert communications could therefore be written in a different vocabulary or even distinct symbolic system from writings meant to be intelligible to a general audience. Though Newton's mathematics-intensive *Principia* would hardly have been intelligible (and therefore not perspicuous) to a generally educated reader in his day, these same representations could better capture his theories for the expert audience (and therefore be more perspicuous for these readers). Linguistic propriety, then, was defined by the use of perspicuous language in a given context.

The boom industry in the popularization of learned texts after 1710 also drew on a recognition that the measure of perspicuity and standard for propriety changed among audiences. For the *Principia*'s general principles to be intelligible to an audience of non-mathematicians, they had to be stripped of their mathematical underpinnings, simplified, and represented in a vernacular vocabulary. This relationship held true not only for scientific disciplines, but also for humanistic ones. Even John Locke's *Essay Concerning Human Understanding*, which touted an ideal of universal, linguistic intelligibility, benefited from Addison and Steele's popularizing efforts, so that his wisdom might reach an audience not up to consuming a philosophical treatise but who could stomach a series of short essays. The popularizers occupied a position similar to translators of ancient texts. In much the same way that "Knowledge of what passed in the famous Governments of *Greece* and *Rome*" found its way to those who could not read Greek or Latin, Addison explains, popularizers communicate the productions of all branches of modern philosophy into an easier-to-understand language.[26]

III. PEDANTRY

In his *Preliminary Discourse* to the *Encyclopédie*, D'Alembert defines the eighteenth-century age of philosophy as one that has thrown off the "yoke of pedantry." Goldsmith's *Enquiry into the Present State of Learning in Europe* characterizes the eighteenth-century attitude towards learning as one in which genius was rescued from "the shackles of pedantry."[27] As one recent critic has suggested, being tarred with the brush of pedantry was among the worst insults the century could give a writer because it was punishment for what were deemed bad literary manners.[28] "Pedantry" connoted the opposite of "propriety"; pedantry is a display of language inappropriate to the current context. George Berkeley explains that those who would affect a philosophical point of view in ordinary conversation "would deservedly be laughed at." If philosophers affect such a style "in common talk[,] it would without doubt appear very ridiculous." "The common use of language" thus ought to "receive no manner or alteration or disturbance" from philosophical theories, but this should not stop philosophers from investigating and writing about such theories.

If common conversation was, following Addison and Steele, defined as that which took place among the "tea equipage" alongside "Bread and

Butter," then such a conversable setting should not be witness to scholarly talk. As Samuel Taylor Coleridge later explains, language should be confined to its appropriate context; violating this convention of sociability characterizes pedantry. Coleridge notes that the standard definition of the pedant was the "man of letters, who either over-rating the acquirements of his auditors, or misled by his own familiarity with technical or scholastic terms, converses at the wine-table with his mind fixed on his musaeum or laboratory ... the latter pedant instead of desiring his wife to *make the tea* should bid her add to the quant. suff. [as much suffices] of thea sinesis [China tea] the oxyd of hydrogen saturated with the caloric [boiling water]." Coleridge offers this example to show the man of science could be as jargony in his use of words as the humanist. At the same time, he also makes a larger point about the appropriateness of language to a given context. Since pedantry is the label for the misuse of language in a given context, Coleridge argues, it could occur in any situation. Those who brought the language of marketplace negotiation into the library, either because they wanted to boast of their associations with the busy world or because they had difficulty thinking of any but financial matters, would be pedants of their own sort.

Coleridge's target here is "the mere man of the world, who insists that no other terms but such as occur in conversation should be employed in a scientific disquisition, and with no greater precision." Such an individual "is as truly a *pedant* as the man of letters":

[I]f the pedant of the cloyster, and the pedant of the lobby, both *smell equally of the shop* ... the odour from the Russian binding of good *authentic-looking* folios and quartos is less annoying than the steams from the tavern or bagnio. Nay, though the pedantry of the scholar should betray a little ostentation ... a well-conditioned mind would more easily ... tolerate ... learned vanity, than ... contemptuous ignorance.[29]

Coleridge echoes Kant's *Anthropology* on the same point ("a *pedant* [can be] a scholar, a soldier, or even a courtier. The scholarly pedant is ... the most tolerable"[30]) as he also carries forward Jonathan Swift's earlier opposition to the adoption of fashionable marketplace slang – the use of words such as "Sham, Banter, Mob, Bubble, Cutting, Shufling, and Palming" – on occasions that called for more polite or technical language. Swift argues that writers and speakers were tempted to import such low talk "to avoid the dreadful Imputation of Pedantry; to shew us, that they know the Town, understand Men and Manners, and have not been poring upon old unfashionable Books in the University."[31] These writers use slang to combat the worry that the technical language of theology would alienate their audience. Alternatively, some feared that if scholarly terms were to catch on, the English language itself would be contaminated into a jargony parody of itself. Though Coleridge and Swift are often found on opposite sides of questions about linguistic propriety, both agree that deliberate attempts to avoid appearing scholarly were misguided.

Fears of pedantry, and the linguistic contamination it implied, spread across disciplines. For example, during the late eighteenth and early nineteenth centuries, when chemists across Europe reformed the system of chemical nomenclature to give elements and compounds most of the names we know them by today, debates raged over the desirability of renaming substances which had been well known by other names for centuries. Irish chemist Richard Kirwan argued that scientists should not give quotidian compounds, such as water, technical chemical denominations because renaming "tends to the subversion of the received language of all sciences, and even of common life." He expressed the fear that scientists would no longer be able to make themselves understood to the rest of the world when speaking about something as primary to human existence as water. Or, worse still, if the scientists' new denomination for water did catch on, it would debase the English language *in toto*. In the latter case, everyone would be expected to speak of "*hydrogenated oxygen* or *oxygenated hydrogen*" instead of water, "and instead of *ice* we are to say *decaloricated hydrogenated oxygen*, and for *steam, caloricated hydrogenated oxygen*." The country would thus be condemned to babble a scientific discourse that mocked the kingdom's native tongue.[32]

Kirwan's reservations derived in part from a century of criticism by those who wanted to define *all* neology and terms of art as by definition pedantic and thus intellectually separatist. Scientists were as vulnerable as humanists to charges of obscurity linked to their linguistic choices. The worry was that the remoteness of their language underscored how little they accomplished of relevance to the workaday or fashionable worlds. Their argots could be and sometimes were interpreted as a formalization of the already suspect condition in which scientists talked only to themselves because they had nothing to say to the rest of the world.

However, as the succeeding chapters discuss, natural scientists ultimately seem to have made effective choices in coping with this divide because they embraced a two-tiered division of intellectual labor, in which specialists developed a language for communicating with one another, and, subsequently, a popularizer represented scholarly knowledge to a wider readership while asserting that this popularization was a simplification and not the work itself. By adopting systems of local perspicuity, disciplines established boundaries around themselves, putting a linguistic barrier between their work and the lay reader. By claiming the necessity of such a division, these disciplines also arrogated to themselves the aura of expertise that defines the modern intellectual disciplines and professions. Humanists enjoyed less success in adopting a double system of perspicuity. Increasingly over the course of the eighteenth century, the learned world had a weaker pull in the humanities than in the sciences, as the disciplines that worked on and in natural languages were made synonymous with general intelligibility.[33]

To begin to address these questions of linguistic propriety, as well as those pertaining to the divide between the learned and conversable worlds, I turn first to Newtonian physics, the discipline whose struggle with these questions defined the grounds on which writers across the intellectual disciplines both debated the value of technical languages for the advancement of academic fields and simultaneously argued for the necessity of translating technical findings into a language that a lay reading public could readily comprehend.

CHAPTER 3

Physics and its Audiences

Nature and Nature's Laws lay hid in Night:
God said, Let Newton be! And all was Light.
— Alexander Pope, "Epitaph for Sir Isaac Newton" (c.1730)

When Alexander Pope turned his pen to writing an epitaph for Isaac Newton, his task was formidable: How does one capture the blazing glory of the first man knighted in England for scientific discovery? How does one account in two short lines for the apotheosis of the man who wrote the charter for modern science? True to form, Pope succeeded admirably, capturing in his eulogistic couplet the effects of both Newton's astronomical advances and his optical discoveries, as well as their perceived effect on the world at large. By his death in 1727, Newton was in the eighteenth-century imagination a divine figure indeed, earning widespread poetic praise atop his longstanding accolades from the scientific world. The reigning metaphor of the enlightenment – the bringing of light into the darkest recesses of nature and the human mind – was given literal form by Newton's writings on light and color.

But Newton's ability to illume nature and nature's laws was not so easily perceived in 1687, when he published his first major work, *Philosophiae Naturalis Principia Mathematica* (*Mathematical Principles of Natural Philosophy*). The eventual, startling popularity of Newtonianism in England and abroad belies how difficult, technical, and unreadable Newton's own published work often was. How, then, do we reconcile the fame accorded Newton in his own lifetime with the difficulty the reading public had throughout his life in understanding his mathematical principles of mechanics, dynamics, and optics? We could begin by assuming that this is the way science and genius work – a scientist solves an important, difficult problem, and the world reveres him for it. We would then cite the cases of Albert Einstein and Stephen Hawking as examples. But this answer proves unsatisfactory. Scientists only rarely solve problems that have been pressing on the minds of most of the world. Newton certainly did

not. Neither did Einstein or Hawking. Newton's renown did not therefore rise of its own accord out of a public perception of Newtonian physics' innate merit or usefulness. Neither did it arise out of a perception of
Newton's difficulty alone; seventeenth- and eighteenth-century writers
were generally inclined to dismiss or ignore rather than endorse difficulty
as a sign of greatness.

In this chapter, I demonstrate that Newton's reputation grew because
difficulty itself was translated by his followers into a commercial product.
By surveying the many eighteenth-century popularizations of Newton's
work, I show how Newtonian physics benefited from a publicity machine
that brought Newton's obscure genius to market, laying putative applications of Newton's physics before a public expressly taught to appreciate
its profundity. Audiences were given peeks under the curtain that veiled
Newton's complex mathematical gymnastics, but were also told that there
were limits to how much they could understand unless they embarked
upon years of mentally taxing and physically draining study.

In other words, Newtonian physics' singular, persistent success in
gaining public approbation relied at first on its proponents' and practitioners' careful separation between – and emphasis on – the technical
aspects of physics, available only to the most talented mathematicians,
and the components that could be translated into popular form, available to almost anyone. This distinction initially filtered out those who
could *do* physics from those who could be taught to *admire* its unique
preciseness in describing the physical world. The barriers between these
realms were initially constructed through Latin and (more importantly)
through mathematics, the natural and artificial languages, respectively,
of the learned world.

Forms of physics made for popular consumption generally represented a
distortion of Newton's work.[1] Indeed, popularizers often linked Newton's
theories to demonstrations and applications in engineering and mechanics
that predated Newton by decades – even millennia. But we can also see this
disconnect between theory and application as an example of what today
we might call Newtonian branding or trademarking. The direct link between Newton's equations and, for example, the workings of the so-called
six simple machines (pulley, lever, wedge, inclined plane, balance, screw)
whose description dates back at least to Archimedes and whose mathematics was a dominant focus of research and teaching across Europe over
a hundred years before Newton's work, was less important than the
ability to associate a visual demonstration with the brand represented by
Newton.[2] The individuals writing these popularizations defended that

distortion through an emphasis on its value as intellectual entertainment or as a stepping stone to deeper knowledge. This chapter traces Newton's early resistance to having his work wholly absorbed by public culture, a crucial stage in the development and reception of natural philosophy that set it apart from both moral and political philosophies of the early- to mid-eighteenth century.[3] By presenting Newton's work to a wide public, Newton's popularizers paradoxically sharpened the distinction between the learned and the conversable by calling attention to the divide.[4] Thus, physico-mathematics became a crucial testing ground for the movement of knowledge from a private, academic realm into a public, social one. The development of physics as a modern field of scholarly research helped define the spectrum between the private world of the scholar and the public one of the non-technical reader.

Tracing the evolution of Newtonian physics' relationship to public culture deepens our understanding of the emergence of modern disciplines. Then as now, most academic disciplines in the humanities and sciences were not structured in the same ways as the disciplines that fed into the professions that are often taken to be paradigmatic, medicine and law. However, the Newtonians' elevation of expertise in physics and its applications followed, to a significant degree, the pattern of early professionalization in other fields. Focusing primarily on men who served as architects in the Augustan period, Geoffrey Holmes has outlined the form that the developing disciplines based on the liberal arts and sciences took; he describes the coexistence of the professional gentleman-expert (generally university-educated, well-traveled, and well-connected), the young professional (generally without independent means and trained by an established master), and the leisured amateur (more than a dilettante, but not quite a professional in that his talents were not typically turned to the service of others). The realm of the Newtonian natural philosopher might be seen to describe a similar spectrum to the one Holmes outlines for architects; Newtonian physicists ranged from the university professor to the young university fellow or clerk of the Royal Society to the amateur gentleman-virtuoso.

In examining physico-mathematics, however, we need to add to its model the popularizers, the men (and they were almost all men) from varied backgrounds who made their living through book sales and lecture series. They operated as teachers with or without an institutional foundation. Much like teachers more generally in the eighteenth century, these men tended to fall between the cracks both in society and in accounts of its professional makeup. Inside or outside institutions, these men needed to advance on an individual basis their standards for qualification or expertise in order to provide themselves with a foundation from which they could advertise their services. Their own incipient professionalism relied on their credentialing themselves, through their rhetoric and their demonstrations. They thus shared with the more highly placed natural philosophers a need to emphasize the gap between themselves and their audiences.[5]

In order to understand or appreciate Newton's innovations in physics, audiences either had to be shown how to perform the mathematics that demonstrated how the system of the world often worked in ways that were counterintuitive, or had to be taught to take that which contradicted or lay outside the bounds of common sense on faith. Newton followed the former tactic. The popularizers generally adopted the latter. In other words, popular science writers did not promise to teach all the secrets of Newtonian physics; rather, they offered to let their audiences see some of its applications, which would suggest that the disciplinary, mathematical apparatus that lay behind it did, in fact, work. Over time, increasing numbers of these popularizations were aimed at an audience who could make little claim to being members of the learned world and who had little to no knowledge of mathematics. Audiences for the popularizations had to be taught to believe what they could not see; they had to be taught to have faith in the expertise of the physicist. Popularization, in short, was not education.

The gap between popularization and genuine education is evident from the way this training into belief was often displaced onto a rhetoric of taste. Newton's expositors showed their audiences how to recognize useful knowledge and thus exhibit to the world their fine taste in science. This newfound knowledge could be then used in artful conversation. The popularizations that positioned themselves most explicitly with respect to the standard of taste paid particular attention to representative techniques of description and narration that are now most familiar to us from poetry, novels, and popular essays. However, these Newtonian writings did not subordinate themselves to works of imaginative literature. Rather, popular science writings positioned themselves at the center of the evolution of a print culture in which specialized knowledge was transformed into common knowledge through its circulation among a broad readership. Any characterization of eighteenth-century print culture must thus take into account an understanding of how the relationship between knowledge and literary entertainment was worked out on the pages of popularizations of scholarly works.

This chapter begins with the most learned texts that contributed to the rise of Newtonian physics, and then moves on to consider the ways in which physics was presented for the lay reader. The progression is also roughly chronological: over time, Newtonian physics was represented for broader and broader audiences, who were less and less familiar with advanced mathematics.

I. THE IMPORTANCE OF BEING DIFFICULT

Newton's *Philosophiae Naturalis Principia Mathematica*, generally referred to as the *Principia*, was taken as a model of a scientific method that could banish the Stygian darkness from the world of philosophy and usher in a new era of intellectual light. The *Principia* was a mathematical treatise on celestial mechanics. In the first decades of its life as a published work, even when translated from Latin into vernacular languages, it was hardly intelligible to most readers.[6] Even specialists balked at the technicality of Newton's new system: mathematician John Craig averred that "nothing less than a thorough knowledge of all that is yet known in most curious parts of the Mathematicks can make him capable to read Mr. Newton's book."[7] Recent historians have turned up fewer than ten individuals who likely mastered the *Principia* in its entirety before Newton's death.[8] The standing joke in Newton's day among Cambridge undergraduates was that the *Principia* was so difficult that Newton himself did not understand it.[9] And when asked later in life to explain his method of calculation in parts of the *Principia*, Newton had difficulty retracing his calculations – "ever since I wrote that Book I have been forgetting the Methods by which I wrote it."[10]

Given our current assumptions that physics is inherently difficult and by its very nature resists straightforward exposition, it might surprise us to learn that Newton himself does not seem to have thought a difficult presentation was an inevitable consequence of advanced study. In other words, the split between learned and conversable versions of physico-mathematics began in part as a rhetorical strategy on the part of Newton himself. It apparently took *effort* on his part to make aspects of his physics look difficult. He had at first imagined having a popular audience for at least part of his researches. However, partway through writing the *Principia* Newton announced his intention that his work be confined to an audience of specialists.

This announcement came *after* Newton had first drafted a more accessible, less technical-looking version of the third book of his *Principia*. He then rewrote book three with the express purpose of making it well-nigh impossible for a general reader to comprehend. Newton explains the barriers to understanding he had erected as follows:

> I composed an earlier version of book 3 in popular form, so that it might be the more widely read. But those who have not sufficiently grasped the principles set down here will certainly not perceive the force of the conclusions, nor will they lay aside the preconceptions to which they have become accustomed over many years; and therefore, to avoid lengthy disputations, I have translated the substance of the earlier versions into propositions in a mathematical style, so that they may be read only by those who have first mastered the principles.[11]

That is, in order to avoid public conversation on these matters, Newton deliberately puts up obstacles to comprehension in the belief that only those who have achieved a certain level of knowledge could wisely enter into such matters. Newton thereby informs the bulk of his potential readers that they are not up to the task of comprehension of the whole, and he therefore wants to prevent their absorbing only parts of it. He sets up an intellectual divide within an intellectual milieu already partitioned by an ability to read Latin. At the same time, he hints that his propositions, written mathematically and in Latin, might nonetheless be generalized to other fields of knowledge, were readers to be sufficiently convinced of the force of his arguments. However, he does not want to take on the task of convincing such readers himself.[12]

The third book of the *Principia*, to which Newton refers here, explains some applications of his theoretical dynamics and mechanics to our solar system. If we think back to the tribulations of Galileo over his cosmological discoveries in seventeenth-century Italy, we might suspect that Newton's reasons for not wanting a popular audience were clear enough: he sought to avoid the church's opposition. However, this does not seem to have been his motivation, and it certainly was not his justification. Early modern English natural philosophers enjoyed a certain freedom from religious persecution, a freedom the English associated with their Protestant church and elected parliamentary government. Indeed, Newton's *Principia* work was often marshaled in favor of a widely held orthodoxy, an Anglican view of a God-created universe that could display exactly the kind of order Newton described.[13] Newton's letters and published work indicate that his reasons for obscuring his researches had more to do with avoiding *public opposition* from the unschooled than with worry over governmental or ecclesiastical prosecution on charges of heresy.

Upset over potential challenges from non-specialists, Newton had threatened to omit the contents of his third book altogether so that his work would only consist of theoretical physics without any reference to applications that a slightly broader, although still learned, audience would understand or appreciate. Writing to Edmund Halley, the astronomer for whom the comet is named and who had undertaken financial and editorial responsibility in bringing forth the first edition of the *Principia* on behalf of the Royal Society, Newton expostulated, "The third [book] I now designe to suppress. Philosophy is such an impertinently litigious Lady that a man had as good be engaged in Law suits as have to do with her. I found it so formerly & now no sooner come near her again but she gives me warning."[14] Newton refers here to Robert Hooke's accusation that Newton had plagiarized some of the contents of the forthcoming *Principia* from Hooke's own researches.

Upon this threat of suppression, Halley pressed Newton to include the application of his physics to celestial motion. In a letter to Newton, Halley wrote that, "the application of this Mathematical part, to the System of the World; is what will render it acceptable to all Naturalists as well as Mathematici[a]ns; and much advance the sale of [your] book."[15] Halley, navigating difficult financial straits himself, had a vested interest in the sale of Newton's book. He likewise had the savvy to realize that it was the application that would secure its reputation. Only then could Newton's experimental principles not seem wholly speculative or purely mathematical to the audience of the Royal Society. Only then would Newton's work be clearly distinguished from the faults of speculation on unfounded principles and the generation of false hypotheses that he had identified in his Cartesian predecessors. And only then would he ever have an audience of more than a very few mathematicians. Newton apparently thought better of his planned self-censorship and exchanged his threatened suppression for a move that would serve him much better in the long run: recasting book three in more mathematical form.

Newton, probably recalling the controversy that surrounded the publication of part of his optical theory in the *Philosophical Transactions* a decade and a half earlier, was reluctant to expose himself to general scrutiny. Though this early paper on optics generally received acclaim, it also came in for its share of criticism. Newton attributed these derogatory attacks to a lack of expertise on the part of his critics, especially Robert Hooke, who had advanced his own competing theory of optics. Newton's response to Hooke at the time contained a cutting accusation: he upbraided Hooke for entering into intellectual waters too deep for his abilities, "without understanding the grounds on [which] he proceeds."[16] Later in his career, Newton would repeat like imputations against those scientists whom he perceived as lacking an adequate background to respond wisely to his work.

Modern historians have thus suggested that Newton recast book three of the *Principia* in this more technical fashion expressly to differentiate himself from Hooke, whom Newton knew not to have had the requisite mathematical abilities to have proven these findings himself.[17] Whether or not Newton's well-documented frustration with Hooke inspired the change, Newton's alterations had the effect of making the *Principia* more difficult for most readers to follow. More importantly, it articulated very publicly a boundary between those who had the expertise to understand his work and those who did not. Newton thereby placed himself at the core of this group of learned experts, who would require his own tutelage to make progress through his work. Newton likewise refrained from appending his planned mathematical treatise to teach readers how to digest the *Principia*. Only readers who could learn Newton's own peculiar brand of higher mathematics as they went through the *Principia* had a fighting chance of being able to grasp its arguments.

This strategy of concealment is fundamentally different from that of the seventeenth-century experimentalists, such as Hooke or Robert Boyle. The need for privacy in the successful execution of laboratory experiments, from the seventeenth and eighteenth centuries to the present, is well established.[18] Experimental research is predicated on access to specialized equipment and controlled surroundings; by definition, an experimental scientific program requires a division between the scientist's laboratory and the world outside, with entrance contingent on invitation. Thus, the Royal Society's early manifestos claiming that the organization was an open, public institution were necessarily of limited truth.[19] But Newton's concealment went far beyond the institutional practices of laboratories. Although we generally assume that *publication* is an act of *publicity*, Newton sought to limit access to his findings even after the research was published.

Newton thought that he had historical precedent for obscuring his knowledge. The suppressed earlier version of book three, published only after Newton's death, opens by observing that the ancient Egyptians and Greeks hid their knowledge from the "vulgar way of thinking" by "deliver[ing] their mysteries, that is, their philosophy of things ... under the veil of religious rites and hieroglyphic symbols."[20] Newton's attempts at circumscribing his audiences have fewer mystical or religious overtones. It would be hard to imagine such a text being received well in the learned communities of Protestant England. Neither does he explicitly draw out the parallel between himself and the ancient philosophic priesthood. However, Newton's representation of himself and his view of ancient mathematicians have striking similarities. Both engage in masking their researches – by avoiding natural language explanations as much as possible – for the sake of committing them only to specific audiences.

Newton explained in pragmatic terms the advantage of seeking refuge in mathematics rather than struggling with natural language. He noted that he feared that his terms "universal attraction" and "gravitation" would create controversy about the definitions of these terms by those who wanted to quarrel over words. Such quibblers would stir up disputes over whether or not the force we call gravity on earth is the same as forces of attraction between other celestial bodies. Mathematical representations allowed him to prove that forces of attraction among all bodies function in the same way without disputing what generates these forces and whether all such forces have the same fundamental essence. In other words, he used his *"mathematical way"* of representation, "to avoid all questions about the nature or quality of this force, which we would not be understood to determine by any hypothesis."[21] By leaning mostly on mathematics, he strove to avoid such terminological questions by limiting his audience to those who could understand the technical demonstration of how forces worked.[22]

Newton also exacerbated (or encouraged) the difficulty that even mathematicians had in hacking through the *Principia*'s dense mathematical cover. Historians have noted that it was not entirely unusual in Newton's day for mathematicians to leave out parts of their proofs to protect their method. The *Principia* takes this a step farther.[23] As recent students of Newton have pointed out, Newton systematically omitted sections of his mathematical proofs that relied on analytical mathematics (what we now call calculus) rather than classical geometry, troubling his earliest readers, who often turned to Newton himself to have these gaps filled in. Newton's reasons for obscuring some of his mathematics stemmed from his commitment to classical geometrical form over and above the analytical methods associated with algebra and analytical calculus. Not that most (if any) of his readers would have known what to do with the calculus either: Newton would still have needed to fill in a good many details about how his newly invented mathematical process worked.[24]

However, the *Principia* may not have remained mathematically obscure for very long had he used calculus: developments in mathematics on the Continent in the ensuing years (advances better publicized than Newton's own mathematical theories) did make Newton's mathematics quickly come to seem old-fashioned. Thus the *Principia* never ceased to seem recondite to mathematicians. Nineteenth-century scientist, philosopher, and historian William Whewell offers what is perhaps the most poetic and sympathetic account of Newton's insistence on not using calculus as a shortcut to proving mathematical truths, though his classical methods cost him and ultimately his readers considerably more effort:

[W]ho has presented, in his [Newton's] beautiful geometry, or deduced from his simple principles, any of the inequalities which he left untouched? The ponderous instrument of synthesis [classical geometry], so effective in his hands, has never since been grasped by one who could use it for such purposes; and we gaze at it with admiring curiosity, as on some gigantic implement of war, which stands idle among the memorials of ancient days, and makes us wonder what manner of man he was who could wield as a weapon what we can hardly lift as a burden.[25]

Newton's decision to avoid showing analytical processes in the *Principia* was both epistemological and stylistic. He believed in the power and beauty of classical geometry because its relationship to the observed world was clear and provable in a way that other forms of mathematics were not. Newton sought legitimacy for mathematics as a method of representing the physical world by arguing that his mathematics were derived from mechanics: "Geometry is founded in mechanical practice," he wrote in the "Preface" to the first edition.[26] In Newton's formulation, geometry was empirical at the core, a representation of how the phenomena of nature operated. As Whewell later explained, in the eighteenth- and nineteenth-century view, other analytical forms of mathematics demanded that their users close their eyes and ignore the relationship between their operations and the physical world. Their algebraic convolutions did not at all times enjoy the same correspondence with the world they represented that Newton's geometry did.[27] Newton's practice gives the lie to the commonplace notion that mathematical language is transparent with respect to the world and without linguistic artifice, a notion, recounted in James Burnet's *The Origin and Progress of Language* (1787), that "in writing upon certain sciences, such as mathematics, no art of style is required": "the language of mathematics ... requires nothing that deserves the name of style."[28]

Despite – or because of (and here is where the fascinating tension lies) – the limits on the general public's (and most mathematicians') ability to understand his work, Newton's reputation grew steadily from the *Principia*'s publication until well after his death. The first edition, printed "in quarto in a fair letter," became quickly unavailable.[29] Newton began revising for a second edition shortly after the first was issued.[30] As one of Newton's early expositors wrote in his dedication to Newton, "[T]here are more Admirers of your wonderful Discoveries, than there are Mathematicians able to understand the two first Books of your *Principia*."[31]

The *Principia*'s extensive renown was, however, not immediate. There were many steps between Newton's presentation of difficulty and the public reverence for it. Frenchman Bernard le Bovier de Fontenelle, mathematician, secretary to the Académie Royale des Sciences, and erstwhile popularizer of ancient and modern philosophies, wrote in his *Eloge* on Newton that the *Principia* "did not at once receive all the applause that it deserved and which one day it was to receive." Fontenelle attributes this delay to the *Principia*'s succint erudition:

> As it is a very learned work, very sparing in words, and with propositions arising in it very swiftly from the principles, so that the reader is forced to supply by himself all the connection between the two, time had to pass before the public could understand it. Great geometers could do so only after studying it with care; mediocre geometers only embarked upon it when excited by the testimony of their greater brethren; but in the end, when the book was sufficiently well known, all the applause that it had won so slowly broke out on all sides, constituting a single paean of praise.

Fontenelle may have been right about attributing its slow progression through the learned world to its sparing use of explanation. Newton's admirers and critics alike found themselves frustrated over the lack of exposition.

Thomas Birch, Newton's earliest biographer and later secretary of the Royal Society, added to Fontenelle's assessment that in the *Principia* "the consequences flow with such rapidity from the principles, that the reader is often left to supply a long chain to connect them."[32] This chain was long indeed – it required its early readers to write letters to Newton to fill in the missing details. Without access to Newton himself, most potential readers had to wait for knowledge to trickle down before they could slowly absorb it. William Whewell comments that the story of the *Principia*'s delayed reception needs to take account of the time it took for these mathematicians to confirm Newton's work by repeating it. Mathematicians then had to learn to explain it to others and follow up on its implications for further study. As Whewell writes, "The doctrine of universal gravitation, like other great steps in science, required a certain time to make its way into men's minds; and had to be confirmed, illustrated, and completed, by the labours of succeeding philosophers."[33] The path of the *Principia* through the learned world was a long one.

But, although full acceptance of the *Principia* across Europe in learned circles would not come until the second half of the eighteenth century, it was widely discussed and endorsed at least in part by most mathematicians before that point. The *Principia*'s life among the learned was conducted in part through scholarly journals on the Continent. There were three early reviews of the *Principia* in European learned journals, and one by Edmund Halley in the English *Philosophical Transactions of the Royal Society*. Two of the reviews, Halley's and an anonymous Latin one in the Leipzig journal *Acta Eruditorum,* have been praised for their brief, straightforward account of the *Principia*'s intricacies. The two others, which appeared in the *Bibliothèque Universelle* and the *Journal des Sçavans*, are less detailed and less specialized; the former may have been by John Locke, which would explain the absence of mathematical intricacy.[34] The most extensive discussions of Newton, however, were conducted through letters that were not printed until the twentieth century. Thus, English mathematicians engaged in much of their learned conversation privately.[35] They therefore contributed only indirectly to Newton's reputation among a broadly educated public.

Among mathematicians, it was possible to question Newton privately and praise him publicly. Fontenelle's description of the *Principia*'s reception as a "single paean of praise" exaggerates the homogeneity of the response to it. Fontenelle himself had doubts about aspects of it. However, the phrase does capture beautifully the general tenor of Newton's eventual reception into learned culture, especially in England. Newton exchanged letters with Edmund Halley, David Gregory, John Flamsteed, Gilbert Clerke, Christiaan Huygens, John Locke (to whom Newton wrote a simplification of the inverse square law), John Wallis, and others. And mathematicians across Europe exchanged letters discussing the implications of Newtonian physics for their own mathematical work.

The case of Newton suggests that what makes a discipline a discipline with recognizable boundaries is its ability to create specialized knowledge that cannot, by definition, be performed by most persons outside their discipline. In other words, a discipline or a profession constitutes itself by instituting and calling attention to the divide between itself and a broadly educated public. Some of these obstacles to lay participation might have been inevitable in the pursuit of specialized knowledge, but some were deliberately constructed and promulgated as such. The apotheosis of Newton cannot and could not be separated from the process of establishing physics as the paradigmatic discipline.

II. DIFFICULTY AMELIORATED

How, then, do we reconcile Newton's broad popularity with the narrowness of his actual reading audience? Newton owed some of his early popularity – before the book had even a handful of readers – to Edmund Halley, who brought it before the Royal Society and whose favorable summary in the *Philosophical Transactions* generated a stir. Realizing that applications would convince more than the technicalities, Halley also presented King James II with a copy of the *Principia* accompanied by Halley's own explication of Newton's "Solution of the Causes of the Tides in the Ocean," which was later printed in the *Philosophical Transactions*.[36] But even after this early review by Halley, however, the great age of popular Newtonianism was some years away.

As the *Principia*'s contents gradually filtered down through the Royal Society, public lecture series were inaugurated to make visually available the fruits of Newtonian physics to "Persons of all Ranks and Professions, and even the Ladies."[37] Similarly, a host of writers expounded upon Newton's principles for lay and learned readers; they wrote texts that replaced mathematical explanation with more easily comprehended visual examples and more familiar language. They took advantage of the explanatory power of the *Principia*'s laws of force and motion, without reproducing all of the mathematics behind it.

Newton was not the first English scientist ever to have his work publicized or reproduced. Newton's distinction was that he had constructed a world system that had to be transmitted to an audience that was not really expected to understand it in any of its details but rather to appreciate in broad terms its dazzling power to encapsulate in a single, universalizing theory the workings of forces both on earth and throughout the solar system. He gave the world a mathematical vision of divine proportions. But it remained a vision that only the few could understand in its complexity. No one would have said this about Robert Boyle or Edmund Halley or Robert Hooke. This distinction made Newton an iconic figure.

Newton's expositors generally had a clear sense of which parts of the *Principia* reasonably well-educated non-mathematicians could grasp on their own: much of the third book and "several of the *Corallaries* and *Scholia* in the other two."[38] Newton himself eventually pointed to these parts as constituting the shortcut to understanding the gist of his work for a reader not committed to taking in the whole.[39] The popularizers' self-appointed task consisted of digesting the first two books of the *Principia* so that readers could know, broadly and by analogy, the contents of the entire work. At the same time, their insistence on Newton's own genius in devising such a system served to deify Newton, establishing Newtonianism as an intellectual brand with Newton's name as its trademark.

The *Principia* suffered from the problem of much mathematical science: its mathematical theories and experimental observation did not always line up very well. In those cases, Newton laid the stress on the mathematical over the observed truth.[40] The popularizers solved this problem differently: they dropped Newton's mathematical priorities in favor of experimental demonstration. In places where Newton proceeded mathematically, the Newtonian lecturers substituted complex mechanical devices, often of their own invention, to make visual the implications of mathematics. Oxford-trained Newtonian lecturer J.T. Desaguliers justified this shift in emphasis by claiming that the "Truth" of "*Newtonian Philosophy* ... is supported by Mathematicks, yet its Physical Discoveries may be communicated without."[41] Their work downplayed the significance of mathematics to the understanding of Newton's system and replaced it with an emphasis on experimentalism not wholly present in the *Principia* itself.[42] Newton's own preface to the *Principia*, in conjunction with the popular presentation of Newton, led to the perception of Newton as primarily an experimentalist, whose mathematics came after the experimental fact, even though for Newton himself, the mathematics formed the core of his discovery. Without the mathematics, there would be no Newtonian *system*, only a collection of celestial observations recorded over time by many different hands.

However, Newton's disciples discovered early on that they could give the broad theoretical outlines of the system, show a few demonstrations of simple machines, and conclude that these *were* the Newtonian system, or as much of it as was possible given the audience's limitations. The advertising campaign on Newton's behalf simplified and otherwise manipulated the consequences of his work in order to communicate certain of its insights to a wider audience. The general seventeenth- and eighteenth-century understanding of Newton thus relied only indirectly on the contents of the *Principia*. The reading public's comprehension depended more on explanations and demonstrations by other writers and lecturers advertising their work under the umbrella brand of Newtonianism.[43] In their emphasis on the experimental or visually demonstrable aspects of Newtonian physics, the popularizers laid stress on the application of

Newtonian physics to real-world problems in navigation, architecture, and what we would now call civil engineering.

However, it is important to recognize that Newton's physics had few, if any, direct applications to the earth-bound world. Newton's creation of a new telescope useful in celestial observation and navigation was among the few side-effects of his study of optics. Newton's major contribution to knowledge was in a greater understanding of mathematics, celestial mechanics, and optics – in other words, he made advances in what we would now call pure science or mathematics that had no immediate application except in the better understanding of mechanical or mathematical processes. Nonetheless, Newton's name was used by his popularizers to offer a theoretical justification for their developments in applied mechanics that did not, in practice, require Newtonian science to be effected or to be understood.[44] The putative applications advanced by Newton's popularizers were *not* strictly applications of his work.[45] The popularizers' frequent emphasis on application, then, was in part a ploy both to advertise advances in (what we would now call) engineering as "Newtonian" and to drum up further interest in Newtonian physics as a potentially valuable subject.

Newton's expositors rationalized their move away from pure mathematical truth by expressing the wish that their efforts would be understood by their audiences as introductory and therefore incomplete.[46] The popularizers also had a second tactic for justifying their anti-mathematical turn. Desaguliers noted that "sometimes one must make use of such ways of demonstrating as are not mathematically true, to prepare them for what is a little more abstract."[47] They likewise frequently asseverated that through their "publick *Courses*; a great many Persons get a considerable Knowledge of *Natural Philosophy* by way of Amusement" and the attendant hope that some of these persons would go on to study higher mathematics.[48] Whether or not we take at face value such generous desires for their audience's eventual intellectual progress, the Newtonian lecturers emphatically underscored the breach, surmountable or not, between their demonstrations and Newton's own text.

Reading the prefaces to Newtonian popularizations suggests that it was an almost universal convention to emphasize Newton's difficulty. The authors would assert that they would help their audiences get over part of this difficulty, but they would not teach them how to replicate completely or to understand fully what Newton himself had done. Most popularizers did not promise to give their readers the ability to read the *Principia* themselves, only to understand broadly its implications. The popularizers thus crafted a crucial place for themselves not as *educators* in physics but as *mediators* between the mathematical genius of Newton and the public's understanding of it.

The Newtonian lecturers enlisted their new audiences for Newton's *Principia* by making abundantly clear that they aimed at reaching a range of readers, in a range of languages. Some were aimed at more learned audiences than others. The Dutch lawyer and mathematician Willem Jakob van 'sGravesande (1688–1742) prepared one of the earliest paraphrases of the *Principia*, in Latin, for the use of educated readers who did not have sufficient mathematics to take in the *Principia* on their own. 'sGravesande's paraphrase was subsequently translated into English by Oxford mathematician and astronomer John Keill and again by Keill's student Desaguliers, so that Newton could reach a vernacular readership in England. Desaguliers, like Keill, also prepared public lecture series. Desaguliers's lectures were subsequently published as the *Course on Experimental Philosophy*. This work professed that, to follow the written versions of his public lectures, the "common reader" needed to have "very little Arithmetick ... to qualify them for understanding," as long as this reader proceeded methodically and sequentially through the book.[49] Desaguliers adds that he has subtended notes for the more advanced reader who wants to know how to connect Desaguliers's experiments to geometrical postulates. This common reader, then, knew Newtonian physics only indirectly and largely through the words of others.

Many explanations were offered as to why Newton was translated for such wide audiences and why the explanations were represented in a mechanical rather than a mathematical vein. In *A View of Sir Isaac Newton's Philosophy*, the editor of the third edition of the *Principia*, Henry Pemberton, offers his justification through an exegesis of the passage in the *Principia* in which Newton declares that he had deliberately obfuscated what could have been rendered more clearly. Pemberton writes,

The manner, in which Sir Isaac Newton has published his philosophical discoveries, occasions them to lie very much concealed from all, who have not made the mathematics particularly their study. He once, indeed, intended to deliver, in a more familiar way, that part of his inventions, which relates to the system of the world; but upon farther consideration he altered his design. For as the nature of those discoveries made it impossible to prove them upon any other than geometrical principles; he apprehended, that those, who should not fully perceive the force of his arguments, would hardly be prevailed on to exchange their former sentiments for new opinions, so very different from what were commonly received. He therefore chose rather to explain himself only to mathematical readers; and declined attempting to instruct such in any of his principles, who, by not comprehending his method of reasoning, could not, at the first appearance of his discoveries, have been persuaded of their truth.[50]

His explanation parallels Newton's very closely, while adding more detail. Pemberton tells his readers that times have changed, and the moment has come for a grand and global unveiling, "since Sir Isaac Newton's doctrine has been fully established by the unanimous approbation of all, who are qualified to understand the same; it is without doubt to be wished, that the whole of his improvements in philosophy might be universally known."[51] The acceptance of the learned world, and the broader culture's knowledge of this acceptance, makes the time right for the revelation of all. This, of course, sounds as much like rhetorical posturing for the sake of promoting Pemberton's own book as a deeply held sense of England's having reached the precise time for publishing such explanations. His own self-promotion notwithstanding, Pemberton's remarks do reflect the general tenor of the popularizers: they performed a service to those outside the learned world who would "take great pleasure in tasting of this delightful fountain of science."[52] Pemberton puns on "taste" here – commenting on the consumption of this kind of science for entertainment by those who could not ingest it more completely in another form.

From the beginning, then, Newton had two audiences, though they may in places have overlapped – those who could understand the most technical of his writings, and those who could understand some of its potential applications and explanations. The popular acceptance of the technical work was dependent on this second process of explanation, but inside the learned world, the work itself maintained a degree of independence from its public reception. Scientists and mathematicians across Europe continued to debate and to build on Newton's system. In other words, the *Principia* led a double life – one among mathematicians, one amid everyone else.

As a matter of course, over time, Newtonian physico-mathematics began to seem less inaccessible to the well-educated.[53] The *Principia*'s implied demands for an educated audience were translated by some of his later expositors into their own claims to provide such an educated audience for his work.[54] By 1770, William Emerson could assert that the *Principia* is "a book which is universally read by all the world, that pretend to any degree of philosophical learning." Emerson's claims ought to be taken with a grain of salt – he had his own companion to the *Principia* to market. But his 1770 text is one of several from the 1740s forward that take the next step, trying to explain some of the finer points of the *Principia* to an audience composed of more than a few mathematicians. As Geoffrey

Holmes has observed, mathematics was one of the "boom subjects of the late seventeenth- and early eighteenth-century curriculum," which led to a larger audience for technical physics, though it did not come close to abrogating the divide altogether.[55]

III. DIFFICULTY AND ITS DISCONTENTS

The difference between the two audiences, and between the standards of mathematical truth and the standards of taste, was not always perfect – nor was such a recognition always desirable. There were many who were unhappy with the secrecy that the split encouraged. Indeed, the *Principia*'s technical aspects became a target of Newton's non-technical critics. They objected to Newton forming a system not open to public inspection and therefore not capable of being disproved in a fair and public manner. The concealment became a problem because Newton's physics was picked up as justifications for certain philosophical and religious beliefs, beliefs that were difficult to challenge if their scientific foundations were not likewise accessible and therefore vulnerable to assault.

Not everyone saw the light as well as Alexander Pope had by the time he wrote his epitaph for Newton. The small but vocal opposition to Newton in England came out of longstanding suspicions against the learned world and its habit of concealing information in abstruse languages. The learned world, the anti-Newtonians argued, went to great extremes to hide their knowledge from the rest of the world: this is why they cloaked their hypotheses in "Mathematical Dress."[56] Were Newton and his followers to use a more straightforward, expository style, anyone possessed of a little common sense would be able to prove them wrong. John Conrad Francis de Hatzfeld suggested in his anti-Newtonian tract *The Case of the Learned Represented* that the fault of Newton and his popularizers lay precisely in their framing hypotheses that ran counter to all common-sense knowledge about the world. A proposition, de Hatzfeld maintained, could be "built upon both Experiments and Mathematicks, and deliver'd with all the imaginable Elegancy, and may nevertheless be as erroneous as can possibly bee."[57] However, the public lacked the requisite knowledge to be able to see this. De Hatzfeld reversed the very weapon that the Newtonians used on their opponents: he called the Newtonians intellectually bigoted and married to a system that they had long held to, even in the face of better evidence.[58] They were too attached to their own system to recognize the common-sense truths staring them plainly in the face. Despite their mistakes, the Newtonians continued to hoodwink the public because "men of sense" were victims of their own trusting nature. Those who were duped by physico-mathematicians believed what they were taught "because they have trusted the Judgment of those who were the first receivers of them [i.e. Newton's followers], and so have taken every thing for granted without at all examining into the matter."[59] The credulity of the public – not the truth of Newton's system – was what carried the day in Newton's favor, according to de Hatzfeld.

De Hatzfeld was far from alone in his suspicions. George Gordon published two editions of his revealingly titled *Remarks upon the Newtonian Philosophy … Wherein the Fallacies of the pretended Mathematical demonstrations … are clearly laid open; and the Philosophy it self fully proved to be false and absurd, both by Mathematical and Physical Demonstration*. His first edition, Gordon tells us, never achieved much of a readership because certain unnamed champions of Newtonianism conspired against his book. These committed disciples of Newton spread themselves out in the university towns and in London in order that they might "perswade every Body" that his book was "silly."[60] In the preface to his second edition, Gordon holds forth on the learned world's factionalism, which, he suggests, made him unpopular, even before anyone had opened the pages of his book. Gordon goes on to rail against the secrecy and the insularity of the learned world, which protects its members and advances their private causes at the expense of the public pursuit of truth and whose ungentlemanly tactics insure that his book would never be read by those qualified to judge.

Gordon likens the learned world to the political realm, in which corrupt parties covertly manipulate the system for the gain of their members: "he knows but little of the Affairs of the Learned World, who know not how considerable that Party is in it."[61] The reason its proceedings remain secret is that they have put up high bars to entry. In the case of the *Principia*, Gordon suggests, such a quantity of study is required to gain access to it that its initiates expect to be rewarded when they have mastered it:

[T]hose very few, who understand that mysterious System, have not attained that Piece of Learning without a great deal of Study; nor is it to be supposed that Men would put themselves to so much Trouble as that Attainment requires, without a Prospect of being at least esteemed by the World for so uncommon a Piece of Learning … In short, it's plain, that by far the greater Part of those who understand that Philosophy, both value themselves, and are valued by the World, upon that Account; and are by their Passions and Interests consequently engaged in the Party. And at this Rate, how considerable, and how powerful this Party is, I think sufficiently appears.[62]

Once the passions and interests of a scholar have been betrothed to the Newtonian system, he feels committed to defend it, mistakes and all, to the "Eyes of the World."[63] Accordingly, the academic system has its compensations to reward its defenders, just as the "Civil world" does,

[T]he great Men who have the Administration of the Affairs of the Learned World, are capable in their Way, by Interest and Commendations, to reward their inferior Adherents, with an inferior Degree of those Blessings which themselves enjoy, and so engage their Passions and Interests in the Affair also; and thereby bind them to concur and assist in supporting the common Cause: As well as Statesmen can strengthen that Government of which they have the Administration, by putting whom they think most proper for that End, into the inferior Officer of the State.[64]

And for those not lucky enough to gain such high offices, lower ones are opened for them. This distribution of rewards gains their cooperation, and the "implicit Ignorance" of the lesser followers secures them "from being overcome by good Arguments, as Passion and Interest does" the "learned."[65]

Gordon's complex paranoia aside, he did have a political point: Newton developed a party of mathematical followers, to whom he explained, often in writing, details left out of the *Principia*. He also helped these men along in their academic careers: David Gregory became Savilian Chair of Astronomy in Oxford; Edmund Halley later advanced to the same chair; Colin Maclaurin took the Chair of Mathematics in Edinburgh, and William Whiston occupied the Lucasian Chair in Cambridge, all on recommendations from Newton. Newton also endorsed some of his popularizers (Desaguliers, Hauksbee) for paid positions in the Royal Society. Richard Bentley may likewise have been made Master of Trinity College in 1699 "in consequence of the Newtonian sermons which he had preached."[66] These are the very men who most prominently advocated Newton's name and his methods, and their advancement on the basis of Newton's word was well recognized.

The mathematical specifics of Gordon's argument against Newtonian physics are generally unsound. However, Gordon does usefully call attention to the fact that much of Newton's work is based on a blend of mathematical theory and scattered bits of empirical data, which, even taken together, did not entirely meet emerging seventeenth-century standards of experimental proof. Newton published what he thought to be the best solutions for astronomical problems without positively asserting that his theoretical solutions were founded in visible or demonstrable fact. However,

Newton's adherents often did not display the same caution, arguing for
the thoroughgoing solidity and self-evidence of Newton's methods and
findings, when, in his own estimation, Newton's achievements would be
better described as the simplest and most elegant explanations that had
been propounded up to that time rather than established fact.[67]

Newton and his writings exerted a magnetic power over the learned
of England, making them *want* to believe. As William Whewell would
later put it in his *History of the Inductive Sciences*, "The most active and
powerful minds at Cambridge became at once disciples and followers of
Newton." Fontenelle made a similar remark to the effect that the men
of learning in England "recognized [Newton] as their chief and their
master; no rebel would have dared to raise his head, not even a doubtful
note of praise would have been allowed." Whewell and Fontenelle advance their respective comments to demonstrate the compelling force of
Newton's mind. But they may also be read less generously as indications
that it was not just truth but also other forms of intellectual power and
attraction that carried the day in the learned world. After all, the first
individual to make a discovery (and much in the *Principia* had been
realized before) is not always the same individual who gets the attention
or credit for it.

A combination of forces cooperated in advancing Newton's career
and, more importantly, the discipline of physico-mathematics. Newton
attracted what the encyclopedist Ephraim Chambers called a "sect": "a
collective term, comprehending all such as follow the doctrines or opinions of some famous divine, or philosopher, &c ... At present, the *sects* of
philosophy are chiefly reducible to three; viz. the Cartesians, Peripatetics,
and Newtonians."[68] This sense that the Newtonians constituted a school
with its own binding doctrine came frequently to the fore in writings of
the age. In the texts of Newton's advocates, it was made clear that the
correctness of Newtonianism's philosophical positions needed to be seen
as progress that should supplant the stubbornly persistent but nonetheless outdated positions of earlier schools and sects – Aristotelianism and
Cartesianism.

Newton's supporters thus felt it necessary to defend him against charges
that he had hidden information in order to conceal his own faults. George
Pirrie, an Edinburgh teacher, devoted the preface to his 1720 *A Short
Treatise of the General Laws of Motion and the Centripetal Forces* to for-
tify Newton's reputation against the aforementioned Gordon's "most
cunning and subtil Piece of Sophistry that ever was formed on a Physico-
mathematical Subject," a veritable "cheat" on all readers. He follows in the

wake of John Ditton's 1705 *The General Laws of Nature and Motion*, which argues that charges of a misleading secrecy have an implicit moral fallacy. A man of Newton's lustre, of his generosity of soul, could never have been guilty of such a sin of selfishness and would have wanted his work disseminated as widely as possible. Ditton portrays a Newton who supports equal access to knowledge, who wants his work known to those not fortunate enough to have had his education:

> Man is bound to believe that the *Illustrious Author* design'd, what he was pleased to publish, shou'd be known; and that not to a few Persons only who fortunately had the Advantage of an Education; but to all whom Nature had qualified with good Reason, and their own Industry with Skill in Mathematics. To think less than this, is to suppose him capable of envying a Part of Mankind the Knowledge of his Discoveries, which wou'd be no small Affront to a Soul much less than his.[69]

Ditton's Newton is hardly the man who wrote book three of the *Principia*, hammering together mathematical fences to bar access to knowledge. Ditton tries to erase the preface to book three of the *Principia* by imagining a Newton who would endorse an epistemological egalitarianism, an egalitarianism he extends well beyond the learned world, even to the "vulgar." He thereby attributes to Newton an advocacy of Ditton's own work.

Ditton's justification takes a page from Protestant discourse in England, which had set itself up in opposition to the secrecy of knowledge associated with scholasticism and Catholicism. In so doing, he moves the debate over from one about mathematics to one about the use of vernacular languages:

> [S]ome People argue for keeping the Sacred Books in an unknown Tongue: But we pretend to a Protestant Liberty, at least with respect to our Philosophy. And methinks both in the one and the other Case; 'tis unreasonable that those that wou'd make a good Improvement; shou'd be kept in Darkness, for the Sake of them, that wou'd abuse their Light.[70]

This early statement of Enlightenment social philosophy plays up the connection between the freedom of access to sacred books in religion and the freedom of the broad population to have like access to advances in natural philosophy. It becomes for Ditton a matter of English national pride for Newtonianism to be available to those who could read their native language.

Another of Newton's contemporaries, mathematician John Keill, likewise saw problems with the disguising of knowledge while simultaneously acknowledging that such guises did much to secure the professional existence of those who hold onto that knowledge. He advanced his ambivalent position on the respective virtues and vices of professional privacy indirectly by projecting them, as Newton did, onto the early Greek philosophers. Such philosophers, "not being willing that their Opinions should be expos'd to the common People ... cast a Veil over them, by the means of Images and Hieroglyphics ... borrowed from Geometry and Arithmetick." This alleged practice of the ancients came with a high price tag for future philosophers, who could have trouble seeing through "the Disguises that they wrapped [their philosophy] up in."[71] As popularizer, Keill's function was to ensure that the same did not happen to Newtonian natural philosophy, although he does not fully follow through on this promise. That is, he does not offer specific exegeses of the *Principia*'s difficult parts, concentrating instead as the other popularizers did on its simpler and more visual elements.

IV. NEWTON'S MOVE TO THE OPTICKS

The story of the *Principia* is not the whole story of Newton's publishing career. Part of the shift from mathematical to experimental emphasis in the public perception of Newton *was* his own doing. The public/learned polarization traced here with regard to the *Principia* did not remain so pure with respect to his later *Opticks* (1704). The *Opticks*, based on his optical lectures of 1671–72, was written in English and had less difficult mathematical underpinnings. It did much to make Newton's ideas available to more readers by articulating a largely experimental science of color. However, historical accounts that represent the *Opticks* as a wholly experimental and thus generally accessible text overstate the shift in Newton's relationship to his audience. Newton himself may have decided to write a less-than-fully-mathematical account only when his attempts to provide a mathematical optics had at least partly failed.[72] In other words, *Opticks* may have marked for Newton a technical failure more than a thoroughgoing volte-face about public access to science. After all, he never considered the *Opticks* a finished work.

Newton's potential failure aside, the accessibility of much of the *Opticks*, which relies on a considerable amount of mathematical detail, was exaggerated not only by Newton's admirers but by Newton himself. Although the *Opticks* was, as Newton scholars have noted, "the most comprehensive public statement he ever made of his philosophy of science or of his conception of the experimental scientific method,"[73] its being written in English helped the perception of its availability without guaranteeing its full intelligibility. When his *Opticks* did appear in 1704, there was a strong market for popularizations of it, since neither his explanations nor his experiments were universally self-evident or immediately replicable by the generality of readers.

Perhaps what the publication of the *Opticks* ultimately demonstrates is that Newton eventually realized that publishing a book was fundamentally incompatible with the controlling of the ideas contained therein, and that if he were to publish, he needed to make certain gestures towards a readership (or have someone do this on his behalf) in order to secure his readers' cooperation in his text's reception. Even so, these conciliatory gestures were not wholly accepted by his fellow scientists. Newton's opponents certainly did not find its experimental proofs to be self-evident, even when they could successfully reproduce the experiments.[74] One of Newton's eighteenth-century defenders attributes the opposition to the *Opticks* to its deliberate contradiction of tradition, received opinion, and, sometimes, common sense. Newton attracted attacks because he had advanced "a doctrine so strange and contrary to all the received opinions about the nature of light" that it "could not be admitted" by "injudicious people that had imbibed other principles."[75] Newton's long resistance to publishing his optical research stemmed from his frustration with potential opposition. The slower acceptance of the *Opticks* as compared to the *Principia* may be precisely because fellow natural scientists expected to understand and then to reproduce the *Opticks'* experiments, without having the ability to do so because Newton had so abstracted them in his representations; whereas, the *Principia* did not give very many people the impression that they could reproduce it.

Newton's supporters triumphed over his opponents during the early years of the eighteenth century; opposition only helped fuel interest in and the spread of Newton's system. By the late 1730s, the Newtonian physics of the *Principia* and the *Opticks* had become a topic of general curiosity in England and abroad. Philosophers and poets lauded its virtues. The blend of admiration and practical demonstration fed and fed off an ever-increasing interest in Newtonianism. Newtonian physics had trickled far enough down that it was being produced for an audience that had little or no claim to being members of the learned world. The emergence of the divide between the doing of science and the popularization of it appears most evident in popularizations written specifically for women. Though it was a convention of popular texts to include "ladies" in their appeals to potential audiences, the books and pamphlets purportedly written for a specifically female audience underscore most prominently the division between education and popularization, between learning to *do* science and learning to *appreciate* or *admire* it.

V. NEWTON FOR THE LADIES, OR,
THE ROMANCE OF NEWTON

While the divide I have described crossed gender boundaries, the texts that specifically engaged gender as a trope for articulating the division between the two kinds of audiences for Newtonian physics made these boundaries most explicit as they defended or denied female readers access to Newtonian physics. Returning to the opposition of the learned and conversable worlds described in Chapter 2, this section turns to a collection of texts, unambiguously on the conversable side of the learned/conversable divide, that share a number of representational techniques, although they range over several different genres from books of lectures to periodicals to board games.[76] Collectively, they were meant for entertainment at a fairly great remove from the technical work of Newtonian physics. These user-friendly popularizations draw on and develop the narrative conventions of the philosophical dialogue, the conversational essay, and the romance. These texts participated in a cycle between creating public curiosity and responding to it, between creating a market and fulfilling it, in the process showing how readers could be made interested in and incorporated into science. Perhaps most importantly, these texts reveal how the popularizers' techniques of simplification and description could operate for an audience unversed in even the rudiments of science. These texts offer few promises that a reader could move from reading the texts to embarking on a scientific career; instead they often try expressly to prohibit such a movement.

This conversable mode of popularization emphasizes the division between the expert and the consumer. The authors of these works stress their belief that a reader who tends not to turn frequently to books of physics or metaphysics might convert her taste for lighter reading into an interest in natural philosophy. They explicitly prescribe the correspondence between knowledge and good taste and how to move from having a modicum of the former to exhibiting a moderate display of the latter.

The eighteenth-century association between taste and knowledge was frequently strongly gendered. The prolific Benjamin Martin promoted one of his many introductions to Newtonian philosophy by appealing to "any Gentleman or Lady, who is happy enough to have a Taste for Knowledge of the best Sort." Works such as Martin's use the cultivation of the faculty of taste as a way to entreat female readers. Eliza Haywood's *Female Spectator* provides some clues about the alliance between taste and science for readers of the "fair sex". On her account, taste is governed by the reasoning faculty: "nothing can be called a *true taste*, that is not regulated by *reason*, and which does not incline us to what will render us *better* and *wiser*."[77] Consequently, the exercise of the mind leads to the cultivation of the faculty of taste, making women not only wiser but more beautiful, erasing "whatever is a blemish in the mind." Coupling knowledge with beauty not only allows Haywood to cast the acquisition of knowledge as an avenue to wisdom and good taste, but also as an avenue to beauty: the knowledgeable woman is one in possession of a mind "brought nearer to what is lovely."[78] Haywood thereby domesticates the pursuit of learning, making it a female, moral good.

Haywood's addresses to a predominantly female audience sometimes argue and often imply that there are separate schemes for crafting and promoting periodicals meant for a general audience (of men and women), and an audience expressly delimited by gender. Thus natural philosophy written expressly for women would need to look different from natural philosophy for men. Addressing a female audience gave an author license to portray the pursuit of knowledge as a path to entertainment and self-improvement, fully compatible with fine taste, exquisite (mental) beauty, and the latest intellectual fashions.

In Book 15 of her collected *Female Spectator*, Haywood prints a letter by a correspondent who signs himself *Philo-Naturae* (though we cannot rule out Haywood's having written this letter herself) suggesting how women might go about stocking their minds with natural philosophy. With supreme gallantry, this writer begins by delimiting the range of most women's investigations into natural philosophy:

> I would not be thought to recommend to the ladies (for whose use I take your lucubrations to be chiefly intended) that severe and abstruse part [of natural philosophy] which would rob them of any portion of their gaiety: – on the contrary, I would not advise them to fill their heads with the propositions of an *Aldrovandus*, a *Malabranche*, or a *Newton*: – the ideas of those great men are not suited to every capacity; – they require a depth of learning, a strength of judgment, and a length of time to be ranged and digested, so as to render them either pleasing or beneficial.[79]

What the writer fails to mention is that most male readers were not up to the task of reading Aldrovandus, Malabranche, or Newton either. *Philo-Naturae* echoes the claim of all popularizers that a true mastery of these materials requires long and deep study, a process that they realize their audience may want to abridge because of limited time, limited desire, or limited mental capacities. Newton and his illustrious company are bodied forth as examples of that knowledge inaccessible to the untrained, the most prominent group of which is women. The writer softens the blow with a disclaimer that allows but nonetheless regrets a more assiduous study on the part of certain women, since it would isolate them in their closets, away from the men who cherish their presence:

Not that I presume to deny, but that there are some ladies every way qualified for the most arduous labour of the brain; but then I shall find little forgiveness from my own sex to persuade those enliveners of society to any thing which would deprive us of their company for any long time.[80]

The *Female Spectator* advocates a drawing room and a fireside science meant for entertainment and light learning. While this letter's author shies away from recommending physico-mathematics, or indeed much book study at all, he nevertheless suggests that without dabbling in this kind of learning, the mind can never be well-cultivated. The admiration of landscapes has its limits, the writer argues, if the admirer cannot also enter into some of the finer details of plant and animal life. Happily for Haywood's readers' sakes, a crash course is all that is necessary: "One summer is sufficient to make them perfect mistresses, and furnish a stock of beautiful ideas for their whole lives."[81]

The emphasis on botany and natural history over physics or chemistry for women bears itself out in records of women's involvement in eighteenth- and nineteenth-century science.[82] However, there were those who thought of women as part of the audience for the harder sciences and occasionally women who wrote about these sciences themselves. The texts that claimed they were for a female audience in particular increased the emphasis on diversion and entertainment present in some degree in many of the expositions of Newtonian physics and mathematics.

The text that brings Newtonian science most decidedly into the drawing room is a 1737 Italian popularization by the Conte Francesco Algarotti. His book, *Il newtonianismo per le dame*, was rapidly translated into English as *Sir Isaac Newton's Philosophy Explain'd for the Use of the Ladies in Six Dialogues on Light and Colours* (1739) by the English poet Elizabeth Carter.[83] Algarotti follows to some extent the model of Fontenelle's immensely popular seventeenth-century dialogues designed to explain ancient and modern philosophy. *Newtonianism for the Ladies* is presented as a witty flirtation between the author and the Marchioness of E – . In the course of their exchanges, the author gradually wins the Marchioness over to the cause of Newtonianism. Though there is a long European tradition of philosophical dialogues, these six conversations read more like a novel or a romance than a philosophical dialogue in the Socratic tradition. In them, coquetry mingles with science in an effort to make Newtonian natural philosophy attractive to Algarotti's readers.

The romance of *Newtonianismo per la dame* may have been in part a false front for reducing the risk of heresy charges in Italy.[84] In Britain, it would have been the most striking feature of the text, especially when contrasted with previous popularizations. Earlier English popularizations, when they posited a speaker at all, took the form of lectures, without the back-and-forth conversation necessary to Algarotti's instruction. To British eyes, *Newtonianism for the Ladies* would not have looked wholly unlike aspects of the Continental romances that had enjoyed considerable popularity in England. It might not be surprising to learn, then, that Carter's translation went through several issues and editions in the British Isles.[85]

Newtonianism for the Ladies is nothing if not clever. Algarotti sets up an analogy between physics and romance using "the principle of attraction," the chief innovation of Newton's mechanical philosophy and a very suggestive metaphor. In the sixth dialogue, for example, the author patiently explains how Newton has demonstrated that the force of attraction between two bodies diminishes according to the inverse square of their distance, or, in other words, the further apart two bodies are, the smaller their mutual attraction. His female interlocutor takes obvious advantage of this law, playing on the idea of attraction between bodies in her coy interpretation. She remarks,

Considering how very easily People are apt to forget those Objects in their Absence, which made the greatest Impressions upon their Mind when present, I cannot help thinking, said the Marchioness, that this Proportion in the Squares of the Distances of Places, or rather of Times, is observed even in Love. Thus after eight Days Absence, Love becomes sixty four Times less than it was the first Day, and according to this Proportion it must soon be entirely obliterated: I fancy there will be found, especially in the present Age, very few Experiments to the contrary.

The author responds:

I believe, said I, that both Sexes are included in this Theorem ... for eight Days are commonly enough to cure the most vehement Passion. You alone have Power to reverse this Theorem, and make the Remembrance of you ... instead of diminishing, increase.

The now scientifically inflamed Marchioness replies,

No! no! Gallantry must never destroy a Theorem. I ... shall think myself exceedingly happy if I have been able to establish any Thing fixed and constant, in an Affair so inconstant and wavering as Love.

Algarotti aims his racy dialogue particularly at women because he has "endeavoured to set Truth, accompanied with all that is necessary to demonstrate it, in a pleasing Light, and to render it agreeable to that Sex, which had rather *perceive* than *understand*." He tells us he has likewise eliminated all the trappings of mathematics because they would rob his text of its romantic, narrative aesthetic, making it look too scientific and thus unappealing. He replaces mathematics with a decidedly Horatian emphasis on delightfulness, striving to aid readers to "interest themselves in it as they would in a Composition for the Theatre. Is there any Thing (especially where Ladies are concerned) in which a Writer should omit any Endeavours to move the Heart?" Algarotti's appeal to the passions allies bodily and emotional with intellectual pleasures, shading subtly from one into the other in order to attract his readers. We need not naively subscribe to the view that all Algarotti's readers were women to see the particular rhetorical appeal of a pedagogical romance that placed a woman in the position of eager student.

Like Algarotti's text, many eighteenth-century popularizations aver that they will lead to an almost physical experience of the scientific sublime achieved through their appeal to the faculty of taste. Algarotti translates Newton's own writing into a vivid, descriptive theatrical metaphor, one that draws heavily on literature and the skills of literary perception. Algarotti imagines that his characters, as well as his readers, are steeped in English and Italian literature. He calls on this background in order to intensify his description of one of Newton's famed experiments:

Imagine yourself to be in a Place of *Milton's* visible Darkness, or rather still darker a Place, if you will be absolutely deprived of all Light; and this shall be our Theatre of Reasoning and Observations.

Let a Ray of the Sun enter in at a Hole made in the Window-Shutter, and let a Glass Prism be placed horizontally at this Hole, to refract the Ray in such a manner as to throw it upon a Wall opposite to the Window ... That Spectrum, or Image of the Sun, which the refracted Ray is of a figure nearly resembling a Fish at Cards, longer than it is broad, and varied with an infinite Number of Colours, among which the seven primary ones are distinguished and placed in a shining Order, one after another.

> *The jolly Peacock spreads not half so fair*
> *The Eyed Feathers of his pompous Train;*

Nor golden IRRIS *so bends in the Air,*
Her twenty-colour'd Bow through Clouds of Rain.[86]
...

I am very glad to find that *Tasso*, said the Marchioness, who had before a little transgressed against the Laws of Refraction for the sake of his *Armida*, has
amended his Fault, and is at present reconciled to Optics.

The concentrated focus and vivid detail of Algarotti's description borrows
from Newton's own early descriptions of his optical experiments.[87] But
Algarotti layers a literary context atop Newton's description, and he combines this description with a narrative plot line to compel readerly interest.
He thus makes the experiment feel more like a fictional narrative in its
careful attention to techniques for compelling its readers' interest. He acknowledges that it asks the reader to imagine, not literally recreate, these
experiments, thereby figuring the senses as not just portals to scientific
observations but also a means through which to envision the beauty of
these proceedings. The senses are scientific instruments, but they are also
aesthetic receptors.

Having gained their interest, Algarotti asks his readers to consider how
the shortcomings of literature, scientifically speaking, could be rectified by
a more precise idea about the nature of light and color. Here science comes
closest to *belles lettres*, just as the many appropriations of Newton in the
poetry of the day make literature come close to science. Popularization of
ideas through fiction was, of course, not new to the eighteenth century,
but its skillful application to Newtonian natural philosophy did much to
advance the Newtonian cause. Science was not just distraction, but in its
popular form presented as art – akin to an evening at the theater or a well-
manicured landscape.

Algarotti thematizes the process through which his readers become ini-
tiated into the understanding of Newtonian science, highlighting their
movement from the naïve acceptance of received wisdom to the realization of the truth of scientific achievement. In leading her along this path,
Algarotti's narrator first demands that his interlocutor, the Marchioness,
must be willing to accept information that contradicts what she currently
holds to be true, despite her resistance. Only after she has repeatedly shown
an ability to overcome her resistance may she be further inaugurated into
the mysteries of Newtonian science. Algarotti teases the Marchioness by
invoking mystical language, and he speaks only partly in jest:

I do not know whether I ought to introduce you any farther into the Sanctuary
of the *Newtonian* Philosophy. There are in this certain Mysteries still deeper and
more sublime than those to which you have already been admitted. You should

now invoke those Spirits of the first-born Sons of Light, the Guardians of those secret Truths which they imparted to our Philosopher, that they would suffer me to discover to you Things concealed from the Sight of Mortals, and deeply immersed in a gloomy Mist and the most profound Night. You must now entirely divest yourself of those few Remains of Profaneness which may still attend you. Tell me, Madam, what Courage do you feel for Truth?[88]

He calls for her to commit to Newtonian truth wholeheartedly, without reservation, though she has not *seen* a single experiment nor been taught a single mathematical process. Nonetheless, she answers that she feels the same courage in following Algarotti's Newtonianism "that a brave Soldier feels to follow his Captain wherever Valour calls. I follow you without Fear wherever Truth leads the Way." Her characterization of herself as soldier is apt: Algarotti demands that she abandon her previous methods for judging truth and accept on partial faith one he asserts in its place. The Marchioness, figured alternately as soldier and priestly initiate, learns to proceed according to a new set of rules, adopted on the basis of her trust in the new leader she follows, rather than believe her own instincts. Instead of teaching her mathematics, Algarotti demands that the Marchioness turn to her ability to feel ever-greater amounts of trust in her teacher. Belief fills in the holes in knowledge.

Alongside translations of Algarotti, England also had its own home-grown Newtonianism for women. From 1755 to 1765 the prolific popularizer Benjamin Martin published his monthly *General Magazine of Arts and Sciences, Philosophical, Philological, Mathematical, and Mechanical*. In 1759, he began issuing annual volumes that rearranged the contents of his monthly magazine into topical sections.[89] The first of these themed volumes he titled "The Young Gentleman and Lady's Philosophy in a Continued Survey of the Works of Nature and Art by way of Dialogue." In it, he collected his periodical's many fictional conversations on natural philosophy between a fictitious brother and sister. The premise of these exchanges is that the brother Cleonicus has just returned home from college, where he has been highly industrious in studying natural philosophy. At home, he regales the company with his bright and witty conversation, tempting his sister, Euphrosyne, into asking him to teach her more about such philosophy. Euphrosyne's curiosity is piqued because philosophy has been kept from her: hitherto it has been the province of the university and is still "a thing as yet unheard of in private Schools" for boys or girls.[90] Euphrosyne perhaps slightly exaggerates the unavailability of an education in natural science, but happily for Martin's readers, her brother is more than glad to oblige her entreaties for private instruction.

Before embarking on their philosophical journey, this pair discuss the appropriateness of natural philosophy for a female audience. While Euphrosyne laments that it seems too terribly "masculine" for a woman "to talk of Philosophy in Company," Cleonicus replies that

Philosophy is the darling Science of every Man of Sense, and is a peculiar Grace in the Fair Sex; and depend on it, Sister, it is now growing into a Fashion for the Ladies to study Philosophy and I am very glad to see a Sister of mine so well inclined to promote a Thing so laudable and honourable to her Sex.[91]

In other words, much as Haywood had done, Cleonicus emphasizes that science is all the rage around the tea table, and, unusually, it is a fashion that tends towards moral improvement. Also following the *Female Spectator*'s lead, Euphrosyne underscores the difficulty of natural philosophy in its pure form – as it exists on her father's library shelves. Its inapproachability, she explains, stems from the specialization of natural philosophers' languages and the technicality of their methods. Their terms of art and abstruse methods render them, as she says, "for the most Part, unintelligible."[92] Cleonicus replies,

Dear Sister, 'tis the Fate of that Science to be attended with some Difficulties in the Study of it; these are no otherways to be removed than by the Assistance of learned Men and Books. But those Parts of Philosophy which are perplexed with Schemes and Abstrusities, are generally such as may be either wholly neglected as useless to the generality of People; or else may be explained in a more easy and familiar Manner by Experiments. Fear not, *Euphrosyne*, the greatest and most delightful Part of this Science is within the Ladies Comprehension.

Cleonicus, much as Desaguliers and his fellows had done, calls attention to the expertise inevitably required to make any kind of progress in science. Achievement in natural philosophy cannot be detached from a lifetime of study. Anyone else can only hope to be a votary at its altar.

While couched in a tone of lament, Cleonicus' remarks take advantage of the gap between the expert and the lay person common to eighteenth-century popularizations of science. He promises that while the inner circle of natural philosophy is inaccessible to the untrained, with the help of a guide like him, Euphrosyne can deliberately close her eyes to much of it and see the rest simplified through experiments. She may concentrate on the aspects of science that produce delight and receive a limited level of instruction. Cleonicus is, though, somewhat more generous to his female audience than Haywood was; he presents his sister with an abridgement of the *Transactions of the Royal Society* so that she might make her way through the bits that she can understand in her leisure time.

Cleonicus makes an admirable teacher. Prompted by Euphrosyne's uninformed questions, he defines the terms of art of natural philosophy simply but without condescension. He has come home more socially adept than the college gentleman ridiculed in Richard Steele's *Guardian* papers, who cannot slough off his college pedantry and must be pulled aside by the author to be reminded to heed Aristotle's advice, "To think with the wise, but talk with the vulgar."[93] Martin's depiction of a gentle, blushing conversation between brother and sister verges at times on the romantic, even erotic, but we are asked by Euphrosyne to interpret their conversation Platonically, or at least on the model of Socrates or Aristotle, who spent time with students in close conversation amid beautiful landscapes. However, the sheen of innocence is hard for Martin to maintain, and the sexual tension implicit in this pedagogical relationship adds the cast of a romantic plot to these dialogues.

VI. THE PULL OF COMMON SENSE

As the initial reluctance of Algarotti's Marchioness to override the evidence of her senses suggests, the great enemy of Newtonian science was the clamor of common sense, whether it took the form of claims made by fellow natural philosophers or complaints advanced by those unschooled in any system of philosophy. In his highly insightful and very popular *Elements of Sir Isaac Newton's Philosophy*, translated into English in 1738, Voltaire begins his text with the assumptions Cartesian philosophy makes. He takes these preconceptions and explains, point by point, how they are disproved by the Newtonian system of the world. Voltaire notes that in René Descartes' philosophical system, many Cartesian propositions sound wholly plausible; they match up perfectly with common sense. However, they are also wrong. Seeing their errors, Voltaire explains, is not a question of thinking harder about the matter. Concentrated solitary thought will not get one any closer to the truth. Instead, one has to do experiments constructed to explain natural phenomena. Only then can the great pull of false intuition and common sense be counteracted.

Employing structures very similar to Voltaire's, many eighteenth-century works in natural philosophy open by refuting the theories that have preceded them. These sections are sometimes historical, beginning with the ancient Egyptians and proceeding through the age's straw man, Descartes. For example, John Keill's *An Introduction to Natural Philosophy: Or, Philosophical Lectures Read in the University of Oxford, Anno. Dom. 1700* begins with a triumphant historical narrative, showing how the

Newtonian system has been generated out of the strengths of the previous ages of science – from Archimedes through the early experimentalists – while dismissing their respective weaknesses.[94]

The counterintuitive nature of physics could have been an obstacle to its spread. In the present day, we often are not aware of how we come to accept such counterintuitive notions because they are typically handled when we are young by the process of formal education. Contemporary studies on physics education call books that confront students' common-sense ideas and replace them with scientifically correct theories "refutational texts." Refutational texts begin by representing the standard intuitive or received notions about mechanical processes and refute them point by point by showing how current science explains these same processes.[95] Though the term is relatively new, this method of teaching physics (which itself appropriates the centuries-old Socratic method) has been around in physics teaching at least since the eighteenth century. Indeed, in his "History of Astronomy," Adam Smith explains that the central problem for natural philosophers in spreading their ideas lies in "overcom[ing] the prejudices of sense [and] education," and that these philosophers require special techniques for surmounting such obstacles.[96] Newton's eighteenth-century expositors had determined that it was a particularly effective educational or psychological technique to acknowledge and subsequently confront and expose the flaws of common sense instead of immediately embarking on their own counterintuitive explanations as if they would be readily accepted by readers.

The more narrative of the popularizations addressed here generate their plots out of the tension between the reader's received wisdom (whether it be common sense or Cartesian philosophy) and the truth of Newtonian natural philosophy. The reader, or, in the case of the dialogues, the naïve interlocutor, is gradually led from relying on her mistaken common sense towards believing in a Newtonian experimental philosophy. These texts depend on assuming a resistance in their audience that can be overcome by contradicting their received wisdom. In some of their most captivating moments, these texts perform the same Socratic magic as many a compelling story or dialogue: they construct their plots so that they surprise their audiences and reverse their expectations.

Such texts often begin with cases that their readers will go along with without considerable explanation in order to gain readerly trust before moving on to increasingly counterintuitive theories. For example, the ingenuous Euphrosyne has difficulty understanding how the earth can revolve around the sun without its occupants seeing or feeling the motion.

To show her that her senses (and her common sense) can easily deceive her, her brother Cleonicus takes her to the local miller's. He then asks her to stand on the rotating mill. As the mill turns around, Euphrosyne has the illusion that she's standing still and that the stationary parts around her are moving. She is thus led by not-so-subtle analogy into the knowledge that the sun can move around the earth while the inhabitants of the earth perceive that the sun moves around them. Martin then moves from this elementary case to increasingly more complicated ones that challenge received wisdom to increasingly great degrees.

J. Newbery follows much the same procedure in his duodecimo book on natural philosophy for children, charmingly titled *The Newtonian System of Philosophy Adapted to the Capacities of Young Gentlemen and Ladies, and Familiarized and Made Entertaining by Objects with which they are Intimately Acquainted: Being the Substance of Six Lectures read to the Lilliputian Society.* The Lilliputian Society is a fictional group of boys and girls taught by a precocious young natural philosopher, Master Tom Telescope. He wants to replace card playing, this most pernicious of entertainments, with a "diversion" that will serve the children better. Master Tom leads the children from the card tables to a more wholesome pastime: natural philosophy. He adverts that learning natural philosophy as recreation ultimately has the same moral and intellectual function as acquiring like knowledge through "serious and elaborate study."[97] Though he later suggests that this is not so for the more serious student, for the moment all that is "abstruse and difficult" will be deferred for future study.[98]

Felicitously, Tom Telescope has a Socratic victim in his crowd, the naughty Tom Wilson. The urges of Wilson's common sense are too strong to be subdued by the dictates of good behavior. He protests against Master Tom's counterintuitive lectures on mechanics. In the lesson on inertia, Wilson bursts out in laughter when told that a top would continue to spin forever were it not for friction. He expostulates with Tom Telescope, "I know by daily experience that they drop, of themselves, without being touched by any body."[99] Young Wilson is duly chastised and treated to an explanation of how the force of friction will ultimately slow down the top. Wilson's impertinent antics are gradually subdued as his recognition of Tom Telescope's expertise deepens, and he begins "to consider himself as a fool in comparison of our Philosopher."[100] Wilson's shame in recognizing himself as a fool stands in for the reader's own feeling that his resistance to Tom Telescope's truth is melting away as Tom's authority expands.

These texts draw the reader through a counterintuitive process, in an effort to overcome what Adam Smith called "the natural prejudices of sense." Their success hinges on the ability to demonstrate a series of basic principles that allow the student or the audience to trust that the Newtonian system does indeed fit together, in the absence of the ability to understand a full mathematical proof.

VII. PARTING WORDS

[T]he Marquis de l'Hôpital ... used to ask the English who visited him, *Does Mr. Newton eat, or drink, or sleep like other men? I represent him to myself as a genius, an intelligence [e]ntirely disengaged from matter ...*
This work seemed to be the production of a genius or a celestial intelligence rather than of a man.
– Thomas Birch, "Sir Isaac Newton," in *A General Dictionary* (1738)

The image of Newton as a great man of his time was carefully drawn by his followers, admirers, and popularizers, and this portrait of Newton served a particular end: it was a way to gain public acceptance of scientific work that was often difficult and counterintuitive. By imagining Newton as an intelligence infinitely far above and wholly divorced from common understanding, his promoters could underscore the gap between Newton's theories and the ability of their audiences to understand. The practice of representing Newton's discoveries as, in the words of one expositor, "the works of a Genius rather divine than human," served a specific, political program: Newton's supporters and those who profited from his work needed to generate trust in their audiences for a system whose results were only partly visible to them, and even when they were visible, often ran up against common-sense views of the world.[101]

The result was not to keep a lay public entirely or permanently out of physics but to place emphasis on the gap between the expert and the audience. Only through the expert could novices acquire specific skills, in order that, if these novices persisted, they could themselves hope to achieve a degree of expertise. In the gap between expertise and lay knowledge dwelled both the physical demonstration of mathematical principles and a good deal of trust.

One of the more extreme (and thus illustrative) statements of such a reliance on trust came in a late-century popularization written by Margaret Bryan, who ran her own school for girls and published her lectures on natural science for her female pupils. She contends that mathematicians and astronomers fulfill their professional function by knowing in intimate

mathematical detail the characteristics of the heavenly bodies and the refraction indices of light. As long as some of their predictions can be shown
through observation, then lesser students of the science ought to take the
rest on faith in the experts. After all, such advanced mathematics

do not come within the sphere of knowledge I wish to conduct my pupils into,
being unnecessary to their peculiar province in life to comprehend all the phenomena they prove; more especially as we are furnished with the result of them
all, which we are enabled to apply to our [e]ntire satisfaction. The study of mathematics would be a misapplication of your time, which might be justly attributed to vanity and ostentation, and be considered unbecoming your character
as females, by employing that time which is more usefully occupied in pursuits
adapted to your situation in society, and as the validity of astronomical com-
putation may be proved by those instruments I have provided, aided by your
reason.[102]

Audiences not explicitly gendered female were not subject to such strong
authorial claims about their "situation in society" and the impropriety
of having advanced technical skills. In less drastic ways, however, most
popularizers, regardless of the audience specified, said or implied that
a lack of desire, ability, or access to advanced mathematical education
meant that male readers were likewise permanently limited in their access
to Newtonian physics and needed to make the same leap of faith.

I have been arguing here, *contra* much recent work on the popularization of Newtonian science, that physics' success in gaining this recognition as the most exact method of describing and explaining the world
depended on the early emergence of a gap between those who could learn
to participate in these mathematical disciplines and those who could only
be taught to admire and appreciate the hard sciences at a great remove.[103]
This divide sliced between those scientists and mathematicians invited in
to the inner, mathematical sanctum of Newtonian physics and those who
were merely asked to delight in the science from a polite distance but who
could never directly contribute to its advancement. This separation of intellectual powers is writ large across Newton's own writing, as well as that
of his many followers and popularizers. Science-for-tea-table-pleasure and
science-for-the-advancement-of-learning were treated as two very different
species of knowledge.

This chapter also runs against conventional wisdom in Newton studies in that it emphasizes that these popularizations – dependent as they
were on so-called real-world applications of Newtonian physics – generally depended not at all on Newtonian physics. As Peter Dear notes, it is
not at all clear that engineering feats are proof of scientific theories: "the

history of science shows time and again [that] it is sometimes unclear that the world even contains the natural objects referred to by the theory supposedly being 'applied.'"[104] Further, most of the practical problems solved in the popularizations that were attributed to the insights of Newtonian physics and mathematics could be – and had been – solved with classical mathematics; Newton's theories had little to do with them except as a force for galvanizing interest in the subject more generally.

Indeed, most eighteenth-century popularizations of Newtonian physics perform a function similar to the modern popular science magazine or science museum – they implicitly or explicitly argue that a side effect of the degree of specialization of modern science is that the public is placed in the role of spectator rather than participant. The modern popularizer of science reports on science and scientists, so that the spectator can learn *about* science – at a remove.

CHAPTER 4

Philosophy's Place Between
Science and Literature

In his *History of England,* David Hume devotes a short eulogistic paragraph to Isaac Newton:

In Newton this island may boast of having produced the greatest and rarest genius that ever arose for the ornament and instruction of the species . . . From modesty, ignorant of his superiority above the rest of mankind; and thence, *less careful to accommodate his reasonings to common apprehensions: More anxious to merit than acquire fame: He was from these causes long unknown to the world; but his reputation at last broke out with a lustre, which scarcely any writer, during his own lifetime, had ever before attained.*[1]

Though the two men never met, the Newton that Hume portrays resembles no one so much as Hume himself, or at least the way he would later represent himself in his deathbed autobiography, *My Own Life.* In it, Hume pictures himself as a man who, like Newton, refuses to bow to "common apprehensions" in pursuing his work, waiting patiently for his fame to catch up with his merit. Hume even describes himself using the same metaphor of the delayed, feverish reputation he had used to portray Newton: "I see many symptoms of my literary reputation's breaking out at last with additional lustre."[2] Despite the correspondence in Hume's descriptions, however, neither their professional lives nor the reception histories of their books followed such parallel tracks. Hume ultimately became known for pandering to popular taste, deliberately forsaking studies too difficult for a general reader to understand.

Unlike the *Principia*'s author, Hume came to foster the belief that a popular and a scholarly work could be coextensive, that a single book could both advance a discipline and be readable by a broad audience. This widely shared and perhaps flawed assumption directed both the tenor and the content of moral philosophy in England for the remainder of the eighteenth century. If the previous chapter told a success story about a discipline (physics) that partitioned itself off from a public audience and then gave that public a limited role in ratifying and appreciating its work, this chapter shows what happened to a discipline (philosophy) that refused to put in place that same insulating divide between professional and public readerships. The insistence that a public audience be able to read productions within the field of moral philosophy contributed to its divergence in practice and in public perception from more scientific fields, such as physics, which continued to respect a distinction between expert and lay readers. My study of this divide between the way physicists and metaphysicians came to regard their relationship with their audiences demonstrates that while some of the distinctions among the ways scholarly fields present their work are axiomatic, arising from fundamental differences in the objects of study, more of them than we might assume are conventional, developing under specific social, cultural, and institutional pressures.

The purpose of this chapter is not to repeat Hume's own story of the transformation of his career from one in which he rejected abstruse philosophy in favor of a more accessible means of philosophizing. Rather, this chapter revisits Hume's own narrative of his career, which generations of readers have often taken at face value, in order to show how and why Hume came to the assumptions that he did. In so doing, this chapter unsettles the belief that the turn that moral philosophy took in eighteenth-century England was natural or inevitable. My method for raising these questions depends on expanding the archive of materials that contextualize these questions. In particular, I examine the reviewing journals of the period, including both articles about Hume and those not about him, in an effort to establish more concretely the culture's standards for philosophical prose. When read in this context, the work of Hume and later philosophers of the British eighteenth century takes on a new cast, one that bespeaks a strategy and a relationship to audience that is very different from that adopted by Newton and his popularizers.

For modern audiences, Newton's and Hume's respective fields of study may seem to have little in common. Physics and philosophy now fall under separate university faculties, they use unrelated methodologies, and their objects of study differ markedly. We think of the people who study physics and the people who study philosophy as constitutionally different, formed from different molds, born under different signs. However, the gap between their two fields was not so wide in the eighteenth century. I show that at the outset of his career, Hume saw strong parallels between a career as a moral philosopher and one as natural philosopher. In response to the mistakes he perceived in earlier systems, David Hume began life as a professional philosopher looking for a scientific method that would allow him to achieve a revolution in metaphysics analogous to the one Newton achieved in physics.

In the years when Hume began writing, both natural and moral philosophies were widely considered "sciences," because both focused on what the encyclopedist Ephraim Chambers called the "perception of the intrinsic characters of habitudes of sensible objects."³ Natural philosophy and mathematics concentrated on the quantities, powers, and properties of sensible objects. Metaphysics and moral philosophy regarded abstract qualities of these same objects and their relation to human happiness.⁴ Hume's philosophy fell into the latter category; it aimed to delimit the fundamental powers of the human mind and describe their operation in moral decision-making. Efforts in moral philosophy and epistemology thus could fall well within standard eighteenth-century definitions of a science and could be subject to the scientific method. Hume believed this strongly: to underscore his association with Newton's scientific method, Hume subtitled the *Treatise* "an attempt to introduce the experimental method of reasoning into moral subjects."⁵ He proceeded on the belief that reasoning in morality could be as scientific – as systematic – as reasoning in mathematics.⁶ He wanted not only to promulgate a new theory, but also to renovate entirely the way philosophy was done in Great Britain. And Hume, like John Locke before him and Thomas Reid after him, believed physics was *the* model for reshaping all the disciplines of philosophy.

Though Hume did not proceed mathematically, he did write a treatise in many ways as technical and specialized as Newton's *Principia*. However, while Newton recognized that the advanced knowledge required to read his book would bar entry to many readers, Hume did not share this belief. Instead, Hume hoped that the general reader would find his or her way to the *Treatise* and teach him or herself to understand it.⁷ When Hume perceived that his *Treatise* had failed to find the appreciative audience he imagined, he reevaluated his philosophical project. After drawing attention to himself by publishing essays modeled on the popular periodical, Hume took it upon himself to become his own popularizer – adopting a more essayistic language and publishing in 1748 the more accessible and considerably shorter *Enquiry Concerning Human Understanding* and in 1751 the *Enquiry Concerning the Principles of Morals*.⁸ These shorter works abandon the systematic ambitions of the earlier *Treatise*; they do small justice to its program.

Hume never returned from his more conversable styles to a technical philosophical undertaking. Late in his career Hume disavowed his early *Treatise* altogether. He did not want it included in the posthumous edition of his works. That is, Hume insisted that the technical *Treatise* did not have a place in modern moral philosophy or epistemology and could be replaced entirely by more popular forms. To renew the contrast with Newtonian science, we should note that even after he had written more accessible works on physics and on other fields, Newton never disavowed the *Principia*. Indeed, it came to be revered as the pure repository of his ideas, before their technical content had been thinned out through popular presentations. Ultimately, I argue, Hume's decision to popularize his own work and his abandonment of the gap between the expert and the general reader contributed as much to the modern division between physics and philosophy, and by extension between the sciences and humanities, as any difference in the two fields' subject matter.

Hume's distaste for his early writings was widely shared in the eighteenth century – his contemporaries writing moral philosophy in England likewise urged that the discipline of philosophy should become one based on common sense that would be easily understood by a broad readership, rather than one derived from technical study that would have meaning to only a few.[9] Discussions of the development of Hume's philosophy have, from the eighteenth century forward, been bound up with considerations of his initially negative reception history. This trend takes its cue from Hume himself, whose autobiography concerns itself more with the popular successes of his books than with his life story. While committing this autobiography to paper, Hume was also drafting his last will and testament, which specified that the autobiography generally referred to as *My Own Life* be prefaced to all future editions of his work because he wanted his philosophy read through his own account of it. The limited view the *Life* gives of Hume as a self-constructed man of letters gives an incomplete and distorted picture of his philosophy and its development.[10] Curiously, historians, philosophers, and other readers of Hume have not often pressed hard on Hume's narrative of his publication history. How could Hume have made the "mistake" of believing the *Treatise* would appeal to an audience of more than a few experts? And how did Hume decide that style is what prevented the *Treatise's* success?

Hume's move away from specialized philosophy and its connection to literary style can be better understood by supplementing his own commentary on his career with the work of his reviewers and other writers concerned with similar questions. Periodical reviewing was a crucial factor in the development of British letters in the eighteenth century. Hume's own notion of his readership was developed in a print conversation with articles in learned journals, reviews in the popular press, and the writings of other philosophers. Hume's reviewers and critics picked up on Hume's own struggle over readership in their commentary and responded to it. In turn, his later writings indicate that he was a good reader of criticism leveled against him, modifying his writing accordingly.

Hume was not alone in his regard for reviews; philosophers throughout the century were explicitly concerned with who their readers were and how to reach them. Philosophers were taken with the possibilities of print culture and the wide sphere of readers it could reach. Hume's publishing career and those of his contemporaries were extended negotiations with print culture and its institutions; reading Hume in the larger context of eighteenth-century print culture and the pressures these circumstances exerted on the liberal arts and sciences allows us a fuller picture of the interaction between technical subjects, markets, and reading behavior in the humanities. Comparing Hume's career and Newton's shows how the emerging gap between physics and philosophy helped establish the difference between the scientific and the literary.

I. THE REVIEWING JOURNALS

Hume's sense that a wide audience should be able to read philosophical productions was not formed in a vacuum. The sense that more than a few readers, including readers outside academic settings, should be able to pick up, understand, and buy a book of philosophy, was perhaps best articulated by the reviewing journals in the first half of the eighteenth century. Though much attention has been given to the rise of regular reviewing in the 1750s with the advent of the *Monthly Review* and *Critical Review*, little has been written about earlier reviewing journals in England. The reason for this neglect is easily explained: the predecessor journals to the *Monthly* and the *Critical* did not generally turn attention to novels, drama, and poetry and have thus been of less interest to historians of literature. What little we know about these journals tends to come from the occasional, individual review of a book – such as Hume's *Treatise* – that continues to attract the notice of modern scholars. Historians of the *Monthly* and *Critical* have also tended to misunderstand the goals of the predecessor reviewing journals because they interpret them according to our current understanding of what a "learned" publication would be. For example, one recent scholar of the *Monthly* and *Critical* downplays the significance of the *Memoirs of Literature* (1710–14, 1717) and *The History of the Works of the Learned* (1735–43) in shaping the market for books and creating a role that the *Monthly* and *Critical* would come to inhabit. She notes that these predecessor journals addressed themselves to "erudite works with small potential audiences."[11] While it is true that these earlier journals did not pretend to cover every work printed in English, the statement that they aimed to speak to a "small potential audience" is misleading because it relies on our current, very narrow sense of what "learned" means, not on an investigation into these journals.

To study these journals is to return to a moment when "literature" might still include most works of science or philosophy. The early journals that called themselves "learned" or "literary" aimed to identify significant literature published in the eighteenth century, not to review scholarly publications for tightly defined, coterie audiences. Taken as a genre, these earlier monthly or weekly publications served as important a function as later periodicals, in both tracking and shaping the development of English letters. These early review journals articulated and gave examples of what constituted the "literary" during the first half of the eighteenth century. As such, they can provide us with crucial information about the vexed category "literature" and the "literary" before textual criticism took the form in which we now know it.

Frank Donoghue has shown that reviewing affected the reception and the writing of novels in the 1760s. Earlier journals such as *The Literary Magazine* also had their influence on both writers and readers in the first half of the century.[12] Instead of addressing themselves strictly to those who knew the learned languages, these journals targeted an audience that wanted to acquire literature, to seem familiar with the best recent books. While they do not address the most popular forms of literature, these journals are nonetheless market-minded; they express little interest in coterie publications for academic or otherwise narrowly expert audiences. Quite the opposite is true, in fact: they tend to rail against books too hard for a broadly educated reader to understand, and they heap praise on authors who make learned topics clear and useful to such readers.

These journals' need to reach a wider audience had much to do with the circumstances of publication: their success was contingent on their sales. And some of these journals did prosper for a time; their lifespans ranged from a few years to a couple of decades. Reviews had been regularly published in England, beginning in 1699 in *The History of the Works of the Learned*, a monthly journal edited by "Mr. Redpath" that lasted until 1712.[13] Michel de la Rouche edited the weekly *Memoirs of Literature* (1710–1714; 1717). The next major forum for reviews came in 1728 when Andrew Reid began editing the *Present State of the Republic of Letters*. In 1735, *The Literary Magazine; or, Select British Library* began to appear in monthly installments under the editorship of Ephraim Chambers, the author of the *Cyclopaedia*. In 1736, *The Literary Magazine* added the subtitle "The History of the Works of the Learned," borrowed from the aforementioned 1699–1712 journal of the same name. From 1737 to its termination in 1743, this journal merged with the *Present State of the Republic of Letters* and was published by their united proprietors under the title *The History of the Works of the Learned*.

The close connection between the "literary" and "learned" in *The Literary Magazine* and its successor is striking. The stated mission of the publication, beginning in 1735, was to give "an early, accurate, and impartial account of the most noted and valuable books and pamphlets publish'd in Great Britain and Ireland" and "also, a succinct detail of such controversies as arise in the Republic of Letters; a View of the State of Learning; and a Catalogue of the best Books published in Foreign parts." It embarked on such a plan because, its 1735 preface noted, the size of the "British Empire" meant that its citizens were scattered in the four corners of the earth, far from "those Marts of Learning" where books were published. Like Addison's *Spectator* No. 529, the preface considers the commercial distribution of print matter – learned or not – central to its reception; this journal aims to overcome the limited knowledge readers in remote parts would have of new books by bringing them to its readers' attention and digesting them on its readers' behalf. The journal does not purport, as the *Monthly* and *Critical* would later do, to review *all* books published in English or in England, only those it deemed necessary to bring to the attention of "those addicted to study," and it wanted likewise to appeal to those who read casually for "agreeable and useful amusement," "people of much leisure, who read *pour tuer le temps*."[14]

What, then, does "literary" mean for these journals? For the *Literary Magazine* and *The History of the Works of the Learned*, both "literary" and "learned" were defined in relation to the study of books recently written in modern languages. These journals tend to elide "learned" and "literary," making them synonyms while simultaneously leaving out very technical kinds of mathematical learning and any works published in Latin. The "learned" does not include books written in what they call the "learned languages," unless they have been translated into English or French. They have restricted their journals to what at least one article calls "polite learning," which does not encompass the whole of the republic of letters because it leaves out disciplinary writings meant for fellow experts.[15]

As both the initial subtitle of the journal, *The Select British Library*, and its later appellation, *The History of the Works of the Learned*, reveal, the publishers imagined their publication not as an ephemeral and therefore disposable periodical, but rather as a work meant to be kept as a historical record, or library catalogue, of literature published in English. In the preface to the December 1735 installment, the editors compare their goals to those of the *Historical Library* of Diodorus of Sicily and the ninth-century book *The Library* by Photius, in which these authors recorded and commented on the important writing of their day. They identify their more recent forbears as the editors and publishers of the French *Journal des Sçavans* and its imitators across Europe. The *Literary Magazine* notes that the journal writer needs to take on the task of the critic and the guidelines that inform criticism, "decency, good manners, probity and religion," while at the same time avoiding the "air and language of a censor or judge," tasks that remain the "undoubted right of the *Public* ... the only sover[e]ign judge of the reputation of an author, and the merit of his compositions." These standards focus on the polite rather than the scholarly aspects of writing; for them, "literature" meant writing for a broadly educated public that could be deemed useful for a generality of readers and that observed certain stylistic mores. These twinned values – usefulness and an elegant prose style – figure prominently in the magazine and define the category of polite learning, or literature, for this journal.

The journal aspired to serve a profitable function, namely to tell the general reader what he or she needed to read in order to appear "learned." The *Literary Magazine* served the desire that Tobias Smollett's ramble novel *Peregrine Pickle* suggests every member of a conversable company has, to claim that he or she is likewise learned. Throughout its run, the journal reviews or comments on several books that also support this desire, books which try to overcome the "discouragement to learning" caused by the seeming "Impossibility of making any considerable Progress in Knowledge, without a constant and laborious Attendance upon Study" when there is so much to know.[16] One of the works under examination in 1739, John Boswell's *A Method of Study; or An Useful Library*, breaks down knowledge into its chief branches, which ramify into a series of basic texts that the would-be learned should know in order to overcome "the Difficulties of Learning."[17] The idea of a "useful library" raised here and in the preface to the journal's inaugural issue pops up throughout the journal's eight-year run, and it predates the notion of a literary, non-biblical canon. A "library" was not always a physical collection of books, but often signified a catalog or list of books, with which a member of polite society should be familiar. "Library" in this sense went hand-in-hand with a conception of "literature" as the learning that a member of polite society should possess.

A survey of the works reviewed reveals much about the kinds of books these journals considered literary and the ways in which they embodied the qualities of usefulness and readability (see Figure 1). In 1735, approximately one third of the works discussed at length were biographies, memoirs, or histories in English or in French, works that were generally praised for their lucidity. Another fifteen per cent were either English translations of ancient writings or commentaries on them or their authors, emphasizing the utility of good English translations and expositions of the ancients. The number of reviews of historical and biographical materials remained fairly constant over the 1730s, as did the number of articles on natural philosophy. Three of the forty-six books reviewed in 1735 were recent volumes of the *Philosophical Transactions of the Royal Society*; two more articles treated popularizations of science or science textbooks. These journals' reviewers avoided commenting on the most specialized articles in the *Philosophical Transactions*, noting that their contents could not be adequately abridged in the short space of a magazine article. They also neglected to review any works of science or mathematics that were not aimed at the broadest of audiences. This absence is striking because it points to the gap between the "literary" and the technical; it deems "literary" only those works of natural philosophy and mathematics that an inexpert reader could enjoy reading, not ones that advanced these disciplines. The review articles emphasize the verbal qualities of the scientific works they review, stressing how their prose style aids readers' comprehension.

Works on philosophy and morality figured almost not at all in this first issue, though they were more significantly represented in the succeeding issues. In 1737 eight philosophy books were discussed out of a total of roughly fifty-three books, and six articles commented on new works of theology or morality. The numbers are similar for 1739, the year Hume's *Treatise* was reviewed.

What, then, were the qualities that these reviewers were looking for in such writing? We might take an article from December 1739 as a characteristic example, a review of *An Essay towards demonstrating the Immateriality and Free-Agency of the Soul*. This pamphlet's author, identified by the journal as Samuel Strutt, was also the writer of the well-known attack on Hume's *Treatise* in the journal *Common Sense*.[18] The fact that *The Works of the Learned* approved of Strutt's writing and not Hume's is not incidental: Strutt's critical and philosophical agenda aligns fairly neatly with that of *The Works of the Learned*,[19] which remarks that Strutt has "handled his

Kinds of works reviewed/years	1735	1737	1739	1741	1743
Histories of countries, regions, and institutions	9	6	3	2	4
Biographies, memoirs of modern persons	7	3	2	1	2
Travel narratives	2	1	2	0	1
Translations of ancient writers	3	0	1	1	1
Commentaries on ancient writers and/or their writings	4	7	2	1	0
Grammars/dictionaries/histories of ancient or modern languages	4	1	0	0	0
Biblical history and commentary	5	3	2	5	4
Accounts of church politics	1	0	1	0	0
Works of religious instruction, morality, theology, sermons	1	5	0	4	3
Moral philosophy, logic, epistemology, metaphysics	0	8	2	2	2
Extracts/summaries of the Philosophical Transactions of the Royal Society	3	2	1	0	0
Popularizations of science/science textbooks	2	4	6	2	2
Medicine	3	5	2	2	0
Miscellaneous collected works; miscellanies in verse and prose; collected letters	2	4	2	1	4[i]
Calls for subscribers to writings in Latin, French, or English	0	0	4	0	0
Instruction on how to become learned	0	1	1	0	1
Legal commentary	0	1	0	0	0
Fictional correspondences	0	0	1	0	0
Epic poem on the invention, science, and progress of music	0	0	0	0	1
Constitution of the Freemasons	0	0	1	0	0
Geography	0	0	0	1	1
Identifying antique medals	0	0	0	1	0
Total works reviewed	46	51	33	23	26

[i] One of these works, *Acta Germanica; or, the Literary Memoirs of Germany*, might also be classed in part under science textbooks. The June 1743 issue of this journal describes the *Acta* as collected work of "what is deemed most valuable and curious in the several literary Memoirs published in different parts of *Germany* and the *North*," translated into English. It ranges over the subjects "Agriculture, Alchemy, Algebra, Anatomy, Animal Oeconomy, Philology, Geography, Gnomonics, Hydraulics, Hydrology, Levelling, Literary History, Logic, Manufactures, Mechanicks, Medicine, Metallurgy, Meteorology, Mineralogy, Opticks, Pneumatics, Pneumatology, Surgery, Zoology."

Figure 1 An anatomy of the kinds of books reviewed in the *Literary Magazine, or, the History of the Works of the Learned*. Single works that are the subject of more than one article are only counted the first time they appear.

Subject with a Perspicuity that one does not very often find in Treatises of this Nature. We can every-where understand him, if we cannot in all Things agree with him; tho' I think he is throughout a rational as well as a clear Writer." The reviewers remark often on the plainness of his exposition and of his illustrations, readily accepting Strutt as their "teacher" on the subjects he addresses. Strutt does not challenge received wisdom about the operations of the soul and its free will; rather, he gives a straightforward and clearly worded defense of standard philosophical positions, ultimately derived from Plato and Aristotle, on ideas, existence, matter, and motion, all of which leads to a reiteration of the doctrine of free will and the immateriality of the spirit derivative of Descartes. The *Essay's* strongest quality is the ease with which it conveys standard philosophical notions to the mind of the reader, making these ideas intelligible and usable. Strutt and his reviewers share the guidelines for philosophical writing that Hugh Blair would later explain in his *Lectures on Rhetoric and Belles Lettres*, namely that philosophical writing must above all be perspicuous. In contrast, they find difficult vocabulary and language distracting, complaining about books that indulge overmuch in technical vocabularies, which cause the general reader to "lose sight of the subject," wishing that such "oracles" could be delivered "in plainer phrase."[20]

As we shall see, it is with these standards of plain phrase and the appeals to utility in mind that the journal would later review and consequently reject Hume's *Treatise* as too difficult, too technical, and not immediately useful. This standard of "literary," too, comes to dominate English philosophy in the eighteenth century at the expense of a more scientific or technical method of representation. When they are pitted against one another, the ideal of the man of letters writing in a literary style triumphs over and ultimately sacrifices the ideal of a scientific philosophy.

In journals such as *Works*, we see again the contradiction of plans for general enlightenment in eighteenth-century England. The journal celebrated learning but insisted on linking it to the literary value of accessible prose style. Hume's professional life enacted the struggle between the enlightenment goal of sharing knowledge widely with a reading public and the desire to generate advanced knowledge that, by definition, only a few could understand. His career is thus largely defined by these two opposed demands, which we might call the literary and the scientific, demands that Hume and his critics sometimes acknowledged as mutually incompatible but more frequently tried to reconcile with varying degrees of success. In this regard, he is a central exemplar of the enlightenment in Great Britain.

II. FINDING AN AUDIENCE: THE *TREATISE*
AND ITS REVIEWS

The *Treatise* is a vast book that asks an equally prodigious question: through what mental processes do humans come to understand and to interact with their world? We need not believe that Hume found the best answers to these questions to recognize the importance of the *Treatise* in the modern discipline of philosophy. What matters instead is that philosophers in the generations after Hume found the *Treatise* groundbreaking and considered it foundational both to their own work and to their disciplinary field. Immanuel Kant, who agreed only in part with Hume, wrote in his *Prolegomena to Any Future Metaphysics*, "I openly confess my recollection of David Hume was the very thing which many years ago first interrupted my dogmatic slumber and gave my investigations in the field of speculative philosophy a quite new direction."[21] The *Treatise* exposed gaps in ways of thinking – philosophical and otherwise – about the world. After Hume, philosophers needed to account for those rifts. Even those who set themselves in opposition to Hume and his approach have pointed out that without the *Treatise*, they could not have formulated their own questions or their own answers in the ways they did.

Given the scope of Hume's project and his eventual influence, a modern reader would be loath to expect that his proposed scientific investigation into human nature would be dispatched effortlessly. Nonetheless, despite the fact that Hume knew enough to warn his readers that his methods and results would not be obvious or easy, he wrote at first with only a limited awareness that his work was not for all markets. Before the eighteenth century in Europe, the distinction between philosophical works meant for popular consumption and those intended for fellow philosophers and students was often well marked. Aristotle's writings, for example, were divided between popular works in an elegant, readable style and more systematic treatises in less golden prose.[22] The latter, learned works passed on within learned communities by students of Aristotelianism are primarily what survives of the Aristotelian corpus. The same sort of divide between books that were intended for a popular readership and those aimed at learned readers is often very clear in Continental literature, from the Renaissance through the end of the seventeenth century. During this period, writers generally wrote in Latin to limit their audience to learned readers and wrote in vernacular languages to garner an audience not literate in Latin. Dante and Galileo perhaps provide the most famous cases of authors choosing the vernacular in order to reach the widest of audiences.

A little closer to Hume's time, Descartes composed his 1637 *Discours de la méthode* in French, addressing it directly to a general reader as a guide to reforming mental conduct on the model of the author's own internal transformation: "I only propose this writing as an autobiography, or, if you prefer, as a story in which you may possibly find some examples of conduct which you might see fit to imitate as well as several others you would have no reason to follow." Descartes advertises that his book has "opened some windows and let the light of day enter into that cave" into which the lesser philosophers of his age had retreated. However, the book that succeeded the *Discours*, Descartes' *Meditationes de prima philosophia*, came out in Latin, not French. In the *Meditationes,* Descartes explains why he had written the former book in French and the latter in Latin, noting that because the *Discours* had not been a "complete discussion" of his topic, it was suitable for vernacular exposition subject to the general "judgments of readers." However, in the *Meditationes*, he tells us that he uses a less easily understood method, "far from the ordinary route" of writing, and that he "did not think it would be useful to explain it in French in a discourse that *might be read by anyone*, for fear that those of feeble intellect would think it permissible for them to make the same attempt." A firm believer in the "infirmity and weakness" of human nature, Descartes suggests certain kinds of writing that must remain within the exclusive domain of the Latinate reader because readers without that level of education would lack the intellectual training to follow his work well enough not to mistake its meaning. Even worse, the dim-witted reader might try inaccurately to imitate his method. In other words, Descartes wrote in Latin to hide certain information from the vernacular reader for at least some of the same reasons that Newton used both Latin and mathematical representations: neither man wanted the inexpert reader to be able to enter a public conversation about his writing.

In seventeenth-century and early eighteenth-century England, the distinction between which kinds of philosophy should be written in Latin and which in the vernacular was not so well delineated. Francis Bacon wrote his scholarly 1605 *Advancement of Learning* in English, but he later expanded upon the first part of it in the 1623 Latin *De Augmentis Scientiarum*. Bacon's alternation between Latin and English was repeated by Thomas Hobbes, who published much of his political philosophy in Latin and in English, often publishing the same work in both languages. Both Hobbes and Bacon wrote serious, difficult, and sometimes controversial philosophical books in English, establishing in England a tradition of vernacular technical philosophy alongside systematic Latin treatises.

Bacon and Hobbes seemed not to share the later assumption of Locke's and Hume's generations, that because a work was written in English, any broadly educated reader of the English language should be able to understand it. This phenomenon seems a particular development of the 1690s that continued through the end of the eighteenth century.

Hume's *Treatise* bespeaks a confusion about who could constitute the audience for technical metaphysics. In his Advertisement to the *Treatise*, Hume lays the *Treatise* at the feet of the "public," whose approbation he seeks and whose praise he considers "the greatest reward."[23] But Hume did not have an unlimited public in view. Hume distinguishes his targeted reading public from "the vulgar" and from the even less appealing "rabble without doors," who can only eavesdrop on the "noise and clamour" of philosophical dispute. At the same time, he aims to reach an audience that is not limited to those who fall under the rubric of "learned." He wants to claim the study of ethics and epistemology for a larger audience. He exhorts the "generality of readers" to suffer through the "pains requir'd to enter into these arguments." He urges them to persevere with him through all that is "abstruse" and through all that contradicts "the common receiv'd notions."[24] He holds the belief that most of his readers have imbibed certain standard notions from prevailing philosophies and popular prejudices, and because of this, readers will find it difficult at first to understand his philosophy because it challenges this received wisdom. Throughout the *Treatise*, Hume explicitly stakes the success of his undertaking not on his appeal to fellow philosophical scholars but on his ability to convince general readers that the bulk of their common-sense beliefs are simply wrong.

General readers, or, more properly, writers for periodical presses who reviewed books on behalf of the "common reader," were not persuaded. Copies of the *Treatise*'s first edition – and there was only one edition in Hume's lifetime – still lay on his publisher's shelves at Hume's death in 1776. Why did readers in his own time not come to recognize or revere his book the way philosophers of later centuries would? The reviews contemporary to the *Treatise* suggest that Hume – in contrast to his model, Newton – failed to establish and exploit a gap between expert and general audiences for his work.

When Hume published the *Treatise* in three books, from January 1739 to November 1740, England did not yet have a periodical committed to reviewing every work that came into print, as it would later have in the *Monthly* and the *Critical*. Despite the irregular nature of reviewing, six periodical commentaries about the *Treatise* did appear within a year of its publication, in the English journals *Common Sense* (1740) and the *History of the Works of the Learned* (1740); the French-language journals *Bibliothèque Raisonée* (1740 and 1741) and *Nouvelle Bibliothèque* (1740); and the German *Göttingische Zeitungen von gelehrten Sachen* (1740).[25] Their collective existence gives the lie to Hume's famous remark that the *Treatise* "fell deadborn from the press." Indeed, the periodical press could have offered Hume an avenue to attract readers in England and abroad. This route, however, did not lead Hume very far: the periodicals' generally negative reaction does indicate that while reviewers had picked up his *Treatise*, they did not recommend that readers follow their lead and do the same.

These six early commentaries share a sense of the *Treatise*'s remoteness from common apprehension, a sense that was likewise expressed by at least one of Hume's philosophically-minded friends who had much trouble making his way through the *Treatise* and asked Hume to "beat it ... into [his] head."[26] Common to the reviews was a conviction that the *Treatise* could not achieve an audience much beyond "the Learned, who are the proper Judges of its Contents."[27] Even the generally sympathetic *Bibliothèque Raisonnée* demurs in the face of Hume's complex metaphysics, noting that "our author ... does not get beyond his depth. We, however, will get beyond ours if in order to examine his principles ... we try to grasp all the details he introduces."[28] The editors of *Common Sense* found it necessary to prefix the remarks they printed on Hume with a warning that those "that never have employed their Thoughts about" philosophical subjects should skip these remarks, as they were "designed for the Learned," a category comprising only a subset of the journal's readership.

Reviewers' concerns about the abstruseness of Hume's work echo the doubt about his work's difficulty occasionally voiced by Hume himself in the *Treatise*. Hume joined in the general chorus of his age against metaphysical systems that did little more than exhibit the philosopher's taste for deep paradox. He wanted to lift philosophy out of a Hermetic tradition in which secret philosophic meanings were deliberately shrouded from general readers by a veil of jargon. However, according to Hume, such a task would not be straightforward because, even when not deliberately obscured, philosophical truth could be difficult for the untrained to perceive. The standard prejudices of the generality of readers blinded them from seeing into the intellectual depths where philosophy dwelled. If philosophical truth existed, Hume argued, "'tis certain it must lie very deep and abstruse."[29] "Refin'd or elaborate reasoning" remained necessary to the progress of "all science and philosophy." Hume saw his philosophical mission as one of teaching his readers how to go with him into these depths. Hume wanted it both ways: he wanted to advance the science of human understanding in a highly technical manner, and he wanted common readers to understand him without needing to become philosophers themselves.[30]

Despite its abstruse method, Hume framed his book as a work of general literature, not as a technical document for specialists. He adopted conventions from literary forms, much like those we would find in a periodical essay or a novel, including extended lyrical episodes in first-person narrative as well as offhand addresses to a general reader. These gestures invited his critics to take seriously the *Treatise* as a work making a claim on a range of readers. Hindsight allows us to see that Hume misjudged his audience. Through such signals, Hume asked reviewers to read his *Treatise* within an interpretive paradigm that did not fit well with the technicality of most of the book. The *Treatise* generated for its reviewers expectations about accessibility that were foiled by the method and structure of much of the work. Hume's desire to straddle the divide between learned and conversable within a single work sabotaged his book's reception.

Reviewers and Hume's fellow philosophers exploited what they took to be the inherent contradiction between the explicit difficulty of and the stated desire for clarity in Hume's writing. The *Works of the Learned*, for example, takes up hints Hume drops in his *Treatise* about the difficulty its readers will have in getting through it.[31] The reviewer wholeheartedly agrees with Hume's assessment of the difficulties to which metaphysical writings are vulnerable and finds Hume guilty of plunging himself into all of them. The review concurrently mocks Hume's tone, taking his all-too-earnest self-revelation about his difficulty in solving philosophical conundrums as grounds to derogate (in a scathingly ironic tone) the entire endeavor. This reviewer exposes the central structural device of the *Treatise*: Hume takes his readers through pages of intricate, unsuccessful solutions to philosophical problems, declares these problems virtually impossible to solve, and then claims he will nonetheless solve them to the satisfaction of all.

Among moral philosophers in the centuries since Aristotle, Hume's structure is a standard one: a philosopher begins with a question, moves through previously unsuccessful answers, and when the reader has begun to despair that any solution is possible, the philosopher reveals his own superior solution and its justification. Or, sometimes, he denies that any solution is possible. Such a format is useful and even engaging for those familiar with a discourse and who can follow the many levels of the discussion. The method takes readers through the history of the current question and asks them to think with the philosopher through the analysis of the question. It enables readers to see the procedure in action and in intimate detail, in much the same way that mathematicians sometimes present their work by first pointing out errors in previous solutions to a problem before working through the proof of their own answers. However, this procedure can be off-putting for the uninitiated reader, for whom it is often easier to see the solution without the complex, architectural blueprint of the apparatus that supports it. It is a strategy far better suited to the expert reader than the general one.

The *Works of the Learned* reviewer complains ad nauseam about the *Treatise*'s structure. He finds it a form of "horrible Cruelty" to the untrained reader, for whom he believes the *Treatise* reads like a collection of sphinxine riddles. The review takes Hume to task both for this method and for the technical language he uses to execute it, while accusing him of pretending to write for nonspecialists and then defeating these very expectations by not enlightening his readers about the "dark sayings" he invokes.

Though the reviewer turns his fierce humor to brilliant effect, he also recognizes that his own ability to elicit a reader's laughter depends on Hume's attempt to speak to the expert and nonexpert reader simultaneously.[32] The reviewer takes full advantage of his masterful close reading abilities to magnify the internal inconsistencies within a piece of difficult writing that claimed to speak to a general audience. He gives a reading of the final chapter of the *Treatise*'s first book, in which Hume takes his famously lyrical turn, dramatizing the despair wrought on him by a philosophy that seems so remote from commonly held beliefs. The relevant passage, excerpted in the review, runs as follows:

I am first affrighted and confounded with that forlorn solitude, in which I am plac'd in my philosophy, and fancy myself some strange uncouth monster, who not being able to mingle and unite in society, has been expell'd from all human commerce, and left utterly abandon'd and disconsolate. Fain wou'd I run into the crowd for shelter and warmth; but cannot prevail with myself to mix with such deformity. I call upon others to join me, in order to make a company apart; but no one will hearken to me. Every one keeps at a distance, and dreads that storm, which beats upon me from every side.[33]

The *Works of the Learned* quotes at greater length than I have here, in order to show that the melancholy Hume must have realized the implicit problems in writing a book that alienated the author from his projected readers. Although this passage puts on display Hume's famously literary style, the reviewer correctly perceives in it a disconnect with Hume's highly learned aims, opening Hume to ridicule rather than admiration. By lifting Hume's purple prose from its context, the reviewer amplifies the piece's self-pitying gestures. He then writes derisively of Hume's philosophical disheartenment:

What Heart would not almost bleed? What Breast can forebear to sympathize with this brave Adventurer? For my part, I cannot, without the utmost Emotion and Solicitude, take even a transient Prospect of the Dangers and terrible Catastrophe to which he is exposed.[34]

The reviewer notes that Hume pulls himself out of this despondency shortly before concluding book one. He then mock-panegyrizes Hume's recovery: "However, after all, as it becomes us to mourn with those that mourn, so it is but fitting we should rejoice with such as are joyful." The review concludes by bidding adieu to this briefly happy Hume:

I will take leave of our Author while he is in this chearful Mood, in this agreeable Situation; for, by looking forward, I perceive him extremely ready to relapse into profound Meditations on incomprehensible Subjects, and so into Scepticism, Chagrin, and all that gloomy frightful Train of Ideas from whence he is but this Moment emerged.

Throughout his article, the caustic reviewer calls for less skepticism and more consolation. In these demands, the article repeats a common refrain of the mid-eighteenth century. Oliver Goldsmith may have put it best in an article in the *Public Ledger*: "Philosophy can add to our happiness in no other manner, but by diminishing our misery: it should not pretend to encrease our present stock, but make us oeconomists of what we are possessed of," yet the average philosopher does just the contrary, "dissipating [his] own cares by spreading them upon all mankind!"[35]

Goldsmith's remarks suggest that an emphasis on application – whether it be instruction for living or solace for life's inevitable misfortunes – qualified a philosophy book for general interest in the eighteenth century. Here, too, Hume's was found wanting. The *Bibliothèque Raisonnée* intimates that much of the reason Hume was not picked up by a general readership was that the current interest in ancient and modern metaphysics in Europe bred reading tastes incompatible with Hume's philosophy. The journal noted that "throughout Europe, for nearly a half-century now,

the taste for philosophy has become more dominant and more widely cultivated," an interest fed by philosophers in England "who have tried to
make philosophy more useful by teaching men to know themselves better
than they previously did."[36] In other words, this reviewer believes (without
specifying which came first) that philosophers have begun to pay attention
to the common-life applications of philosophy, and more general readers
have become more interested in philosophy. One recent scholar has tanta-
lizingly suggested that the eighteenth-century reader grew to expect that
a philosophical book would provide moral comfort that would stand in
for the kind of advice once gleaned from religious texts.[37] While perhaps
not enough evidence exists to make this assertion too firmly, reviewers
did come to expect that all books for a general audience should offer both
reliable moral instruction and a guide to good taste and that philosophers
target their books at a general audience. It comes as little surprise, then,
that eighteenth-century philosophy books were expected (by reviewers) to
provide guidance in morals and taste. The burgeoning popularity of philosophy books likewise makes it clear why Hume could have believed a
philosophy book would have gained the attention of the broadly educated
reader, but his challenges to such a reader's expectations often made his
particular appeal ineffective.

The 1740 *Bibliothèque Raisonée* review indicates that the *Treatise* was
doomed to failure because Hume's own philosophical abilities did not
guarantee a readership capable of following him or interested in his goals:

We wish with all our hearts, that the public judge of these matters as the author
hopes: but it is not without fear that *the common reader* complains again that his
metaphysics is a little obscure and that he could have shed more light on the matter. It is sometimes unfortunate to have too much spirit and insight. As one does
not condescend to the level of the common man, one is not heard, and it is a sheer
waste of time to speculate, as the common man does not notice such sublime
beauties. However, when one wants to reform the ideas of almost all mankind,
and trace new paths to the very eyes of philosophers, it would be natural to make
oneself heard with a language that is simple and clear, one that everybody can
easily understand. Without that, it is impossible to communicate ideas, and even
less for them to be appreciated. Morality, principally, must be taught with the
greatest simplicity. A metaphysician who believes in demonstrating the principles
of Natural Law, by way of rendering them abstract, wastes his time and effort.[38]

The *Bibliothèque* sympathetically notes that Hume's ambition is incom-
mensurate with his method: changing the minds of both philosophers
and the common reader requires an author to "condescend to the level of
the common man." Moral philosophy, as the field closest to application
to daily life, requires fewer "sublime beauties" and more straightforward
clarity. The same journal's later review of book three recommends that

only those concerned with the "abstractions and subtleties of metaphysics" even bother to approach a book that the reviewers find themselves unable to understand completely or to "render intelligible" in a short space. The reviewers' emphasis on application provides a useful point of comparison with the reception of Newton. The establishment of Newtonianism as an intellectual brand also depended on connections, however tenuous, to real-world applications. The key difference is that Newton himself did not undertake to display such applications to a general public, instead relying on interpreters and popularizers. In contrast, Hume's frequent gestures toward a general readership raised the expectation that the value of his work might be found in its application, an expectation that Hume's expert researches did not fulfill.

Taken together, these reviews berate Hume's *Treatise* for being incompatible with both common sense and the philosophical tastes of their time. They outline for Hume what he would need to do in the future to make his work palatable to the broad readership that he had so desired for the *Treatise*: he needed to find a way to make his work seem of a piece with the other kinds of writings popular in the eighteenth century. In order to do this, he would need to challenge readers' expectations much less.

Hume's letters and his future published writings indicate that he took these admonitions very much to heart.[39] His response to reviews came to shape his philosophy over the succeeding decades. The core lesson Hume extracted from his reviews was that he should not have assumed that he could advance the field while still remaining broadly intelligible. The *Treatise* did not fit within the contours of the literary culture Hume had hoped to reform.

III. MORAL PHILOSOPHY VS. MORAL INSTRUCTION

Samuel Johnson perhaps best depicted his century's sense of the divide between specialized and broadly accessible discourses when he wrote, "In morality it is one thing to discuss the niceties of the casuist, and another to direct the practice of common life."[40] Johnson's lines also capture well the ambivalence of his era to the pursuit of technical, academic knowledge: it is difficult to love a nicety. Hume admitted the greater attraction of personal, moral instruction over abstract philosophy while strenuously asserting that the latter still had a place in public discourse. In the third book of his *Treatise*, written before but published after the *Works of the Learned* review, Hume notes that:

There is an inconvenience which attends all abstruse reasoning, that it ... requires the same intense study to make us sensible of its force, that was at first requisite for its invention. When we leave our closet, and engage in the common affairs of life, its conclusions seem to vanish, like the phantoms of the night on the appearance of the morning; and 'tis difficult for us to retain even that conviction, which we had attain'd with difficulty. This is still more conspicuous in a long chain of reasoning, where we must preserve to the end the evidence of the first propositions, and where we after lose sight of all ... received maxims, either of philosophy or common life.[41]

In other words, philosophical reasoning that is remote from any direct moral application has difficulty taking root in a reader's mind, especially if it does not simply repeat "received maxims." Hume had justified the elaborate epistemological apparatus by explaining that he had provided the scaffolding for applications in morality. Just as the third book of Newton's *Principia* won him a greater audience because it suggested the relationship between his mathematics and the universe we inhabit, Hume intended his third book to show the link between his philosophy and the everyday lives his readers pursued. His third book does not seem to have been much more successful in winning over readers than the earlier two. His readers found him too speculative and too skeptical throughout; his philosophy did not pay sufficient attention to how *useful* its readers would find it in going about or thinking about their lives.

Despite the *Treatise*'s claim that it was a speculative and not an instructive document, Hume's critics worried that gullible readers could understand just enough of Hume's *Treatise* to hurt themselves spiritually. Hume had anticipated such accusations and defended himself on the grounds that he only raised the specter of religious doubt for the sake of discussion.[42] Few, if any, found such remarks about Hume's academic detachment very convincing, another side effect, perhaps, of Hume's gestures towards a broader audience. Many found his writing unsettling to the foundations of Protestant theology. Hume's lifelong inability to gain a university position has generally been attributed to his printed challenges to religion.

The *Common Sense* reviewer put the case against the *Treatise*'s moral tenor most strongly. His comments on the *Treatise* attempt to counteract the "*mischievous* Effect" Hume could have upon the "Opinions or Morals of Mankind." He suggests that his worry springs from Hume's dangerous incomprehensibility:

[I]ndeed, I should have taken no Notice of what he has wrote, if I had not thought his Book, in several Parts, so very abstruse and perplex'd, that, I am convinced, no Man can comprehend what he means; and as one of the greatest Wits of this

Age has justly observed, this may impose upon weak Readers, and make them imagine, there is a great Deal of *deep Learning* in it, because they *do not understand it*.[43]

This unnamed reviewer exhibits a keen awareness of the power the recondite text might hold over its readership; such a text could seem to promise secrets unavailable to the casual reader. He worries that the wrong kind of reader might get his hands on the book and understand only enough to know that the book deals a severe blow to religion. Such a reader, the reviewer fears, might believe Hume's assault on religion was successful because its obscurity made it seem deep. This interpretation is summarily dismissed by the review as a red herring: the *Treatise's* rhetorical complexity is not caused by the immense learnedness of its author – as the weak reader might assume – but rather by its author's linguistic inexactness and faulty reasoning. Just as the anti-Newtonians had done to Newton, the reviewer accuses Hume of a crime against the trusting nature of readers: Hume advances his blasphemous views under cover of hazy language. "It is a Most *flagitious Crime*," he writes, to render philosophy "obscure and perplexed ... *designedly*, for the sake of any *private View*."[44] For this writer, Hume's philosophical behavior has crossed the line from the mildly ungentlemanly into the decidedly criminal. Hume's interest in bending the uninformed reader's mind towards his reprobate private opinion associates him with religious enthusiasts and corrupt politicians. The writer fashions himself as the protector of readers, saving them from the influence of Hume's anti-social tendencies. The best defense, he suggests, is not to read Hume's book.

The more generously inclined *Bibliothèque Raisonnée* included a less acerbic but equally alarmed warning about Hume's potential danger to readers. The reviewer writes that he does "not even know if [Hume's] method does not harm religion, against [his] intent ... It is known that the heart incessantly seeks pretexts in order to avoid obedience; and what pretext more plausible than the one that emerges from obscurity of works published with the intention of teaching elements of virtue."[45] What emerges from this review is the fear that readers will apply what they have read and possibly misunderstood, whether or not the author intended that they should do so.

Behind each of the *Treatise's* reviews lay the assumption that most readers will not read in a detached, contemplative mode, even when reading abstract philosophy. Everything – no matter how speculative or obscure – could be taken to heart by the projected general reader. This manner of reading becomes pernicious when moral action or religious beliefs hang in the balance. The Hume of the *Treatise* did not seem to have absorbed the lesson that generations of scholars had before him: scholarly work that directly affronts the standard belief system would not be well received. But neither had he learned the lesson of Newton, who used the expert language of mathematics to protect his work from doubters.

Periodical essays and reviews frequently commented about what books could or could not do to the morals of readers, especially "the young, the ignorant, and the idle."[46] These groups in particular were thought to lack a thorough defense against what they read. (Arguments of this ilk seem to have been based on anecdote and conventional beliefs about the inexperience of the young, not on a systematic collection of empirical evidence about reading behaviour.) The essayists and reviewers argue that the young lack "common sense," the bulwark sensible minds use to brace themselves against the attacks of those who would mislead them. Reviewers often put learning in opposition to both common sense and received morality, with the latter two offering safer havens for their readers' minds.

"Common sense" gained support as the gold standard against which writing and behavior could be measured over the course of the eighteenth century. The Common Sense school of philosophy, whose most famed exponent was Thomas Reid, gained ground by responding to Hume and certain of his predecessors. For Reid and his philosophical compatriots, common sense was "the complement of those cognitions or convictions which we receive from nature; which all men therefore possess in common; and by which they test the truth of knowledge, and the morality of actions." This definition combined the two prevailing, general meanings of "common sense" in the eighteenth century: 1. "The endowment of natural intelligence possessed by rational beings; ordinary, normal or average understanding; the plain wisdom which is everyone's inheritance"; and 2. "The general sense, feeling, or judgement of mankind, or of a community."[47] Common sense was often positioned as the antithesis of learning, and in their mutual struggle, common sense was portrayed as the inevitable victor. Reid used Hume's attempt at elevating learning above common sense and received morality against Hume.

Although Reid wrote his major philosophical works after Hume had published his better-received and more straightforwardly worded philosophical *Enquiries*, Reid orients much of his writing as a response to the unpopular *Treatise*, which he takes as the undiluted statement of Hume's epistemology. He wanted to show why philosophers needed to reject Hume's method and instead align philosophical and common-life ways of thinking. These efforts offered him considerable success: Reid's work was received more eagerly than Hume's initial publications. Reid also gained university positions and had students and followers to a degree Hume never had in his lifetime. But his popular success was predicated on a repudiation of the difficult, the technical, and the obscure. It also entailed counteracting the idea that the learned world should harbor knowledge unintelligible to the general reader. He was even willing to revise history to make this argument, claiming – impossibly – that Isaac Newton's philosophical principles had advanced the cause of common sense.

In *An Inquiry into the Human Mind, on the Principles of Common Sense* (1764), Reid claims Newton for the realm of the commonsensical, lifting him out of the learned world in which he had conducted his researches. Reid writes that:

The man who first discovered that cold freezes water, and that heat turns it into vapour, proceeded on the same general principles, and in the same method, by which Newton discovered the law of gravitation and the properties of light. His *regulae philosophandi* are maxims of common sense, and are practised every day in common life; and he who philosophizes by other rules, either concerning the material system, or concerning the mind, mistakes his aim.

It seems that by 1764 Newtonianism had been so successful that its counterintuitive elements were no longer recognized as such. Reid's wording suggests that Newton's discoveries could have been made by almost anyone following through on the same general principles always at work in making it through the day. Indeed, Reid argues elsewhere in his *Inquiry* that genius typically has very little to do with "useful discoveries"; "more frequently," he avers, "they are the birth of time and of accidents."[48] Reid portrayed his own task – and Newton's – as the somewhat workaday one of clearing the ground for the course of progress.

The *Critical Review* roundly applauded Reid's efforts, writing of the *Inquiry*: "This is a sensible, and, we think, candid, attempt to restore the intimate connection that ought to subsist between two very old acquaintances, we mean philosophy and common-sense. We wish that the ingenious author had attacked a more formidable performance than the *Treatise of Human Nature*." The *Inquiry* enjoyed great acclaim in its own time and was reprinted often in Great Britain and America through much of the nineteenth century. Reid's *Inquiry* triumphed over the *Treatise* for obvious reasons – it paid closer attention to its audience's own predilections and tastes in reading material and it spoke to a wider audience than Hume had managed to reach.

An appreciation of Hume's method ran counter to the prejudices of a wider reading public, who tended – as even a brief sampling of responses to Hume shows – to believe that what is possible at all in language is possible in commonsensical formulations. Reid catered to this latter view, arguing that common sense precedes philosophy and ought to serve as its foundation. Common sense and common life also ought, Reid asserted, to serve as the testing grounds for philosophy. If a philosophy could not be directly commuted into a sensible practice in the "common Conduct of Life," it was "foolish and ridiculous."[49]

This belief in the power of common language to address philosophical questions was and is still bolstered by a host of eighteenth-century writings on the topic. Authors from John Locke to Hugh Blair averred that when language is held strictly accountable to the ideas underlying it, both language and ideas will be transparent to their readers. That is to say, critical investigations into subjects not easily made tractable to straightforward (or straightforwardly worded) solutions ran counter to the stated aims of enlightenment. For at least this brief moment in history, popular pressure and philosophical epistemology coincided – in theory. Rhetorical clarity was the hallmark of the way empiricist and common-sense philosophers thought of themselves. When clarity was not possible, inquiry was inadvisable.

Reid's philosophy dealt in elegant and often witty formulations of what was already known to many of his readers intuitively. He wrote that "there are hardly any human notions more clearly, or more universally understood" than those addressed by his philosophy, endorsing the belief that sound philosophy should be, like true wit, "what oft was thought, but ne'er so well expressed." Reid wanted to explain rather than repudiate the foundational beliefs held by his readership. Defending the idea that "whatever is, is right" is fine for a poem, but rings a little hollow in a philosophy. Reid's philosophy only made a place for itself by portraying itself as a response against Hume; without making Hume into a straw man, Reid hardly had a philosophy.

Reid used the common signification of words both as the starting point for his philosophy and as the standard by which he then measured his philosophy. Needless to say, his philosophy often seems tautological, assuming that which it later says it has proven. By embracing this circular logic that equated assumption and proof, Reid largely avoided the contradictions inherent in the ideal of enlightenment in which Hume's *Treatise* had become (at times, hopelessly) entangled. While Hume had struggled with reconciling advanced study with expository presentation, Reid rejected the notion that there should be philosophical pursuits so specialized that an untrained reader could not easily gain access to them. (Reid did allow the loophole that if someone could convince him otherwise, he would gladly alter his opinion. He never did change his mind.) Consequently, in his own work, Reid reduced the technical content of moral philosophy.

For Reid, any closeted study was by its very nature contrary to the goal of enlightenment. Fond of metaphors of light and darkness, Reid took apart Hume's metaphor of enlightenment in an effort to discredit Hume's philosophy:

> [Hume] ingenuously acknowledges, it was only in solitude and retirement that he could yield any assent to his own philosophy; society, like daylight, dispelled the darkness and fogs of scepticism, and made him yield to the dominion of Common Sense. Nor did I hear him charged with doing any thing, even in solitude, that argued such a degree of scepticism as his principles maintain. Surely if his friends apprehended this, they would have the charity not to leave him alone.

This response to Hume concentrates on what Reid takes as the *Treatise's* central mistake: the disjunction between philosophical and commonsensical ways of thinking. The argument was not original to the *Inquiry*. In *A View of the Principal Deistical Writers of the Last and Present Century* (1755–56), for example, John Leland had intoned in his survey of Hume that "a man who argueth against common sense, however subtil and ingenious he may otherwise be, should also be inconsistent with himself."[50] In much the same spirit in which Samuel Johnson allegedly refuted Berkeleian idealism by kicking a stone, Reid shows that Hume could not have lived his life in accordance with his philosophy because it would have been physically impossible to do so. His response to Hume, entertaining throughout, includes this particularly witty paragraph:

> It seems to be a peculiar strain of humour in this author, to set out in his introduction, by promising, with a grave face, no less than a complete system of the sciences, upon a foundation entirely new, to wit, that of human nature; when the intention of the whole work is to shew, that there is neither human nature nor science in the world. It may perhaps be unreasonable to complain of this conduct in an author, who neither believes his own existence, nor that of his reader; and therefore could not mean to disappoint him, or to laugh at his credulity.

Reid's success here turns on his humor, on his ability to point up and exploit inconsistencies in a rhetorical vein that closely resembles that of the *Works of the Learned* review. Neither Reid nor the *Works of the Learned's* author suggested that he had discovered a quality of Hume's philosophy that Hume had not already explored for himself. Rather, both reject Hume's divide between certain kinds of philosophy and life by showing that if we begin with the premise that these two fields cannot be thought of separately and that therefore there should be no learned world, then Hume's philosophy, which depends on a semi-independent speculative realm, can lead only to paradox and self-contradiction.

On some level, Hume would likely have approved his critics' starkly drawn opposition between received wisdom and philosophical investigation. But he saw this split between everyday and philosophical ways of thinking as a strength rather than a weakness. His desire to keep the two separate, however, was not endorsed by his reviewers, who perhaps perceived Hume's own ambivalence on the topic. Nor was it for the most part picked up on by fellow English philosophers of his own century. The confusion or conflation of moral philosophy and moral instruction defined the eighteenth-century reception of philosophy in Britain. It also prepared the path for the Common Sense school's adoption of a moral philosophy based on a universal, shared moral sense, while dealing a setback to the idea of philosophy as a learned, expert pursuit.

IV. STYLE AND SUBSTANCE

It is crucial to note that the eighteenth-century attacks on Hume drive home their points through brilliantly turned phrases and biting humor. Their ability to raise ridicule and its bedfellow, unsympathetic laughter, lie at the heart of their critical technique. Periodical reviews and common-sense philosophy both represented themselves as, at least in part, forms of entertainment, meant to delight as much as instruct. Reviewers and other commentators profited by amplifying the author's perceived shortcomings; they maintained an audience not simply by providing information but also by offering merriment at the reviewed author's expense. As Samuel Taylor Coleridge would later write, "a Review, in order to be a saleable article, must be *personal*, *sharp*, and *pointed*."[51] And reviews operated in the conservative vein of most satire by reinforcing communal norms with an appeal to broadly-based beliefs.

In the eighteenth century, the cruelty of satire was justified on the grounds that it had a moral purpose as well as being *très amusant*. In deriding its object, satire could act as a corrective to wrong-headed thinking. Any philosophy "shocking to common sense," Reid argues, demands "the ridicule and contempt of sensible men."[52] One of Reid's and Hume's predecessors, Anthony Ashley Cooper, the third Earl of Shaftesbury, had explained to his era the important effects of satire and ridicule in his philosophical writings: by pointing out the faults of those that diverged from the *sensus communis*, satire served the necessary function of enforcing moral norms and good taste.

If, according to Shaftesbury, "to philosophize" was "to carry good breeding a step higher," philosophy's chief burden was to explain the norms of widely sanctioned behavior.[53] For Shaftesbury and his would-be well-bred followers, satire could exert a pressure on offenders against widely held beliefs by nudging them back in the direction of the *sensus communis*. Shaftesbury's justification for satire was seconded by satirists par excellence, such as Jonathan Swift, who argued that mockery could serve as a corrective by holding a "mirror up to nature," forcing its targets to see themselves and correct their faults. Shaftesbury's or Swift's theoretical justifications for satire were themselves consistent with the practice of satirists and reviewers, who were often the same person. In his *Inquiry*, Reid explicitly throws his lot in with Swift, arguing that any philosophy not built on widely shared beliefs – the *sensus communis* – "mak[es] mankind [into] Yahoos." Yahoos were, of course, the human abusers of God-given mental faculties that Swift had portrayed in *Gulliver's Travels*.[54] Reid finds philosophy like Hume's liable to create the same kind of woefully misguided humans.

Very much a part of the philosophical culture of Swift or Shaftesbury although not himself prone to such satiric outbursts, Hume wrote a polite, even amused, letter to Reid after the appearance of the *Inquiry*, acknowledging the cutting remarks at his expense with good humor and noting that "It is certainly very rare, that a piece so deeply philosophical is wrote with so much spirit, and affords so much entertainment to the reader," though he does not pass up an opportunity for some subtle criticism of Reid, nonchalantly mentioning that "some obscurities ... still seem to hang over your system." In print and in his letters, Hume responded to his early reviews and his reception by other philosophers explicitly and implicitly from the early 1740s through the remainder of his career. He picked up on French and English reviewers' suggestions that the *Treatise* was a "juvenile" production; Hume would later note more than once that in publishing the *Treatise* he "had been guilty of a very usual indiscretion, in going to the press too early."[55] Following his reviewers' advice, he cultivated what he thought was a more developed, less juvenile style for presenting his ideas.[56]

This style was that of the periodic essay, made popular by Joseph Addison and Richard Steele's *Spectator*, published six days a week between 1711 and 1714 in issues of two to four thousand copies each.[57] The *Spectator* essays adopted a prose style meant to imitate the easy flow of spoken conversation, a style that allowed effortless transitions among topics, did not demand argumentative rigor, and relied heavily on the appeal of anecdote, example, and analogy. As Addison styles it, the periodical essay is defined by its "wildness of composition," the irregularity in its movement.[58] Addison and Steele compensate for the desultory structure of each essay by focusing their content on topics already familiar and therefore easy for their readers to follow. They rely often on the classical proverb or story as a touchstone from which to begin a witty exposition, spiraling out from there in associative chains.[59]

The now-forgotten Vicesimus Knox (1752–1821) noted in his 1782 *Essays Moral and Literary* that over the course of the eighteenth century, essays had come to "convey the idea of regular treatises." If the proliferation of philosophical essays in the decades from the 1740s forward is any indication, Knox's observation seems accurate. Essays had certain advantages over longer, more systematic works – they paid keen attention to a readership by dividing large topics into smaller, easily digested pieces.[60] Though Addison and Steele had pioneered the short, philosophically inclined essay, Hume's many essays came to shape the genre of the philosophical essay in the mid-eighteenth century. Hume's 1741/42 volumes of essays inaugurated a period in his career during which he seems to have concentrated much more closely on his style and vocabulary.[61]

In 1748, Hume returned to the topic of the philosophical essay and its readership in the first of his *Philosophical Essays*. This collection came to be known as the *Enquiry Concerning Human Understanding* and represents Hume's formal reworking of book one of the *Treatise*, alongside a number of new themes, in popular form. In the first of these essays, he takes up directly a number of the criticisms leveled at him, especially those regarding the difficulty of his philosophy. He responds to what he perceives as the difference between philosophical works that aim to direct the practice of common life and those that try to explain the underlying mechanisms of human reason. The former category, he acknowledges, has always been more popular, because its goal is to cajole a reader into complying with moral standards he already knows are right by appealing to his sentiments rather than his reason. In attempting instead to cultivate his reader's reason, Hume recognizes that he will inevitably have a hard time making his writing touch the imagination and thereby offer sufficient pleasure to justify the reader's efforts. He hopes, however, that the essay can bring some of the rhetorical flowers of the former category to the latter.

The *Enquiry*'s essays abandon the comprehensive ambition and systematic proceedings of the *Treatise*. Rather, the *Enquiry* strings together "twelve loosely related philosophical essays," with a common theme, the "importance of experience and casual inference in establishing our ideas."[62] As Leslie Stephen would later describe it in his still-standard review of eighteenth-century philosophy, in writing the *Enquiries*, Hume "mangled the earlier 'Treatise of Human Nature' with singular want of parental affection. Part is rewritten, and much is altogether omitted."[63] On the one hand, Hume committed this near-infanticide on his *Treatise* because he took his critics' accusations of obscurity to heart. On the other, he had not entirely abandoned the idea that philosophical writing required a certain level of difficulty.

Written in direct rebuttal to Hume's critical reception, the *Enquiry*'s first essay visits the question of philosophical difficulty, debating whether the difference between lucid and obscure philosophical writings is simply a matter of style or whether the difference inheres in the subject matter itself. Hume hovers between admitting philosophical abstraction cannot be explained without resorting to a highly learned approach necessarily difficult to read and an assertion that he will manage it anyway by dismissing much of what he has to say. While the essay had advantages for recreational readers, it was not a particularly good form for advancing a field of study through a systematic analysis. The loss of the systematic *Treatise* in the more literary *Enquiry* meant also a decline in the rigor and depth of English moral philosophy in the eighteenth century.

The Hume of the *Enquiries* had "thrown together" various "loose hints" about a topic while leaving out a "full explication" of its related "principle and all its consequences" because it "would lead ... into reasonings too profound and too copious for this enquiry."[64] Much as the editors of *Common Sense* did in prefacing the commentary on Hume's *Treatise* with a warning to the inexpert reader, Hume put up signposts in his *Enquiry* for his readers just before the philosophically deep sections, suggesting that "readers of a different taste" should neglect these sections because they are "not calculated for them."[65] He pursued a similar strategy in his second *Enquiry*, the *Enquiry Concerning the Principles of Morals*, which amounts to a redaction of the moral arguments drawn from all three of the *Treatise*'s books.

Hume's management of difficulty in the *Enquiries*, especially the second, proved highly satisfactory to his contemporaries. William Rose, editor of the *Monthly Review* and a friend of Hume's, led his January 1752 issue with a review of Hume's second *Enquiry*, celebrating its lucidity:

The reputation this ingenious author has acquir'd as a fine and elegant writer, renders it unnecessary for us to say any thing in his praise. We shall only observe in general, that clearness and precision of ideas on abstracted and metaphysical subjects, and at the same time propriety, elegance, and spirit, are seldom found united in any writings in a more eminent degree than in those of Mr. *Hume*. The work now before us will, as far as we are able to judge, considerably raise his reputation.[66]

Rose's comments reflect the fact that Hume's reputation as a prose stylist had been on the rise through the 1740s with the publication of his volumes of essays. However, later academic philosophers have generally found the *Enquiries* a less significant philosophical achievement. That is, while Hume suggests that speculative philosophy can be represented in easier terms, his attempts to do so necessarily leave out the more detailed and technical parts of his philosophical maneuverings. They lean more on stories from classical and modern literature meant to serve as anecdotal support for their points. The *Enquiries* do not examine the philosophical history of the questions at hand, nor do they offer carefully reasoned arguments to justify their assertions. Chapters sometimes break off by stating that a full proof is beyond the scope of the present work. The *Enquiry* thus makes palpable Hume's growing sense of the trade-off between learned and literary writing.

To replace logical proof, each *Enquiry* repeats its central premises a striking number of times, as if Hume wanted his message to become gradually familiar to his readers so that by the end of each book, they would have accepted the premise without ever having been confronted with it head-on. If a popular book, then as now, is a book that has one central idea repeated over and over again, in the *Enquiries* Hume had found the key to popularity.[67]

V. THE LIMITS OF STYLE

But while some of the change between the *Treatise* and the *Enquiries* was indeed a matter of prose style, we can see that the term "style" also served as a smoke screen, masking deeper divergences in structure and content. An evaluation of style weighed heavily in eighteenth-century criticism, whether the critique be of a work of *belles lettres*, political theory, or mathematics. Condemning a work's style was *the* way to discredit its content – muddied language was taken as the sign of muddled thinking. Across eighteenth-century fields of study, objections to bad writing look strikingly alike – complainants allege that their opponents seek cover under verbal dispute and false paradox and that they retreat behind rhetorical ornament and empty phrasing. They likewise maintain that if such bad writers were flushed out into the open, it would be clear that they were trying to pass off high-flown nonsense as truth. The formulaic quality of such critiques is not a coincidence because the actual style of the work was often not what was at stake. Those who hurled accusations of weak or cryptic style did not usually base them on a rhetorical analysis of their opponent's language. Nor did the accusers inevitably or even generally write in a clearer style than the one they derided.

"Style" could take in a range of qualities about a work of literature, only some of which had anything to do with style. As we have seen, stylistic criticism of Hume was often as much about questioning Hume's ideas as his writing. It should thus not surprise us that Hume's adoption of a more conversable mode of communication did not keep readers from complaining about his writing. Indeed, when he became more readable, he also became more controversial. Religious pamphleteers and assorted other detractors now had much easier access to Hume's writings and so – these writers feared – did more vulnerable readers. We might take George Anderson, an army chaplain who attempted to have Hume excommunicated from the Church of Scotland, as a representative case.[68] He responded to Hume after the appearance of *Enquiry Concerning the Principles of Morals*, a book widely lauded for its readability. Nonetheless, in *An Estimate of the Profit and Loss of Religion ... with References to Essays on Morality and Natural Religion* (1753), Anderson took Hume to task for his style. Anderson denounced all philosophical language, calling it an "artificial mist of cant and jargon," arguing that works of modern philosophy are, even at their best, much less effective than the abilities of the average agrarian citizen to comprehend the fundamentals of morality. "Rustic souls," he writes, "whom Gentlemen of education judge to want a turn of mind for the *moral science*, may be as judicious, more moral, more honest, and more useful members of society, than men full of learning, who unload their own heads of useless and hurtful notions, to fill the empty heads of others, to very little, or to bad purposes."

Anderson might have found some minor disagreement from those in the Shaftesburian school, which elevated gentlemanly good breeding above a provincial outpouring of a pastoral morality, but, in general, his point would not have been especially controversial at mid-century. Indeed, Samuel Johnson devoted one of his 1750 *Rambler* papers to supporting the truism that men of all sorts often write much better than they live, because men suffer from the "imperfection of matter and the influence of accidents" when exposed to the life outside their closets.[69]

The canned nature of Anderson's argument notwithstanding, in calling up this familiar reproach against men who do not live up to what they write, Anderson conflates the practice of morality with its study. He does so in order to argue that the study is unnecessary to the practice. This is hardly a well-targeted criticism of Hume at an intellectual level. Hume himself would likely have agreed with Anderson's basic point about the difference between the study of the current moral system and its practice; he notes in the *Treatise* and the first *Enquiry* that he writes to cultivate the reasoned understanding of moral principles, not to direct moral action. Hume conferred great value on common sense and habit because they allow us to get on with the business of everyday life. He did not, however, see common sense as the solution to epistemological problems. But, of course, Anderson's critique, while often intelligent, is hardly meant to appeal mainly on the grounds of intellection. It treats practical application as the only test of learning.

The thrust of Anderson's attack is intended to challenge the learned world's right to a semi-autonomous or self-governing existence. Hume's defense – that he had in mind the cultivation of reason rather than the prescription of behavior – would hardly have held water for Anderson, who asked about modern philosophy: "To what purpose all this *galamatias*, this gibble gable, senseless stuff? To what end is this unreasonable railing against reason? Is it to shew that the terms reason and reasonable are too old for modern philosophers?" Anderson did not situate his argument against modern philosophers in relation to the early eighteenth-century ancients vs. moderns debates (perhaps best memorialized by Jonathan Swift's "Battle of the Books"). He seems not at all interested in elevating ancient learning above modern. However, he does share with such earlier arguments against modern philosophy a fundamental suspicion of the eighteenth-century learned world and all its newly developed institutions. Anderson makes a move characteristic of the second half of the eighteenth century, opposing common sense to scholarly efforts, a confrontation in which the former generally emerged the victor. Although he couches his attack in the familiar vein of a complaint against the "abuse of terms," his true aim here is to challenge the learned world as such.

Criticism of style was thus often part of a rhetorical protocol for discrediting one's antagonists or predecessors. Such accusations went hand-in-hand with the allegation that one had used a learned language to obscure information from those who could know no better. From the Renaissance humanists forward, part of the process of rejecting one's predecessors or competitors in a field of study required advertising that one had put that study on a stronger – because clearer – linguistic foundation. Thomas Sprat's great manifesto for the Royal Society, for example, argued that in pursuing their new approach to philosophy, the society also advanced a "natural way of speaking ... preferring the language of Artizans, Countrymen, and Merchants before that of Wits or Scholars."[70] Needless to say, the Royal Society's prose hardly looks like the speech of seventeenth-century mechanics and farmers. Sprat's depiction of a society turning away from the scholarly language of its predecessors smacks of a pastoral fantasy about a return to a simpler state – in this case a linguistic one – as a way of understanding the natural world free from the corruptions that the learned world had introduced over many centuries. As one recent scholar has noted, seventeenth- and eighteenth-century "accounts of style are seldom neutral or accurately descriptive. They are the result of animus, or controversy, or party politics, or religious dispute. What so many of these writers give us is not a program or manifesto for how they themselves intend to write but an account of how their opponents write."[71] And their opponents, by their accounts, wrote badly.

Critiques of the style of philosophical writings invoked age-old rants against the abuse of rhetoric familiar to readers of Socratic dialogues. Seventeenth- and eighteenth-century writers frequently include "sophistry," the arch-enemy of the straight-speaking Socratics, in their litany of criticism against poor writing. In the seventeenth century, Francis Bacon, John Locke, and their many exponents advanced a program of clear writing, though few of them could, strictly speaking, be considered models of the kind of anti-rhetorical clarity they espoused. Locke in particular had founded a generation of writers who argued that by paying attention to the direct connection between words and the ideas underlying them, philosophers could avoid both jargony obscurity and the dangers of rhetorical flourish. The general interpretation of Locke in the succeeding century held that if words were held strictly accountable to the ideas that underpinned them, philosophical and rhetorical clarity would result. This watered-down version of Locke's *Essay*, advanced in England by Locke's consummate essayistic popularizer Joseph Addison, became a rallying-cry of eighteenth-century criticism.[72]

Beginning in the late seventeenth century, English metaphysicians positioned themselves explicitly not only against the Aristotelian tradition of doing philosophy that had grown up in the universities but also against all the trappings of learnedness associated with the university. Books perceived as learned were suspect because they smacked of associations with the long discredited schoolmen and casuists, whose primary fault was their frequent recourse to verbal dispute in the absence of empirical evidence. Though they allied themselves against this tradition, English philosophers of the enlightenment never effectively freed themselves from the constraints and assumptions of their philosophical heritage. While arguing that the schoolmen did not do philosophy, only quibbled over words, eighteenth-century philosophers continued to believe that by reforming the use of words, they could still solve philosophy's problems through language correctly deployed. The common claim of eighteenth-century philosophers – that they had found an empirical approach not reliant on linguistic quiddities – did not effectively detach the philosophy from the language used to represent it because the same philosophers continued to argue that their meaning and therefore their effectiveness as philosophers lay in the words they used.

VI. LANGUAGE AND THE DISCIPLINES

The notion that an English prose patterned on conversational speech, properly regulated, could be the vehicle of philosophy gained currency from Locke's time forward. But alongside this belief ran another, perhaps articulated best by George Berkeley in 1708, about the difficulty that the non-scientific disciplines faced in sharing the vocabulary of everyday life:

Herein Mathematiques have the advantage over Metaphysiques & Morality[,] Their Definitions being of words not yet known to [th]e Learner are not Disputed, but words in Metaphysiques & Morality being mostly known to all[,] the definition of them may chance to be controverted.

The short, jejune way in Mathematiques will not do in Metaphysiques & Ethiques, for y[e]t about Mathematical propositions men have no prejudices, no anticipated opinions to be encounter'd, they not having yet thought on such matters. [T]is not so in the other 2 mention'd sciences, a Man must not onely demonstrate the truth, he must also vindicate it against Scruples & establish'd opinions w[hi]ch contradict it. In short[,] the dry Strigose rigid way will not suffice.[73]

That is, mathematicians do not have to contradict their audience's preconceptions about their terms because such terms are expressly set apart from and defined in contradistinction to everyday language. In contrast, metaphysicians are put in the position of having to defend their language from the claims of all users of that language who claim a mastery of it. Practitioners of non-mathematical, technical disciplines must contend with the commonplace notion – in Berkeley's time and in our own – that language is language is language. The operative belief in this case is that common speech embodies common sense, and that anything worth saying can and therefore should be said in broadly accessible terms. This is the heart of the critique of Hume's *Treatise* by Thomas Reid and the attack on his second *Enquiry* by George Anderson: knowledge is not knowledge if it cannot be comprehended in commonsensical terms.[74]

Twentieth-century ordinary language philosophers have leveled a similar critique at technical disciplines more generally: technical work must have been ultimately – at its origin – based on ordinary understandings of the world.[75] This search for intuitive origins or even a consistent language of common sense entails problems very much like the ones Berkeley spells out, namely that expert languages often operate differently from commonplace usages, even if they had at one time overlapped.[76] One of post-Lockean philosophy's tasks – as well as that of post-Newtonian science – has long been to point out the assumptions and presumptions lying behind common sense and its unilateral advocates. The particular problem of eighteenth-century moral philosophy was the belief that if the object of study was common life, the language used to represent it should similarly be that of common life. In many ways, the eighteenth-century debate over moral philosophy became a debate over the philosophy of language, because both had become inextricably bound up with disagreements over the language of philosophy.

If we hearken back to the development of Newtonian physics, we can see more concretely the distinction between the use of language in mathematical disciplines and its use in non-mathematical, ordinary language disciplines. Newton wanted to keep his writing in mathematical terms to avoid arguments from those who would dispute the meanings of vernacular language. Because what he argued ran counter to the received wisdom of his times, he wanted to avoid exposing himself to common-sense critiques from those who lacked the background to understand his reasoning. As long as mathematicians could vouch for the truth of technical writings, Newton had no need to express his work in another form. His would-be detractors were frustrated by his insistence on mathematical formulations as the essence of his natural philosophy. They wanted to dispute the meaning of his philosophy in a vernacular language so that they could do exactly what Newton had feared they would do, namely, bend his terms to suit their meanings. While almost anyone in the eighteenth century could mount an uninformed critique of Newtonian physics, they could hardly challenge his theory at its origin without a high level of expertise.

When Locke and Hume discussed the mathematical sciences, they acknowledged that it took time for work in the natural sciences to filter down to those who did not practice those disciplines. However, they did not adopt the same standards for their own writing. Eighteenth-century moral philosophers adopted a radically different tack with respect to their audiences: these philosophers and their reviewers argued that a broadly educated reader *should* be able to understand their writing in its original form. Though the Royal Society occasionally paid lip service to the same ideal, the major innovations by its participants hardly lined up with it. Moral philosophers largely refused – in theory and in practice – to differentiate among kinds of audiences and participants.

In our own era, the comparison between moral philosophy and natural science as disciplines may seem a false analogy precisely because we believe that their objects of study demand such different approaches. It is clear at the outset that there is no philosophical language directly equivalent to mathematics; a philosopher's language will overlap more with the language of common life than a mathematician's symbolic representations will. Then again, some branches of philosophy have since taken up symbolic logic and like forms of representation, and other once-humanistic fields have employed statistical, graphic, and other non-vernacular approaches to their objects of study. These techniques aim at a scientific exactness. In other words, attempts to model philosophical disciplines on mathematical ones have certainly not ceased. Part of the controversy then as now is whether or not philosophy, and other non-mathematical disciplines, should look for a technical language that either approximates mathematics or is in another way similarly removed from conversational languages.

The success of any discipline at being perceived as scientific seems to lie in the degree to which it can escape (and gain acceptance for this escape) from a thoroughgoing reliance on what Berkeley had called "words ... known to all." Newton's intuition that he should rely on nonvernacular representation – even in the cases when it was possible to do otherwise – has proven over time to be an effective technique for arrogating to a field of study professional status and public respect.

None of this is meant to reduce the difference between physics and philosophy simply to language. Of course the objects of study in physics and moral philosophy are different. And this will affect how they are studied. Arguing against these premises would be misguided. However, it is equally mistaken to believe that the way disciplines represent their work follows as naturally from the object of study as night follows day. Understanding in any field is inextricably linked with representation. This chapter and the previous one have shown that the representational forms (mathematics, statistics, visual or virtual models, vernacular languages, and so on) a discipline has at its disposal inevitably affects how it views its object. By making choices among these methods, a scholar simultaneously limits the kinds of work that he or she can do. Physics is not by definition more specialized than philosophy. However, the insistence that the language philosophers use must be broadly intelligible pushes philosophy away from specialization.

Perhaps needless to say, the language a discipline uses affects how specialized it seems to those outside it. If the history of professionalization has taught us anything, it has demonstrated that professionals create their status by proving to the outside world that they can perform and are certified to perform tasks that nonprofessionals cannot. This insight has been marshaled often enough by those who believe that the need for a barrier between professionals and nonprofessionals has been constructed needlessly to help the professionals at public expense. Those who have argued against the need for specialized languages in the humanities – in the eighteenth century and now – suggest that anyone who insists that research cannot be presented in broadly accessible language creates artificial linguistic barriers to public understanding, either 1. to create the illusion that the practitioner has knowledge that others do not have, or 2. to hide knowledge from the public. Both arguments may sometimes be true, and they need not only be true about the humanities. Newton seems to have done both on occasion. The respective cases of Hume and Newton have shown why narrowly demarcating one's audience may have benefits for advancing a discipline. There are also other possibilities for why a disciplinary language might be necessary. Hume's philosophical writings have shown us that restricting a discipline to ordinary uses of language restricts what it can say, even if the practitioners of a discipline themselves do not or do not want to recognize this restriction.

Eighteenth-century moral philosophers could have removed themselves from the ebb and flow of vernacular speech by following a program that insisted on a professional language, if not a wholly separate representational system. Seventeenth-century philosophers such as John Wilkins had considered versions of such a project, imagining ideal philosophical languages to facilitate natural and moral sciences. However, moral philosophy and epistemology did not develop in that direction; instead, they found themselves tangled up in a project of making conversational language work for technical purposes. John Locke wanted a philosophically exact language, but he wanted that language to be derived from commonplace usage and subsequently to fix such usage in place. Locke aimed for a conversational style that would nonetheless embody the exactness of a technical terminology. His popularity was great, but his success in achieving his goal was mixed. In the preface to the second edition of his *Essay*, Locke noted "my meaning, I find, is often mistaken, and I have not the good luck to be every where rightly understood." He offered two possible explanations for his being misunderstood: his readers were not reading carefully enough, or he was not clear enough. He leaned toward the former explanation: inattentive readers. He did not allow for a third possibility, which is the one Berkeley describes: language has multiple meanings built into it, and any attempt to make coextensive an everyday diction and a precise terminology will inevitably be less than perfect because it will invite the same range of interpretations that the language as a whole allows. A paradox thus threatened Locke's project of enlightenment: he wanted to have the advancement of knowledge represented only in a language that never outpaced the comprehension of a broadly educated audience; and he wanted to fix the usage of that language in place while not sacrificing the flexibility required in a conversational, vernacular language.

Taking up these same incompatible premises in his *Treatise*, Hume thought he had set aright the unstable parts of Locke's program: he thought he had found a new linguistic and epistemological foundation for philosophy that lay well within standard uses of the English language. His detractors responded by saying that he decidedly had not met these requirements and instead had made more complex the philosophical jargon that had long plagued the field. (One of his reviewers remarked that he would have saved his readers "a lot of work," if he "had thought to add a glossary."[77]) In the spirit of his era, in response to such criticisms, Hume expresses much of his later reaction against his early philosophy in terms of its faults in style rather than in its content. In his autobiography, he writes, "I had always entertained a notion, that my want of success in publishing the *Treatise of Human Nature,* had proceeded more from the manner than the matter."[78] But we can recognize that reducing the difference between Hume's two kinds of writing to stylistics does not do justice to the structural difference between the two kinds of work. Much of his readers' trouble in reading the *Treatise* turned out not to stem from Hume's style as such (as many critics have demonstrated, his individual sentences are generally very lucid), but rather to the philosophical method bound up in the language: he used many complex procedures and coined many terms of art.

Thomas Reid tried again, as Locke had done, to turn to the language of common life and tried to use the standard meanings of words to do philosophy. He did so more doggedly than anyone had before, believing that words should be taken at face value in their vulgar signification.[79] Reid's common sense philosophy seems an inevitable consequence of mid-century print culture. If the broadly educated reader was the measuring device for literature, then a philosophy that explained how the broadly educated reader judged the world made intuitive sense. The fault of Reid was not in what he chose to investigate, but rather that he did so at the expense of other kinds of thinking.

Reid found that the chief fault of Hume and his fellow offenders against good sense was that they adopted a "language of a different structure from the common," corrupting the "language, by using words in a way which the purity of the language will not admit."[80] Reid's alternative was to take what he believed to be the common senses of words as given in everyday usage and to generate a chain of assumed premises based on them. The justification he gave for his premises was twofold: first, the structure of language itself showed that certain principles were innate to the way humans thought, and second, his foundational premises were based on what "every man of understanding" believed. The former category was hardly self-justifying: what Reid had written about the structure of all languages was not accurate, even when limited to only the languages known in Britain at that time. The latter category had its own set of problems: Reid himself pointed out many mistakes that philosophers might be led into by relying on the structure of language; he found as many faults as strengths in common language for doing philosophy. What "every man of understanding" believed thus constituted a slippery foundation for Reid. Common sense or common language – much like common law – changed in interpretation over time, even over the pages of Reid's philosophy books. Most often, Reid operated on the basis of assumptions about the way languages and beliefs worked and took these assumptions as proof.

At moments in reading Reid, one is tempted to indulge in the ungenerous feeling that his work seems a philosophy of mediocrity, one that endorses a lowest common denominator as a standard measuring device for human activity. He frequently begs "our leave to think with the vulgar" and declines to rise above this level.[81] For Reid, the steady march of tradition sets the pace of innovation in knowledge; attempts to outpace tradition lead to the usual mistakes of overeagerness and overrefinement. Reid calls standard usage the "arbiter of language."[82] For Reid, tradition reposed in language, and only through widely accepted changes in usage could innovation be introduced into language and therefore into philosophy.

The strongest critique of Reid and of the kinds of criticisms typically leveled against speculative thinking remains the introduction to Immanuel Kant's *Prolegomena to Any Future Metaphysics*. Kant scorns Reid's penchant for appealing to the "opinion of the multitude," and he degrades Reid's school's tendency to treat common sense as an oracle to which it appeals for truth. The common-sense philosophers would have disputed both of Kant's criticisms of them – neither opinion nor oracular pronouncement is their articulated standard for judgment. Nonetheless, Kant identifies a kernel of truth: their philosophy uses a set of assumptions about what constitutes the common sense of mankind to dismiss other kinds of philosophy. "Chisels and hammers," Kant writes, "may suffice to work a piece of wood, but for etching we require an etcher's needle."[83] By insisting that common language – the repository of common sense – be the guide for philosophy, Reid commits a crucial mistake. Requiring that all the old assumptions remain in place and all the same imprecise linguistic tools be used cripples the kind of innovation that a new science demands.

Kant gives a precise analysis of why Hume's speculative metaphysics needs to be housed in a long and sometimes difficult book: Hume needs first to call into question "alleged knowledge previously acquired" to show that judging the world through this knowledge has its limitations. He needs to make fine distinctions between the foundation for his new science and the thought patterns that his readers have acquired as "second nature" by "long habit." The *Treatise*'s difficult "long-windedness" may "discredit the book" but its "dryness" and "scholastic precision" are "unavoidable" in an effort to separate everyday assumptions from the practice of a new, technical philosophy.[84]

Following along the same lines as Kant, Thomas Reid's student Dugald Stewart saw the problem of using everyday language for philosophical purposes perhaps better than any British thinker since Berkeley. Stewart is now little recognized, but his analysis of common sense is both more sophisticated and more self-conscious than Reid's. Stewart identified the inevitable pitfall of using natural languages for technical work, namely that

the imperfections of words constitute the principal obstacle to our progress, nor is it possible to advance a single step without struggling against the associations imposed by the illusions of metaphorical terms, and of analogical theories.

However, at the same time, he identified the faults of attempts to come up with a philosophical language modeled on mathematics, such as those proposed by the French thinker Étienne Bonnot de Condillac and the German Gottfried Wilhelm von Leibniz. Their attempts to "reduce reasoning in all the sciences to a sort of mechanical operation, analogous, in its nature, to those which are practised by the algebraist, on letters of the alphabet" were flawed because vernacular languages depend on their flexibility to have meaning in different contexts: "*the whole* of the words about which our reasonings are conversant, admit, more or less, of different shades of meaning."[85] Stewart asks for a balance between a "technical phraseology" and the words in which "all mankind, whether wise or ignorant, think and speak alike."[86]

Though Stewart himself does not explicitly express this, his writings lead to the conclusion that ultimately, academic philosophy would need to depart from strictly commonplace usage if it were to aspire to the status of a science. Even if the language and behavior of common life were the object of moral philosophy, they *need not* be its sole method. If philosophy were to be done at an advanced level, they *could not* be its sole method.

Dugald Stewart valued Hume's *Treatise* for the same reason Reid had attacked it: it contained the most exact description of Hume's new epistemology. This was an insight that German philosophers found long before British ones. While we need not subscribe to the belief that Kantian philosophy was the pinnacle of eighteenth-century thought, we can nonetheless note that the efflorescence of the German academic thought that underpins much of the way we still think about ethics, aesthetics, history, and morality – inside and outside the university – acknowledges a strong debt to Hume's *Treatise*. The careers of German philosophers, however, diverged from Hume's. While Hume's priority was to be a man of letters, Kant had the sense that a philosopher could write technical works and then write a popular exposition or overview, without renouncing the original work, even in the face of critical reviews. He acknowledged that the two kinds of works serve different functions and different audiences, in much the way Newton's *Principia* was read by experts and his popularizations were read by lay readers. Following the analogy with Newton, we might even speculate that the support that Kant and his predecessors had from the German university structure contributed to his ability to imagine these two kinds of audiences for himself – certainly the institution of the academic discipline of philosophy had a stronger presence in Germany much earlier than it did in England.

In publishing the *Treatise*, Hume ran up against the fundamental difference between disciplines that do their work on and in natural languages and those that work on physical objects or through mathematical representations. The precondition of describing the findings of physical science in ordinary languages is that such formulations inevitably will be incomplete: the essence of the work is given up in the transition from mathematical to linguistic representation.[87] The vernacular description of the work is acknowledged to be a series of metaphors that can be shaped to conform to the level of understanding of the projected audience without affecting the original results. Thinking in language comes after the mathematical or experimental fact and is, or is presumed to be, radically autonomous from science itself. This distinction between the expert and the lay audience persists in physics and its fellow material sciences. Modern physicists continue to argue that elegant, verbal formulations of their work can and should be used to foster public understanding of what they do.

By contrast, in the humanities in the Anglo-American tradition, findings and their representations to an audience are thought to be bound up together in one and the same language. The entanglement between the work itself and its linguistic presentation gives rise to the assumption that because one can understand a vernacular language, one should be able to understand all things written in it. But the problem with this assumption is that it discounts the histories, traditions, and methods that develop in expert discourses and their constituent terminologies. Although specialized vocabularies are intertwined with the language of common life (if indeed such a common-life language exists as such), they are not identical to it. The popular prejudice against disciplinary jargons likewise adumbrates a host of suspicions. Such wariness is founded on a hazy but nonetheless powerful anxiety that texts written in expert idioms are hiding important knowledge from the vernacular culture for diabolical or at least potentially exploitative purposes. The widespread distrust of legal language is the paradigmatic example, but other disciplines, especially in the humanities, have likewise long contended against similar misgivings. The sciences and humanities have thus long displayed asymmetrical relationships to natural languages.

This is perhaps why, even after the successes of Hume's later more popular writings, his *Treatise* did not, at least in the public sphere, follow the trajectory of Newton's *Principia* by becoming more valued because it was more inaccessible. The difference seems to lie in a combination of their respective disciplinary practices and the language they used to present their work. In the eighteenth century, Hume was much less successful in rising above accusations that his learnedness was a smoke screen with nothing substantial behind it than Newton was, in part because Newton and his followers consistently argued that their proof lay outside linguistic description. The Newtonians emphasized other kinds of proof and of truth. By insisting that his philosophy was grounded in his language, Hume positioned his philosophy wholly within the realm of his ability to command belief based on verbal arguments. And because it ran against received opinion and received religion, its task was formidable – and largely unsuccessful in persuading an audience.

By the early nineteenth century, the many failed claims by philosophers that they had found the true, scientific way of doing philosophy made the eighteenth-century parallels drawn between moral and natural science seem strained. While many still held out the hope that a scientific method could eventually be applied to other fields, Stewart argued that there had come to be a *de facto* division between the hard sciences and fields that would become the social sciences and the humanities. He thus proposed a repartitioning of the system of knowledge into fields that addressed "matter" and those that addressed the "mind." William Whewell made a similar case in his *Philosophy of the Inductive Sciences* (1840), suggesting that though we might ultimately argue for a continuity among sciences based on a shared, inductive method, the physical and biological sciences had set themselves apart in their level of achievement through these methods as detached from language. And, over the course of Whewell's writings on the history and philosophy of science, the disjunction between material sciences and other fields of study becomes more apparent than their continuity.

Stewart argued that the progress of natural philosophy was much easier to see than progress in the sciences of man. In large part, this was for reasons much like those that Berkeley had suggested: findings in the humanities were mixed up with the "casual associations" embedded in the language used to explore and to communicate them. In topics that came "home to their business and bosoms," philosophers and readers alike were most likely to be led astray by the layers of connotative meaning attached to individual words. Stewart describes the net result of this asymmetry between the sciences and humanities succinctly, as well as the effect that this asymmetry has on their perceived value:

The consequence is, that while the physical and mathematical discoveries of former ages present themselves to the hand of the historian like masses of pure and native gold, the truths which we are here in quest of may be compared to *iron*, which although at once the most necessary and the most widely diffused of all the metals, commonly requires a discriminating eye to detect its existence, and a tedious, as well as nice process, to extract it from the ore.[88]

That is, scientific and mathematical truths stand out because they are clearly distinguishable from the traffic of common life and language, while those in moral philosophy do not. He follows on this metallurgic metaphor to argue that because they rely on circumstances external to vernacular language – in particular, visual evidence or mathematical proof – the physical sciences have a command over the imagination that moral philosophy has never had because it has not been presented as a separate object, visual or otherwise, to the imagination. Moral philosophy is always tied up with previous associations and "inveterate prejudice," or, as Stewart writes, "improvements in moral and in political science do not strike the imagination with nearly so great force as the discoveries of the mathematician or of the chemist." Only a "certain class of learned authors," Stewart argues, have given us any hope that the study of philosophy could likewise make advances over time, and even so, this potential for progress is not always clearly discernable.

Stewart's remarks point to the fact that eighteenth-century philosophy in Britain demanded that philosophy be a form of popular literature at the same time it endeavored to be a science. The pressure put on broadly intelligible and even attractive linguistic formulations subtracted from its ability to be perceived as a science. Though Hume showed inklings of this realization in his first *Enquiry*, he continued to want it both ways. Stewart, too, believed that the concurrence of a common language and a philosophical one might be possible were certain ground rules to be generally accepted.

None of these philosophers held the belief that gained some currency on the Continent that moral philosophy should find a vocabulary remote from common usage; instead, they came gradually to accept the idea that their findings would always struggle against common apprehension and would always be subject to criticism from those who did not grasp the discourse. They grew to admit that external factors would inevitably alloy the purity of the discipline, devaluing its results. While Locke had tipped his proverbial hat to the more rapid advances of physical scientists in his own time, Stewart positively gives up the race, deciding that his discipline would always seem "less splendid," even when it was more useful. Stewart's feelings on this matter also make the adoption of a common-sense approach seem sensible – if the discipline would always struggle against common sense, perhaps it seemed best simply to embrace it and go from there.

With the rise of academic philosophy in nineteenth-century Britain, following on the success of the eighteenth-century Scottish universities, support for an academic philosophy that departed from a popular form gained momentum. A technical philosophy that did not make claims on a popular audience became a more plausible idea when housed inside the university. Hume's reputation as a philosopher suffered in nineteenth-century Europe because he was perceived as degrading his early, pure pursuit of knowledge in an effort to become popular. This perception of Hume is largely his own fault; he wrote often about literary fame and literary reputation in reference to himself and (as we saw in his discussion of Newton) other men of science and of letters. T.H. Huxley, for example, wrote that

Hume exhibits no small share of the craving after mere notoriety and vulgar success, as distinct from the pardonable, if not honourable, ambition for solid and enduring fame, which would have harmonized better with his philosophy. Indeed, it appears to be by no means improbable that this ... was the cause of his gradually forsaking philosophical studies, after the publication of the third part of the *Treatise* ... and turning to those political and historical topics which were likely to yield ... a much greater return.[89]

Nineteenth-century evaluations of Hume as a panderer to both common taste and his own passion for fame largely ignored the circumstances surrounding his writing. These comments were made in an era in which the universities were taking on greater importance in England and offered a partial haven for the technical pursuit of humanistic knowledge. Following this line of reasoning, scholars in the nineteenth and twentieth centuries resurrected Hume's *Treatise*, regarding it as a landmark in the history of philosophy. They valued it for the very reasons that readers in Hume's own time ignored or disdained it.

Though the eighteenth century's essayistic turn did not become a lasting means for doing philosophy, the damage had been done.[90] A century of emphasizing that the essence of philosophical systems was embodied in the language in which they were expressed – as opposed to residing in their method, in their object of study, or in some kind of data – established the perception that moral philosophy should be judged by literary standards. By expressing the desire that a philosophical language be modeled either on the vocabulary of vulgar, everyday use or on the best literary prose stylists (both standards took their turns, often in the same work), philosophers invited reviewers external to their field of study to pronounce judgment on how well they had succeeded. And these judgments largely relied on their rhetorical qualities. Though the later nineteenth-century university recovered Hume's *Treatise*, the popular perception about disciplines that relied on vernacular languages – a view sometimes shared by those inside the discipline – persisted. While writers for the popular press began to reflect the inevitability that science would remain apart from common understanding, they persevered in the belief that a philosophy book should be intelligible to a broadly educated reader.

CHAPTER 5

Poetry Among the Intellectual Disciplines

The first volume of Diderot's epoch-making *Encyclopédie* (1751) opens with a diagram of the "Detailed System of Human Knowledge," which depicts visually the tree of knowledge described in Francis Bacon's *Advancement of Learning* (1605). The diagram was subsequently copied and translated back into English in the first volume of T.H. Croker's *Complete Dictionary of Arts and Sciences* (1764). This epistemological tree reduces the realm of the imagination, which takes in poetry and its sister arts, to a conspicuously small compass – barely a sixth of the space allotted to the "reasoning" disciplines of theology, ethics, mathematics, medicine, botany, chemistry, and the like (see Figure 2). The image is striking: poetry is nearly crowded off the edge of the intellectual map.[1]

On Bacon's or the *Encyclopédie*'s account, the difference between the respective contributions of the *beaux arts* and the philosophic disciplines to learning ran deeper than their associations with separate mental faculties. The several branches of philosophy and their attendant professors each contributed to the advancement of knowledge by cultivating a narrow plot of intellectual territory. In the eighteenth-century division of intellectual labor, disciplines such as physics, botany, chemistry, and moral philosophy had delimited themselves by each identifying with a particular object of knowledge.[2] The philosophers and scientists in these fields could be recognized as experts in large part because they used and understood particular, expert languages designed to describe their respective objects.

But unlike the subdisciplines of physics and philosophy, poetry had no apparent object of study, no obvious subject to illuminate. The poet's usefulness to the accumulation of wisdom therefore seemed less evident, and poetry's need to vindicate its place among the intellectual disciplines more difficult. Increasingly, poets were pressed to answer the twinned questions: In the division of intellectual labor, does the poet have a share? And does the answer to this question hinge on whether poetry has its own technical

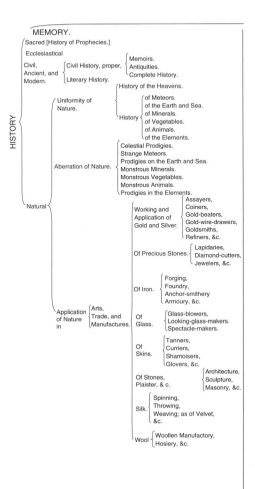

Figure 2 A "Systematical View of Human
Knowledge," from Croker's *Dictionary.*

KNOWLEDGE.

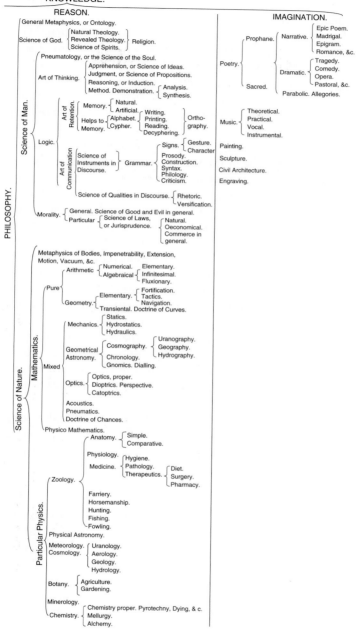

Figure 2 (*Cont.*)

language to represent the poet's knowledge, analogous with disciplinary argots of other fields?

In the opening years of the nineteenth century, William Wordsworth took up this question, asking, if we know what the "Man of science, the Chemist and Mathematician" do, if we know what they contribute to learning, "What then does the Poet?" If intellectual specialization is a precondition of modernity, how does the poet fit into the equation? In this chapter, I return romantic poetry to this forgotten context of the growing division of knowledge.

In western Europe, poetry and education were tightly linked together from at least the middle of the second century BCE, when the Greek language was taught to Roman schoolboys through Homer's *Odyssey*.[3] A student's subsequent education in grammar and rhetoric, which included mastering the conventions of literary genres and making use of literary devices in writing and speaking, built on these poetic foundations. Poetry was the gateway to the Greek language; the Greek language was the portal to other learning. Later, Latin poetry would take the place of Greek in western Europe. And though poetry remained part of courses of study on grammar and rhetoric, it had no explicit place in the universities that grew up in the European middle ages. Like history, poetry was not accorded a disciplinary status of its own.[4] When English began to have its own university courses and departments towards the end of the nineteenth century, the writing of poetry was generally subordinated to the study and criticism of it. The transitional years in the seventeenth through early nineteenth centuries are crucial to the understanding of poetry's place among the intellectual disciplines.

In this chapter, I argue that many of the now-canonical writings of the romantic poets arose in response to the need to provide evidence for poetry's remaining among the intellectual disciplines. Poetry's answer to this pressure was not to become a discipline like physics or philosophy, but to follow a different path, becoming a practice whose specialized role was the creation of common language and universal experience.

In his 1802 "Preface to Lyrical Ballads," Wordsworth characterizes his age as one in which man could be thought synonymous with his professional identity, when he was often first a "a lawyer, a physician, a mariner, an astronomer, or a natural philosopher."[5] His 1814 political pamphlet *The Convention of Cintra*, whose ostensible purpose is to criticize the British government's policy towards the Spanish and Portuguese as set out in a controversial treaty between Great Britain and France, offers in more elaborated form Wordsworth's misgivings about a world intellectually divided against itself, predicted by Francis Bacon's epistemological scheme two hundred years before. Although his specific reference to Francis Bacon was left out of the *Convention* when it was printed, Wordsworth's manuscript notes indicate that he conceived parts of the *Convention* in direct response to the uses to which modern writers had put Bacon's writings:

Lord Bacon two hundred years ago announced that knowledge was power and strenuously recommended the process of experiment and induction for attainment of knowledge. But the mind of this Philosopher [Bacon] was comprehensive and sublime and must have had intimate communion of the truth of which the experimentalists who deem themselves his disciples are for the most part ignorant[.]

These truths of which the experimental philosophers are ignorant, Wordsworth explains, reveal that in specializing their minds for the sake of "rapid and eager advancement" of science, philosophers allow their "more noble" faculties, especially their imagination, to "lag behind in proportion."

In Wordsworth's reading, Bacon was the inadvertent founder of what late-eighteenth-century economists would call "the division of intellectual labor." Bacon's recommendations for the advancement of science, as Wordsworth describes them, have been abused; Bacon's emphasis on the experimental has been replaced by an emphasis on the technological and industrial. Wordsworth calls the current age's lopsided interest in applied science over other kinds of studies "the cause indirectly of a course of obtuse and mechanical thinking on moral investigations and ... a source directly of degrading moral habits" in the "mind of the individual" and in the "general mind of the age"; in other words, "while we have been making large encrease of gains on one side these gains have withdrawn our attention from great loss on the other."[6] The imbalance between reason and imagination represented so strikingly in the *Encyclopédie*'s depiction of Bacon's tree of knowledge has become Wordsworth's target.

When Sir Philip Sidney composed his *Defence of Poesy* over two centuries earlier, before Bacon began constructing his new system of learning, he wrote from the assumption that his audience already considered poetry a kind of learning. The *Defence* argued that poetry triumphed over the other arts and sciences as a form of knowledge because each of these other branches of learning was bound to a particular object of knowledge. Poetry remained free of all such ties.[7] Between Sidney and the romantics, something changed. The distance we now perceive between the writing of poetry and the pursuit of modern scientific disciplines – the strangeness with which we regard a world view in which poetry could be considered one of the three main forms of knowledge, alongside history and philosophy – indicates to us that the poet has passed from a position among the practitioners of the learned disciplines to an existence within an almost wholly separate literary sphere.

This historical distinction is telling, suggesting that developments over the course of the eighteenth and nineteenth centuries shaped the disciplinary divide we currently take as given. But was this movement inevitable? Modern critics of nineteenth-century literature tend to answer this question in the affirmative, noting that the romantics' resistance to poetry's becoming a discipline on the model of the sciences was the signal moment in which poets first recognized that they had begun inescapably to move towards an autonomous literary realm. But such an observation tends to consider the writings of the romantics through darkened teleological lenses, an optic which filters our vision through our current divided perspective on the arts and sciences.

Recent attempts to compensate for this distortion in our critical scrutiny have primarily attended to the sympathetic attitude romantic poets had towards certain scientific endeavors. Such studies note that, for example, neither Wordsworth nor Coleridge would have considered himself a Luddite: Coleridge read Newton and befriended chemist Humphry Davy; Wordsworth "exult[ed] to see / An intellectual mastery exercised / O'er the blind elements ... almost a soul / Imparted – to brute matter."[8] While useful, this corrective still hits a bit wide of the mark. It misses the fundamental disciplinary question that early nineteenth-century poets themselves articulated: *could* poets hold their place on the plane of knowledge by patterning their field or their language after the structure of the scientific disciplines? After all, Coleridge argues in *Biographia Literaria* that poetry had "a logic of its own, as severe as that of science; and more difficult, because more subtle, more complex."[9] Poetry could be a discipline, or a method, that held together the thoughts expressed by verse, rooted in a practical reflection on language itself.

If we return to the Britain of 1800, we find that poets could be considered specialists, with their own peculiar technical usage, yet they could also stand as the general guardians and perfectors of the English language in its purest and most universal form. In fulfilling this dual, seemingly paradoxical function, poets writing in early nineteenth-century Britain ultimately sound the death knell of the eighteenth-century ideal of a print culture in which practitioners of many intellectual disciplines could imagine speaking directly to a broad, Anglophone audience. The romantic poets put in its place a vision of a *lingua communis* and a common reading public that could be realized only through a certain kind of writing: the compositions of disciplined writers of imaginative literature and poets in particular. Coleridge's "*lingua communis*" and Wordsworth's "real language of men" came to be available only through poetry. Poetry thus began to assume its distinctively modern role: it took on many of the functions of a disciplinary language while still claiming universal intelligibility.

"Literature" for these romantic writers no longer signified all productions of the learned world, as it did for Samuel Johnson when he wrote *A Dictionary of the English Language* half a century before. The overlap of the literary and the learned that had so bedeviled Hume's career ceased to apply. Indeed, Hume's own turn towards a literary mode was a major step in establishing the literary as separate from the learned. In the intervening years, the intellectual disciplines had differentiated themselves to the extent that no individual could be privy to, or even fully understand, the technical discourses of all branches of study. "Literature" came, for the romantics, to stand for the writing which tried to bridge the gap between the learned and the lay reader, and literary language became a language that stood somewhere on the spectrum between learned and conversational languages.

By claiming for the modern poet the ownership of a national language, Wordsworth and Coleridge stake out a role for poets in the division of intellectual labor. Poets become the innovators and caretakers of a national literary language, providing an alternative to vocational and conversational languages at all levels – those belonging to the intellectual disciplines and their practitioners and those deriving from manual occupations and the laborers who perform them. But, in their efforts to combat linguistic divisiveness, Wordsworth and Coleridge underscore the division of intellectual labor and of language in two ways: first, they theorize and thereby deepen the gap between the intellectual strata of society and those who live by agriculture, manufacturing, and trade; and second, they acknowledge and often encourage the distinction between the language of poetic *belles lettres* and those of other arts and sciences. They thus offer a theory of a divided language that mirrors the theories of the division of labor advanced by late-eighteenth-century economists.

As they established a full-time position for the poet, Wordsworth and Coleridge also worked towards separating those who could generate and use a truly poetic language from those who could only learn to appreciate it. The narrowness of both the poetic career and the readership for poetry was trenchantly, if harshly, expressed by Jeremy Bentham: "If poetry and music deserve to be preferred before a game of push-pin, it must be because they are calculated to gratify those individuals who are most difficult to be pleased."[10] Wordsworth's prose writings on poetry are largely directed at finding (or making) such an audience of the difficult to please: "every author, as far as he is great and at the same time *original*, has had the task of *creating* the taste by which he is to be enjoyed."[11] Resist it as they might, their need bespoke its own form of artistic specialization.

The difficulty poets faced in responding to intellectual specialization extended, as it did in other disciplines, to the language poetry used. Though it may now seem counterintuitive to us, the English romantics' attempts at finding their place on a changed intellectual map was characterized as much by an embrace of specialization as a resistance to it. I argue that in attuning themselves to "poetic diction," the early romantics were not merely making an aesthetic observation; rather, they took part in the larger, culture-wide debate about the connections among disciplinarity, language, class, and audience. The romantics' discussions of the language of poetry thus must be understood in relation to the similar controversies over specialized languages raging across eighteenth- and nineteenth-century fields of study, from physics to philosophy.

There are, for example, strong and not incidental parallels between how Wordsworth and Coleridge aimed to transform poetic language in the *Lyrical Ballads* and how, a decade earlier, experimental chemists had reformed their nomenclature. Both chemists and poets aimed to clean up antiquated terms that were no longer perspicuous and replace them with a more supple, progressive linguistic instrument. Despite their occasional claims to the contrary, in their poetry, Wordsworth and Coleridge carry forward the project of eighteenth-century scientists and humanists in struggling to find ideal, representative languages for their work. The parallel does, however, have its limits. Poetry did not – at this moment – become unintelligible to a broadly educated reader, as much of chemistry did. Instead, the poetic theory and often the practice of the English romantics represents a shift from thinking about poetry as consisting of a *specialized language* to consideration of poetry as common language *used in a specialized way*.

I. THE POET'S DISCIPLINE

When the aspirations of the *Advancement of Learning* met the era of *The Wealth of Nations*, poetry had much to lose. In the representations of the English and German romantics, the division of the mental faculties envisioned by Bacon had been realized on a human scale, in which an individual developed one aspect of his mental capacities at the expense of the others. What these poets intimate and what *The Wealth of Nations* does not mention, or could not admit, is that specialization has a momentum of its own and cannot be confined to the fields whose progress it promotes. The poets do not reject Smith's model as a portrayal of the modern world; rather, they ratify his political–economic vision, finding it more accurate than Smith himself allows.

Although Smith strove to achieve a theoretical balance between national prosperity and individual development by coordinating *The Wealth of Nations*, a theory of the population taken as a whole, with *The Theory of Moral Sentiments*, a depiction of the individual, moral human, Wordsworth and his compatriots suggest that operations on the national level threaten the individual development of the sort Smith described in the *Theory*. The opposition between Smith's two major works represents the gap between the success of the nation and the success of the individual, which is the central critique Wordsworth levels at the mass professionalization and industrialization of Europe. At the same time, Wordsworth supports this distinction by calling attention to the distance between his own writing and the lives and language of those he seeks to represent.

In considering the model of the disciplines emerging around them, Wordsworth and Coleridge confronted the question of how, if it were one more profession or discipline among many, poetry differed from the sort of narrow linguistic specialization it endeavored to combat. This problem had already been considered often in mid-eighteenth-century Britain. When Adam Ferguson first addresses the "separation of the arts and professions" in *An Essay on the History of Civil Society*, a crucial precursor to Smith's *Wealth of Nations*, he predicts "that writing may become a trade, and require all the application and study which are bestowed on any other calling." He recommends, though, that these writers combat a tendency to professional mental confinement by engaging themselves wholeheartedly in the currents of the workaday world, to cultivate "the spirit and sensibility of a vigorous mind."[12]

Wordsworth and Coleridge both pick up on solutions that have much in common with Ferguson's, while ostensibly rejecting Ferguson's central tenet that the professionalization of the writer is inevitable. As has often been observed, the English romantics argue that for poetry to solve the problems of men across professions, the poet likewise needs to avoid the pressures that lead to the mechanization of the mind. In order to do so, poets need to insist that, for poetry to be successful, the writing of poetry can not be a profession at all. In his *Biographia Literaria*, Coleridge exhorts the "youthful literati" of his age: "Never pursue literature as a trade."[13] For Coleridge, the repugnancy of writing for money does not arise from the traditional opposition between the man who works for his living and the gentleman who does not need to. Indeed, Coleridge recommends that young would-be writers take up a paid occupation, preferably as clergymen, so that they secure for themselves an education, a social circle, and an income. Rather, Coleridge worries that a poet's dependence on a regular poetic output for income will turn him into a *mere* literary man" defined by "the sale of his works for the necessaries and comforts of life," which requires him to pander to the taste of the market rather than to intellectual or moral standards. Coleridge frequently opposes learning to the mart or market in his writing; the marketplace has its role, but that role is not to assign value to literary production.

As Raymond Williams has noted, the romantic poets' cultivation of the view that poetry is received by inspiration rather than crafted by a learned and practiced artist coincides directly with a need to dissociate the poetic career from other, especially scientific, professions, whose productions might be assigned financial value.[14] In the writings of Wordsworth, Coleridge, and later Shelley, diatribes against mechanization of the physical world are set off against accounts of poetic inspiration. The success of authorship as a profession depended precisely on its denying that it had anything in common with training, markets, and the like. In fact, we can go beyond Williams's analysis to observe that the English romantics' insistence on the disparity between the poet and other men extended not only to distinguishing between their respective careers, but also to describing the variances in the fundamental, bodily constitution of the two kinds of individuals. Out of their professional needs, the poets derived a theory of human difference.

While Adam Smith's *The Wealth of Nations* argued that the distinction between a porter and a philosopher derived only from their respective educations, nineteenth-century poets found it behooved them to assert that a poet could not be created in the same way as a porter or any other tradesman or professional. In the case of the true author, only innate gifts decided what role the author could play in the national economy.[15] As Coleridge wrote, "*Poeta nascitur non fit.*"[16] This resistance to labeling poetry as profession extends into the poetry itself: it is no accident that the poet-figures in Wordsworth's and Coleridge's respective poems are wanderers or travelers, ranging over wide swathes of intellectual ground that could be claimed as imaginatively their own. These poet-prophets had no profession, or had abandoned one.

Wordsworth's and Coleridge's antipathy to defining the poet as a professional stems from a shared desire to locate the "human" – that which lies outside any single profession – in poetry.[17] This, of course, has the paradoxical result of casting poetry in the light of an industry whose special task is to create a human soul, at least for certain classes of readers.[18] This mercantile attitude was underscored by discussions like Coleridge's of the poet's right to sell his intellectual property in the same way the "wine-merchant or milliner" sold his.[19] At moments like this, Coleridge seems not too far from Adam Smith. Indeed, these poets accept many of the fundamental conditions of specialization – the division of the mind into faculties each expressed through different activities and the need for the poet to be a separate kind of thinker from the scientist. At times, the early English romantic poets' declared enmity to professionalization evinces a desire to construct a retrogressive model of social development built around a resistance to specialization, while at the same time acknowledging this model as a product of their own imaginations.

In Coleridge's description, learning and the market are acknowledged to be moving towards opposite poles of the literary field. This is not to say that Coleridge espouses the belief that literary works *should* be inaccessible to the generality of readers: he suggests often that he would rather educate popular taste and therefore alter the market than define his works against it. In other words, he does not (yet) describe the same plane of polarities that Pierre Bourdieu finds in late nineteenth-century France, in which the inverse relationship between market and literary value was actively cultivated by writers. Coleridge's attitude smacks of ambivalence and often frustration over how the quality of books and the quantity sold could be brought into a more favorable alignment. Wordsworth's position is similar to Coleridge's and grows even more so over time. In his 1815 "Essay, Supplementary to the Preface," for example, Wordsworth gives a brief literary history of the popularity (and lack thereof) of English poems, in order to show that popularity serves as a poor measure of quality. In so doing, Wordsworth denounces the very word "popular": "Away, then, with the senseless iteration of the word, *popular*, applied to new works in poetry, as if there were no other test of excellence in ... the fine arts but that all men should run after its productions."[20] The intellectual landscape had not yet fractured in such a way as to oppose formally radical and popular literature. But much as in philosophy or physics, writers had begun to give concerted attention to the gap between popular and learned poetry, with an eye to the desirability of maintaining the distance and using language to do it.

In opposing the reduction of poetry to the lowest linguistic common denominator, Coleridge returns to the same contradiction of the eighteenth-century ideal of enlightenment that Newton and Hume confronted: if the size of the audience that a text reached were the primary measure of its effectiveness at enlightening readers, authors would inevitably need to turn their attention to popularization rather than innovation. Indeed, if literature's primary function was to instruct and delight the broadest of audiences, then, as David Simpson has observed, the creation of knowledge through poetry would necessarily need to be sacrificed to the popularization of it. The emphasis on broad appeal threatened not only politically edgy or formally experimental literature, but also intellectually or linguistically innovative writing. Such standards represented a peculiar problem for Coleridge, who thought the poet's priority should be to advance the English tongue, rather than to translate knowledge into an already-popular idiom. Reducing poetry to the popular would proportionally diminish poetry's claim to remain among the intellectual disciplines. If poetry were to align itself more closely with learning, it would then sacrifice a broad audience. The romantic poets, I suggest, found another possibility: that poetry make a claim neither to be learned nor to be popular, but to occupy a third position, outside both.

While the romantic poets did not want poetry classed as a profession, neither did they mean for it to be regarded as an idle pursuit. Wordsworth's 1815 "Essay, Supplementary to the Preface" argues that those who come to poetry in their youth as "an occasional recreation … in a course of fashionable pleasure" can never be the true guardians of English letters.[21] Nor can those who approach poetry "in middle and declining age" as a form of "religion, for protection against the pressure of trivial employments, and as a consolation for the afflictions of life." As we saw in Chapter 4, these arguments resemble closely those marshaled in the eighteenth century, particularly in Germany but also in Britain, against casual philosophers, here turned against desultory aficionados of poetry.

Wordsworth does not go so far as to argue that there are professional poets or readers of poetry, only that it requires a lifetime commitment of one's "leisure time" to the cultivation of poetry to be a true judge of it.[22] But the "leisure time" Wordsworth describes must expand to replace entirely any other disciplinary or professional occupation – poetry cannot be pursued by those who regard it only when they think "it proper that their understandings should enjoy a holiday." Here we find a definitive statement that the reading and writing of poetry is an intellectual labor coupled with a statement that this labor can only be written about in terms of leisure. To be intellectual work, poetry needs to become a full-time mental engagement. "It is in the fine arts as in the affairs of life," Wordsworth writes, "no man can *serve* (i.e. Obey with zeal and fidelity) two Masters."[23] And business and poetry have difficulty commanding the attention of a single individual simultaneously. Indeed, Wordsworth sees the poet as also neglecting other forms of intellectual labor in order to serve wholeheartedly his single master, the poetic muse.

This begins to sound much like a disciplinary arrangement, yet Wordsworth insists on using the word "leisure" to describe the activity. The need for this mask lies in the inherent problem bound up in the idea of profession – that anyone, possessed of sufficient financial and intellectual means, could apprentice himself to the field. And so the poets employ the older term "vocation" to distinguish between the calling of the poet and other kinds of modern work. A "vocation" could not necessarily be taught; the very word suggested divine ordination. But, as Wordsworth notes, for a vocation to be pursued seriously, *all* of one's time would need to be transformed into so-called "leisure" time.

The solution to Wordsworth's conundrum lies in part in turning away from "profession" towards the central concept of this study, discipline. Wordsworth's writing makes especially available the twofold meaning of "discipline," as being both education and punishment, that the present book has hitherto allowed to remain dormant. The use of "discipline" to refer to a particular branch of study has an organic connection to these other meanings: it is only a short step from creating disciples (in Latin, *discipuli*) to imagining that what they study has an existence independent of specific students, a discipline (*disciplina*).

Discipline is one of Wordsworth's keywords, particularly in his sonnets – not surprisingly, given the formal discipline of the sonnet. For Wordsworth, the word discipline brings together a set of educational contexts connected to lifelong practices: academic, ecclesiastical, and military. The sonnets are also Wordsworth's poems about older forms of discipline: those of religious and military life. Discipline is always, for Wordsworth, self-discipline, that which organizes bare into purposive life, a life drawn forward towards vocation through discipline. And so the poet fears a past where modern "discipline" and "valour" could not withstand the "discipline of swords," and finds a somewhat more congenial dwelling place for his past self in an "Old Abbey" where "by discipline of Time" the inhabitants are "made wise." In the choice among the disciplines of violence (military life), or of waiting and wanting (religious life), or of living in nature (poet's life), Wordsworth inevitably chooses the "simple discipline" of the last. Thus *The Prelude*, a poem about the training of the poet's mind, announces its own completion at exactly the moment when he thinks that discipline has been fully acquired:

> And now, O Friend! this history is brought
> To its appointed close: the discipline
> And consummation of a Poet's mind,
> In everything that stood most prominent,
> Have faithfully been pictured; we have reached
> The time (our guiding object from the first)
> When we may, not presumptuously, I hope,
> Suppose my powers so far confirmed, and such
> My knowledge, as to make me capable
> Of building up a Work that shall endure.

Of course, the irony of this moment is that *The Prelude* never preluded anything; Wordsworth's preparation for his mature "Work that shall endure" proved a lifelong endeavor. But perhaps this unfulfilled promise shores up the common ground between poetic discipline and the military and religious lives from which he had tried to distance himself: a discipline is never complete. It is not, as he had promised himself, ever fully acquired.

II. THE LANGUAGE OF REAL MEN

The professional poet or the serious reader of poetry, described by Wordsworth as an individual possessed of a large store of leisure time, seems at first to jar with Wordsworth's poetic theory, which claims a strong linguistic affinity with a labor-intensive agrarian or seafaring life. Wordsworth's use of the phrase "the real language of men" has, from the beginning, been a stumbling block in the interpretation of his poetry. But although dangerous territory, "the real language of men" demands revisiting. On the one hand, as Jerome McGann warns in *The Romantic Ideology*, we need be wary of "an uncritical absorption in Romanticism's own self-representations," not allowing Wordsworth's "Preface" to dictate how we read his poetry. McGann's thesis follows Northrop Frye's earlier caution that, although "Wordsworth's Preface to the *Lyrical Ballads* is a remarkable document, as a piece of Wordsworthian criticism nobody would give it more than about a B plus."[24] While keeping these admonitions well in mind, I suggest that the "Preface" can be read with another aim in mind: it stands as the major statement on how the early English romantic writers entered into an ongoing debate about disciplinary languages.

Because poetry had to find its way in a changed world, the pressure Wordsworth and Coleridge faced compelled them to describe a new role for poetry as much as to write a new poetry. Wordsworth's prefaces and Coleridge's *Biographia* speak explicitly to this central conflict and cultural strain. Wordsworth's several prefaces exhibit the paradox that the avant-garde continues to face to the present day: a poetic movement begins with a manifesto that claims the art that follows will make the manifesto unnecessary. But it rarely happens this way; readers often perceive a wide gap between poetry and theory. As a political or rhetorical position, Wordsworth's "Preface" thus demands a critical reassessment because it was changes in poetic theory perhaps more than in practice that captured the nineteenth-century poet's orientation with respect to the intellectual disciplines and their uses of language. It was the romantics' alteration in theory that enables our own tradition of poetic criticism; the explicit reart-iculation in prose manifestoes of what constitutes poetic language can be read as a concerted effort to maintain poetry's relationship to the intel-lectual disciplines.

Turning, then, to the "Preface" as a repository of poetic theory, we might note that the rhetorical unit, "the real language of men," has unduly borne the weight of interpretations of the *Lyrical Ballads* that mistakenly insist on the linguistic egalitarianism of Wordsworth's project. Let us then charge headlong into an examination of this phrase. Or perhaps it is more accurate to say "these phrases," as Wordsworth uses "the real language of men" or some small variation on it no fewer than a dozen times in his "Preface" to the *Lyrical Ballads*:

1. "The first Volume of these Poems ... was published, as an experiment ... to ascertain, how far ... *a selection of the real language of men* in a state of vivid sensation, that sort of pleasure, which a Poet may ration-ally endeavour to impart ..."
2. "The principal object ... proposed in these Poems was to choose inci-dents and situations from common life, and to relate ... them ... *in a selection of language really used by men*, and, at the same time, to throw over them a certain colouring of imagination, whereby ordinary things should be presented to the mind in an unusual aspect ..."
3. "My purpose was to imitate, and, as far as is possible, to adopt *the very language of men*; and assuredly such personifications do not make any natural or regular part of that language. They are indeed, a figure of speech occasionally prompted by passion, and I have made use of them as such."

4. "As much pain has been taken to avoid ["what is usually called poetic diction"] ... for the reason already alleged, to *bring my language near to the language of men ..."*

5. "[T]he language of such Poetry as is here recommended is, as far as is possible, a *selection of the language really spoken by men*; that this selection, wherever it is made with true taste and feeling, will of itself form a distinction far greater than would at first be imagined, and will entirely separate the composition from the vulgarity and meanness of ordinary life ..."

6. "And *what language* is to be expected from him [the poet]? – He is *a man speaking to men*, a man, it is true" who has "acquired a greater readiness and power in expressing what he thinks and feels ..."

7. "*[T]he language* which [the poetic faculty] will suggest to [the poet], must often, in liveliness and truth, *fall short of that which is uttered by men in real life.*"

8. "How, then, can his [the poet's] *language differ in any material degree from that of all other men* who feel vividly and see clearly?"

9. "The Poet must descend from this supposed height; and ... *he must express himself as other men express themselves.*"

10. "[W]hile he is only selecting from *the real language of men*, or, which amounts to the same thing, composing accurately in the spirit of such selection, [the poet] is treading upon safe ground ..."

11. "[A]n indistinct perception perpetually renewed of *language closely resembling that of real life* ... make[s] up a complex feeling of delight ... "

12. "I have chosen subjects from common life, and endeavoured to bring *my language near to the real language of men.*"[25]

We are so accustomed to the "Preface" that we tend not to notice what a strange, rambling document it is. On the one hand, close attention to its repetitiveness prompts the observation that the poet doth protest too much. Why emphasize the "real language of men" so often, if the poetry that follows the "Preface" will exhibit this language to the reader? But, on the other hand, as a slogan for Wordsworth's poetry, "the real language of men" has had a career of an unusual brilliance. The words are memorable, and repetition helps them stick. We might observe, following Coleridge, that "the real language of men" at first seems inaccurate; no reading of Wordsworth's poetry yields up a true selection of language that we would expect to find among rustics or sailors. But, following Coleridge again, we might also acknowledge that this is not precisely what Wordsworth suggests we will find when he tells us he has chosen his poetry from the real language of men.[26] Wordsworth's use of this phrase has been largely misrepresented in criticism; readers have tended to remember the sound bite at the expense of the argument that surrounds it. What, then, does the rehearsal of the phrase signify within this preface?

Each time Wordsworth writes "the real language of men," he qualifies it in a slightly new way. By repeating the term, he refines it, building up a definition by degrees. His technique of engendering a technical term by gradually accreting layers of meaning to it was common among eighteenth-century philosophers. For example, we can only understand Hume's "cause and effect" or Kant's "aesthetic judgment" by following the multiple ways these authors use the phrases as their respective arguments develop. Only within a series of local contexts does a general meaning become clear.[27] And although Hume's and Kant's technical terms derive from vernacular languages, their writings impart a meaning to these terms that are not coextensive with the signification of the phrases in the language of common life. Their divorce from commonplace usage is what makes them technical terms. Such terms were always subject to misunderstanding by the untrained or inattentive precisely because they were not invented jargon but common words used in special senses. Wordsworth's "the real language of men" has suffered from many of these same misconstruals, predicated on confusing the everyday sense of the term with Wordsworth's local and technical usages.

If we pursue the definition of the term advanced in the "Preface," we find that Wordsworth's "real language" does, in fact, sever poetic from workaday uses of language. This divide would "form a distinction far greater than would at first be imagined, and will entirely separate the composition from the vulgarity and meanness of ordinary life." This language would use figures of speech that did "not make any natural or regular part" of ordinary conversation; rather, it would be patterned on the speech used only in extraordinary situations. Poetry itself was thus described as a special context, outside the uses of language found in conversation or in prose expositions.

Poetry, like all art, would only imitate or come "near" such language, tendering a mimetic representation of the language of common life filtered through "true taste and feeling." And though this poetry would not indulge overmuch in neologisms (as the languages of the other disciplines did), at the same time it would limit itself to a particular subset of the English language, that deemed most appropriate for representing emotion. Only the poet possessed the "true taste and feeling" necessary to choose this kind of language, and he thus had the responsibility of training his or her readers into understanding and appreciating this language. Or, as Wordsworth writes, "Poets do not write for Poets alone, but for men." Poetry's comprehensibility derived in part from the poet's drawing on modes of expression already well understood, but at the same time, poets had a didactic responsibility, one that Wordsworth and Coleridge chose to take on jointly by advancing a mimetic theory predicated on a linguistic theory.

Although "the real language of men" may sound like an appeal to a popular and broad-based diction, within the confines of the "Preface" it comes to represent a new way of conceiving language. That is, the "Preface" itself does not give us a useful guide to the "real language of men" in the ordinary sense because it becomes so qualified as to have escaped almost altogether its popular signification. "The real language of men" enacts the very process Wordsworth describes: it selects from the English lexicon but configures these choices in such a way that they take on a new signification, apart from conversational or representational uses of language. Thus, what Wordsworth describes is not a separate language, but it is a specialized use of language.

The "Preface" thus argues for a refinement of and reflection on English language only possible through poetry. The romantics represent a shift from a conception of poetry as a different language, to poetry as language used differently.

This shift of linguistic focus, this move from an attempt to find a uniquely poetic vocabulary to an effort to understand how ordinary words function within an extraordinary context, marks the break between poetry and other intellectual disciplines. The poet's language took on the role not of describing things as they were or as they ideally could be, as poetry was once thought to have done and as the languages of physicists and philosophers claimed to do, but rather of exploring the expressive possibilities of language itself. As much as critics have tried to organize theories of romantic poetry around representations of "things," whether the core object be the natural world, or the poet himself, such analyses miss the romantics' refusal or inability to put objects at the center of their profession in the same way that the scientific disciplines had done. If the explicit function of eighteenth-century philosophy, in the train of John Locke, was to identify a philosophical use of language that would embody a direct connection between words and things, poetry's role was to show how language shaped thinking. In other words, the severe logic of language Coleridge describes is not evaluated in terms of imitation or inspiration, because both of these sources lie outside the language being used; the difference springs from an attitude towards language itself.[28]

We thus can see in Wordsworth's and Coleridge's poetic theories a kinship with later philosophies of language distantly derived from German romanticism, which argue, as Wittgenstein later does, "Do not forget that a poem, even though it is composed in the language of information, is not used in the language-game of giving information."[29] At the same time, we need to be wary of pushing this argument too far; the English romantics had not yet detached entirely their theory of poetry from what Roman Jakobson has called the "communicative function" of language. For most of the nineteenth century in Great Britain, poets and critics continued to make the Aristotelian argument that poetry and other forms of art could and did impart factual knowledge alongside aesthetic pleasure. Indeed, following Bacon, epistemological theories in eighteenth-century Britain focused on the intimate connection between pleasure and knowledge.

Perhaps, then, a more appropriate theory of romantic poetry might be derived from the writings of Niklas Luhmann, which describe poetry as a system of communication, one with a different function from ordinary conversation, but nonetheless with a set of communicative goals achieved through representations meant to be shared with an audience. On Luhmann's terms, the "moral-pedagogical function of art" is bound up with its aesthetic function in "providing the world with an opportunity to observe itself."[30] Poetry thus combines factual knowledge with an imagined realm of possibilities, linguistic and otherwise. In the particular case of romantic poetry, the self-observation or self-reference embodied in poetry often takes the form of an examination of language when jarred out of its usual setting and put into poems. Or, in other words, the poetic system moved away from the communicative system of the intellectual disciplines because they came to have different relationships to their languages.

The intellectual disciplines invested their energies in developing specialized vocabularies and systems of signification that would (ideally) strictly delimit the meanings of words and syntactic units to particular and unchanging meanings for the sake of linguistic perspicuity. However, perspicuity did *not* likewise lie at the heart of poetic uses of language. Poetry of the romantic era was not concerned with delimiting the representational possibilities of ordinary or specialized language; rather, it sought to exercise the full expressive potential of such language in a range of linguistic circumstances. In fact, poetic uses of language came to signify the opposite of perspicuous uses. However, as the two systems differentiated themselves from one another, they maintained structural parallels because both took part in a larger network of economic and communication systems that demanded certain equivalent currencies for exchange. In particular, poetry reserved the right to draw on disciplinary as well as other forms of language as raw material for its own investigation into representation.

The need for this particular form of linguistic self-reference at this moment arose out of a change in the conception of poetry's relationship to other professional languages focused around the representation of knowledge. While the eighteenth century did not have an argot that could accurately be called a technical language of poetry to the same extent that it did for mathematics or even philosophy (perhaps not until Mallarmé and Rimbaud in France, or Eliot and Pound in America and Britain, was there an earnest attempt at creating a language for poetry divorced from general intelligibility), a notion of "poetic diction," a set of words, structures, and figures believed to be suited to poetry, did exist in the eighteenth century. This language resembled other, professional languages in that it arrogated to itself a particular set of words belonging uniquely to the poetic context.

As poet Thomas Gray explains in a 1742 letter to Richard West, the vocabulary of poetry — as conceived of in the eighteenth century — fundamentally differs from the language of everyday usage in that it includes a greater proportion of foreign idioms and calques, derivative forms, and words of each poet's own composition and invention. Gray gives a fertile list of examples from Dryden's poetry:

Full of *museful mopeings* — unlike the *trim* of love — a pleasant *beverage* — a *roundelay* of love — stood silent in his *mood* — with knots and *knares* deformed — his *ireful mood* — in proud *array* — his *boon* was granted — and *disarray* and shameful rout — *wayward* but wise — *furbished* for the field — the *foiled doddered* oaks — *disherited* — *smouldering* flames — *retchless* of laws — *crones* old and ugly — the *beldam* at his side — the *grandam* hag — *villanise* his Father's fame.[31]

Though the *Oxford English Dictionary* postdates Gray's writing by over a century, a dip into the OED confirms many of Gray's observations. The OED sometimes (albeit not consistently) uses the label "poetic" for words that occur almost exclusively in poetry or for words that were once more common but have become obsolete except in poetry. The *Dictionary*'s examples stress what is implied in Gray: in addition to the increased frequency of so-called poetic devices — turns of phrase that include alliteration, assonance, metaphor, and so on — in poetry, there are specific words, forms of words, and particular uses of words that belong almost exclusively to the word hoard of poetry. Where, for example, another writer might use "academy," the poet has often instead preferred "academe." (Showing its literary stripes, the *Times Literary Supplement* has in recent decades revived "academe" as an alternative to "academy.") A former plural for "beef" – "beeves" – was dropped by speakers and writers in general but was retained in poetry to refer to oxen or cattle.

Certain prefixes and suffixes are considerably more common in poetry than in other forms of writing, and these forms often exist or survive only or primarily in poetry. To take an example: the prefix "back-" combined with a present participle to make adjectives, as in "back-drawn, -flung, -thrown, -turned," etc, owes its continued existence entirely to verse poetry from Sidney through Elizabeth Browning and beyond. This example speaks also to the general predilection for prefixed verbs and past- and present-participial adjectives formed from these verbs in the poetry of the long eighteenth century. Much of what is lexically distinctive about the poetry of this period, borrowed to some extent from earlier – and sometimes resuscitated in later – English poetry, is embodied in these words. "Up" used as a prefix for verbs is reserved almost exclusively for verse poetry. Tracking the use of such a word can reveal how poets borrow language from other poets, as the word has in practice been reserved for such contexts. For example, *Paradise Lost*'s liquid "uproll'd / As drops on dust conglobing from the dry" echoes, among other verse precedents, Edward Fairfax's 1600 translation of Tasso's *Jerusalem*, "the sweat ... the dust therein uprold."

Perhaps the most frequently derided example of eighteenth-century poetic phrasing is the frequently occurring "finny tribe." However, this stock expression was never reserved for poetry in particular. Throughout the period, "finny tribe" regularly appears as a synonym for "fish" in contexts as mundane as guides to angling, brewing, and using a microscope. (I would not go so far as to say that "finny tribe" does not signal an attempt to produce a rhetorical flourish, as common – or hackneyed – as it may have been. Insofar as the poetic is thought to extend beyond poetry, "finny tribe" thus remains a viable candidate for the label "poetic diction.") In any case, "finny tribe" points out the tendency for adjectives to be the signals for attempts at poetic turns of thought. In other words, innovation in adjectives is a common property of English poetry. A new adjective or noun–adjective pairing compounded of parts whose individual signification is well-known, but whose combination opens up a wider latitude of meaning, can function as a condensed metaphor, packing considerable meaning into a word or two. These adjectival nonce words can, as in the previous paragraph, take the form of participials, but they can also appear in other forms. Sometimes this kind of linguistic novelty in poetry is attributed to verse's requirement for meter or rhyme, but this explanation is insufficient. For example, the use of "changeful" in Dryden's "changeful temper of the skies" (evoking Shakespeare's "changeful potency") does not rhyme – or need to rhyme – with another word, and it bypasses the grammatically more predictable and metrically equivalent form, "changing." This form of compounding, a noun plus the ending "ful," is an established and thus easily understood part of the language, but the specific combination is unusual, virtually nonexistent, outside poetry. "Changeful" thus calls attention to itself and the wide range of meanings it could signify.

During the early and mid-eighteenth century, poets were wont to hold up Dryden as the standard of poetic writing in the modern world (Johnson's dictionary is a conspicuous example of this tendency), it is against this view of poetry that Wordsworth positioned his writing.[32] It may be taken as a long-term measure of the romantic poets' success in influencing poetic taste that so much of Dryden's work has fallen so much out of favor even in university contexts. The much bandied-about term "poetic diction" has come to stand for all the romantics disliked in the poetry of their immediate predecessors. It behooves us, though, to revisit the term because in the eighteenth and early nineteenth centuries, the significance of "poetic diction" was more specific than this. In 1715, Alexander Pope gave an empirical-historical definition of the term – poetic diction is the kind of language we find in Homer. "We acknowledge him," Pope wrote of Homer, "the Father of Poetical Diction."[33] Pope's understanding of Homer was precisely Coleridge's problem with so-called "poetic diction": Coleridge found in Pope's translations of Homer the wellspring of infelicitous language in poetry, "the main source of our pseudo-poetic diction."[34] To Coleridge's mind, Pope's translation of the *Iliad* could best be described as a linked chain of syllogisms that have lost all poetic and sometimes even logical sense. It is "difficult to determine whether," Coleridge writes, "the sense or the diction be more absurd."[35]

Coleridge's criticism echoed Edward Young's earlier strictures against Pope's Homer. Young's "Conjectures on Original Composition" argued that Pope had fallen prey to a "gothic demon" who enjoined him to massacre the *Iliad* with infelicitous phrasing and forced rhyme. However, according to Coleridge, generations raised on Pope had internalized his unfortunate poetic paradigms and had thus forgotten how to read poetry with an ear to sound and sense.[36] Similar feelings gave rise to Keats's "On First Looking into Chapman's Homer," a poem about how discovering George Chapman's sixteenth-century English translation of Homer had freed Keats, who could not read the learned languages, from the tyrannous monopoly Pope's popular translation had had over readers only capable of reading English. "Poetic diction," then, was portrayed as sharing many of the undesirable qualities of an expert language – obscurity and difficulty – without its positive aspects – accuracy and perspicuity.

Pope had not been the only one to support the notion that poetry had its own technical vocabulary unavailable to other writers. Mid-eighteenth-century periodical essays help us towards a more concrete conception of many of the arguments that Wordsworth would later refute. "Poetry Distinguished from other Writing," an essay that first appeared in the *British Magazine* and that is sometimes attributed to Oliver Goldsmith, opens with the argument that poetry differs from prose not on the basis of versification, but rather on the basis of its language:

If poetry exists independent of versification, it will naturally be asked, how then is it to be distinguished? Undoubtedly by its own peculiar expression: it has a language of its own, which speaks so feelingly to the heart, and so pleasingly to the imagination, that its meaning cannot possibly be misunderstood by any person of delicate sensations. It is a species of painting with words, in which the figures are happily conceived, ingeniously arranged, affectingly expressed, and recommended with all the warmth and harmony of colouring: it consists of imagery, description, metaphors, similes, and sentiments, adapted with propriety to the subject, so contrived and executed as to soothe the ear, surprise and delight the fancy, mend and melt the heart, elevate the mind, and please the understanding.[37]

For a poet to paint such word-pictures with a "language of his own," he needs to cover his canvas densely with "tropes and figures … artfully disclos[ing] ideas" through "epithets" and "compound epithets … sounds collected in order to echo the sense conveyed, … apostrophes," and "above all, the enchanting use of the prosopopoeia, which is a kind of magic, by which the poet gives life and motion to every inanimate part of nature." Knowing full well the average rhetoric manual would contain a similar thesaurus from which the prose writer or orator might also choose his figures, the essay's author notes that poetry could and indeed ought to use these linguistic ornaments more liberally than an orator would because the poet appeals to imagination, not to reason. The poet of the mid-century age disdained linguistic sobriety in favor of a Bacchanalian excess of image.

Perhaps more curiously for audiences now, this essay likewise includes a list of specific words that, by their very presence, could convert a sentence into poetry. It begins,

There are many other verbs of poetical import fetched from nature and from art, which the poet uses to advantage, both in the literal and metaphorical sense; and these have been always translated for the same purpose from one language to another; such as *quasso, concutio, cio, suscito, lenio, saevio, mano, fluo, ardeo, mico, aro,* to shake, to wake, to rouse, to soothe, to rage, to flow, to shine or blaze, to plough.

And continues,

> The Latin language teems with sounds adapted to every situation, and the English is not destitute of this significant energy. We have the *cooing* turtle, the *sighing* reed, the *warbling* rivulet, the *sliding* stream, the *whispering* breeze, the glance, the gleam, the flash, the *bickering* flame, the *dashing* wave, the *gushing* spring, the *howling* blast, the *rattling* storm, the *pattering* shower, the *crimp* earth, the *mouldering* tower, the *twanging* bow-string, the *clanging* arms, the *clanking* chains, the *twinkling* stars, the *tinkling* chords, the *trickling* drops, the *twittering* swallow, the *cawing* rook, the *screeching* owl, and a thousand other words and epithets, wonderfully suited to the sense they imply.[38]

The list strikes us now because the inherent poetic qualities of these words seem less than self-evident to modern ears. This rapid litany of participials tends to provoke laughter rather than some more refined poetic emotion. Packed so closely together, these phrases catalog the hackneyed, the overwrought, and the quaint.[39] Or perhaps the premise of this list jars with our sensibilities because we, too, have followed the romantics (in theory) in discounting the idea that words – least of all a seemingly random assortment of phrases – could be by definition poetic and by their very nature inspire both the imagination and the emotions.

Here it might be objected that these verbs do indeed have something in common: they are onomatopoetic. This objection is at best a weak one. Insofar as English users associate sound-words with a particular sound, they can be said to evoke that sound. The feeling that these words correspond to true sounds can be strong, but as linguists have long since determined, the sound-sense association called onomatopoeia has to do with representational conventions, one particularly prevalent in poetry, not a direct correspondence between sound and sonic event. This observation is enforced by the fact that onomatopoeia can still seem to be present when the words are rendered in participial form. The "ing" ending conveys present action in English, but there is nothing inherent in the /ŋ/ or /n/ sound that corresponds to action. Indeed, the identical ending makes the words sound like one another rather than like the individual sounds they represent. Further, the participial-noun pairing in English is at least in part patterned after the Latin poetry on which generations of English writers had been raised, in which the words sound rather different from those highlighted in the passage above, even when they are representing the same sound.

Wordsworth did not entirely part company with those who would define poetry as earlier eighteenth-century writers did, still holding that poetry ought to speak "feelingly to the heart." He likewise retained the idea that a poet's language should be "dignified and variegated, and alive with metaphors and figures."[40] Nor was Wordsworth among the first who objected to much of the language of eighteenth-century English poetry. Addison, for example, assailed the mismatch between language and thought in poetry in the English tradition, writing that "our *English* Poets have succeeded much better in the stile, than in [their] sentiments. Their Language is very often noble and sonorous, but the sense either very trifling or very common." On many counts, eighteenth- and nineteenth-century theories of poetry occupied a continuum, sharing many of the same standards. Addison also shared Wordsworth's view that poetry should avoid the jargony vocabulary of the trades and professions. In his criticism of *Paradise Lost*, Addison faults Milton for borrowing overmuch from the terms of art belonging to astronomy and architecture. By larding his poetry with pilasters, cornices, ecliptics, eccentrics, and trepidations, by following stars dropping from the zenith and rays culminating from the equator, Milton made "hard Things" linguistically *less* rather than *more* palatable.[41] In such cases, Addison regarded Milton's diction as failing to meet standards of linguistic propriety; the language did not suit the circumstances because the expert terminology of physicists or architects was not that of the poet.

By claiming to root his poetry in rural language and then lift it above that context, Wordsworth could anchor himself in a historically rich etymology that predated the specialization of language. But, of course, this move is more rhetorical than substantive. Wordsworth's emphasis on the language of the agricultural classes in his prose accrues new justifications to the familiar premise that the simple language of the country avoided the untruths and exaggerations bound up in a more rhetorically sophisticated language. It is similar to the idea voiced in Sprat's *History of the Royal Society* (1667), which maintains that the Royal Society prefers a prose that imitates a "natural way of speaking ... preferring the language of Artizans, Countrymen, and Merchants before that of Wits or Scholars." Wordsworth's position also bears a close kinship to Joseph Addison's profession of homespun wisdom in *Spectator* No. 177: "For my own part, I prefer a noble Sentiment that is depressed with homely Language, infinitely before a vulgar one that is blown up with all the Sound and Energy of Expression."[42] Likewise, the writings of the Christian disciples were frequently and positively described as hewing closely to the standards of everyday speech; as John David Michaelis notes in his 1771 introduction to the *New Testament*, "The writers of the New Testament in general have never pretended to the beauties of literary language; and St. Paul, who was the most able, has used in the epistles the same expressions, as he would have used in common conversation."

In other words, Wordsworth's valorization of language-minus-professional-sophistication puts him in a well-established anti-rhetorical tradition of plain-spoken truth, popular in England throughout the long eighteenth century. These several sources that lead into Wordsworth's philosophy of language suggest that he wanted to make the same move for poetry that experts in other fields of study had already purported to do for their prose – to begin again with a clean, crisp language, and build it up from the foundations. This brings Wordsworth close to philosophers and scientists of the eighteenth century, advocating enlightenment through linguistic renewal.

But while they thus shared the view that powerful sentiment underpinned the best poetry and that the words used in poetry needed to be different from those used in other, specialized pursuits, the difference between the romantics and their similarly anti-rhetorical eighteenth-century predecessors lay in their beliefs about how language should relate to meaning. The eighteenth-century and romantic modes of regarding poetic language resemble, respectively, what twentieth-century linguists and philosophers of language have called the "cloak" and "mold" theories of language.[43] The cloak theory advanced by Goldsmith or Addison is compactly stated in Pope's "Essay on Criticism": "True wit is nature to advantage dressed / What oft was thought, but ne'er so well expressed." Such views held that language dresses thought but is not coextensive with it. Language garnished thought; it served a decorative function. Like meanings could be dressed up in different fashions.[44] Wordsworth expressly opposes such theories in his poetry and in his prose works, as in his first "Essay upon Epitaphs" (1810):

Words are too awful an instrument for good and evil to be trifled with: they hold above all other external powers a dominion over thoughts. If words be not ... an incarnation of the thought, but only a clothing for it, then surely will they prove an ill gift[.]

Wordsworth, like Coleridge, generally subscribed to a mold theory, in which the words available to the poet controlled not only what he could express, but also what he could think.

The undesirable side effect of such a theory was that words, because they were inextricably linked with habitual patterns of thought, could also keep a poet's mind "prisoner, without liberty to tread in any path but that to which it confines him."[45] If a poet were to confine himself to – as Gray had recommended – "words of an hundred years old, provided antiquity have not rendered them unintelligible," he would be closing off poetry within a cocoon of poetic tradition and language instead of making it a flexible, modern instrument for conveying thought and emotion.[46] On this count, Coleridge concurred with Wordsworth. "Poetic language" embodied a false antiquarianism because it imitated old-fashioned phrasing without worrying overmuch about the meaning; poetic language kept poetry from keeping pace with thought.[47]

In the romantic portrayal, then, the poetic languages of the eighteenth century could never serve the function of the professional argots of other disciplines because, by definition, "poetic diction" refused to exercise the flexibility necessary for language to keep pace with thought. This move is what makes romantic poetic theory so congenial to modern criticism: language is generative, not simply reflective.[48] Rather than representing an object of study, language here creates the object of study, the poem.

III. THE PRISON HOUSE OF LANGUAGE

If poetry could be imagined as having a technical language (rather than a separate system of communication) in the eighteenth century, it could no longer be seen in such a way in the nineteenth. Much of Wordsworth's attack on poetic diction came from his surveying the intellectual landscape more generally, and realizing that poetry functioned – and needed to function – differently from other professional languages. And although Wordsworth's railing against the language of Gray's "Sonnet on the Death of Richard West," which underpins Wordsworth's attack on the artificial language of the poetry of the last age, made the sonnet seem much more removed from the common train of writing than it perhaps was, Wordsworth was not simply tilting at windmills. He might have found a better candidate for his criticism in Gray's 1757 "The Bard, a Pindaric Ode," a poem intricate in style, deep in learning, rich with a peculiar, poetic vocabulary, and difficult for most to read.[49]

Although they did not agree on all points, Coleridge helps us understand Wordsworth's position on the language of poetry more deeply and with more subtlety, suggesting that romanticism was not entirely hostile to the idea of disciplinary language. Throughout his prose works, Coleridge defends the need of science and philosophy to have an expert terminology.

In a letter that appeared in *Blackwoods' Magazine*, Coleridge responds to the question of why a speculative philosopher would need to use uncommon words, or technical meanings for common words:

But why employ words that need explanation? ... Put the same question to Sir Edward Smith, or any other member of the Linnaean Society, to whom you had applied for instruction in Botany! And yet he would require of you that you should attend to a score of technical terms ... Every science, every trade, has its technical nomenclature; every folly has its *fancy-words*; every vice its own slang – and is the science of humanity to be the one exception? Is philosophy to work without tools? To have no straw wherewith to make the bricks for her mansion-house but what she may pick up on the high road, or steal, with all its impurities and sophistications, from the litter of the cattle market?

In other words, for Coleridge, the humanistic disciplines each required a language, as any society needed its cant, any profession its argot.

Poetry was no exception to this rule: it was not prose, and therefore would and ought to contain sentences that "would be vicious and alien in correct and manly prose."[50] The language of conversation differs from that of poetry, "so much so indeed, that in the social circles of private life we often find a striking use of the latter put a stop to the general flow of conversation, and by the excitement arising from concentrated attention produce a sort of damp and interruption for some minutes after. But in the perusal of works of literary *art*, we *prepare* ourselves for such a language."[51] Quoting Milton, Coleridge envisions that poetry could likewise limit its audience by its language: "A poem is not necessarily obscure, because it does not aim to be popular. It is enough, if a work be perspicuous to those for whom it is written, and 'Fit audience find, though few.'"

But if for Coleridge there was a kind of poetic diction required in any form of art, that diction still differed from the technical nomenclatures of other fields because poetry had the peculiar responsibility of guarding "the purity of their native tongue with that jealous care, which the sublime Dante in his tract 'De la nobile volgare eloquenza,' declares to be the first duty of a poet. For language is the armoury of the human mind; and at once contains the trophies of its past, and the weapons of its future conquest."[52] Poetry must preserve the finest qualities of a language while it also serves as a standard for that language. That is, it is poetry's job to discover and fix an ideal, communal language, for, as Coleridge notes, "Anterior to cultivation the lingua communis of every country, as Dante has well observed, exists every where in parts, and no where as a whole."[53] Coleridge resorts to Dante as the authority on vernacular poetry, since Dante represented for him the first great effort to construct a national, literary language.

Coleridge leaves unremarked the other reason that Dante's early fourteenth-century Latin treatise, *De Vulgari Eloquentia*, stands out. Traditional, patristic interpretations of the story of Genesis 11.1–9 tell of the ancient Babylonians' attempt to build a tower to the heavens. When construction begins, all persons speak a single Edenic language, the same one that Adam and Eve had used in communicating with one another and with God. Most interpretations of this story understand God's subsequent action (quoted here in the language of the King James Bible) – "confound[ing] their language that they may not understand one another's speech" and "scatter[ing] them abroad from thence upon the face of all the earth" – as punishment for humanity's hubristic attempt to reach the divine realm and challenge its power. The story of Babel has proven to have extraordinary explanatory power. It accounts for the chaos of human languages in which speakers of different languages cannot converse and in which even speakers of the same language suffer from the communicative difficulties brought about by linguistic ambiguity and language change.

Dante's *Vernacular Eloquence* adds a new twist to an old story by proposing that the biblical story of the tower of Babel is a parable about the division of labor. Dante's interpretation introduces an additional detail: the ancient Babylonians realized that they would need to divide up the tasks of building if they wanted to erect a tower that would truly touch the heavens. As Dante writes, "Some gave orders, some drew up designs; some built walls, some measured them with plumb-lines, some smeared mortar on them with trowels; some were intent on breaking stones, some on carrying them by sea, some by land; and other groups still were engaged in other activities." They continued "until they were all struck by a great blow from heaven." This divine stroke made permanent the divisions among the groups by making each of them speak a different language available only to the others of their profession. As Dante writes, "Only among those who were engaged in a particular activity did their language remain unchanged: so, for instance, there was one for all the architects, one for all the carriers of stones, one for all the stone-breakers, and so on for all the different operations." Furthermore, "As many were the types of work involved in the enterprise, so many were the languages by which the human race was fragmented; and the more skill required for the type of work, the more rudimentary and barbaric the language they now spoke." In sum: the fragmentation of language is a consequence of the division of knowledge.

Of course, unlike the Italy of Dante's era, England in the nineteenth century did have a national language. Coleridge slants, or deliberately misconstrues, the historical circumstances in which Dante wrote to create a context for his own remarks. Much as Wordsworth couches his desire to reform language in a fantasy of returning to a pure linguistic source in rural language, Coleridge attempts to find his own originary wellspring of modern, vernacular poetry in Dante. He does so to call attention to the fact that his vision of the *lingua communis* does not derive from a language anywhere in circulation. It exists nowhere in what his age identified as the learned, busy, or conversable worlds of readers. Rather, it is a language defined by literary production, and by high literary art in particular, in contradistinction to "the composition of our novels, magazines, public harangues, &c." which are "commonly as trivial in thought, and yet enigmatic in expression, as if Echo and Sphinx had laid their heads together to construct" them.[54]

In other words, Coleridge reverses the eighteenth-century association between common sense and common language, finding only verbal obscurity and confusion in popular discourse and linguistic perspicuity in the writings of poets with whom most of the populace had less than passing familiarity. On his account, popular language and the *lingua communis* necessarily lie miles apart, yet at the same time, he identifies the language of poetry not as an expert language but rather as a universal one. Coleridge's selection of the term "*lingua communis*" emphasizes the mistake he saw readers making in understanding Wordsworth's "the real language of men"; he wanted to replace this oft-misconstrued vulgarism with a Latin phrase out of the common run of English speech, thereby calling attention to the removal or elevation of this special use of language from ordinary use.

Coleridge's turn to Dante's poetry as a model for forming a *lingua communis* also calls our attention to the fact that such a language is meant to be written rather than spoken. Coleridge's idea of a common language is one that nobody would ever speak, entirely a construction on the page, emphasizing its removal from the common train of conversational life, even when it references or represents that life. This further accentuates the intellectual divide implicit in Coleridge's vision of language: it requires a high level of literacy. Indeed, Coleridge devotes much of *Biographia Literaria* to demonstrating that an intellectual elite will always stand in contrast to those who were "Rudely disbranched" "From the tree / Of Knowledge, ere the vernal sap has risen," as he put it in his early poem "Religious Musings" (lines 265–67). Poetry served as the central vehicle for expressing this socioeconomic, educational difference, for both Wordsworth and Coleridge.

For his part, Wordsworth argues in his three "Essays upon Epitaphs" that the individuals whose social circumstances rudely disbranched them from the tree of knowledge are permanently marked by this break, retaining a "rudeness of expression" throughout their lives. And after their death, their epitaphs would perpetually "personate the deceased, and represent [them] as speaking from [their] own tomb-stone[s]" in equally "uncouth" language. While finding inspiration in this "monotonous language," Wordsworth's many negative epithets for this particular "language of men," before it is mitigated through the poet's intervention, speaks volumes.[55] The poet again protests too much in arguing that he has not "affect[ed] any superior sanctity" in regarding the language of the lower orders, because, indeed, this is the primary message of his remarks, as he notes the "striking" formal faults in the written compositions of English rustics and provincials. Reading the tombstones he (allegedly) finds in English villages, monuments that he considers the main written expression of certain classes of men, Wordsworth points to "the homeliness of some of the inscriptions, the strangeness of the illustrative images, the grotesque spelling, with the equivocal meaning often struck out by it, and the quaint jingle of the rhymes."[56] Even as Wordsworth inaugurates an exchange between the language of the laboring classes and the language of poetry in his essays, prefaces, and poems, he sharpens the division between the way language is used in poetry and its use in conversation, and between the way language is used by members of the intellectual classes and its use by those of other social classes. Indeed, Wordsworth's linguistic juxtapositions across his poetic oeuvre point to the gap between poetic and other forms of communication more forcibly than his eighteenth-century predecessors ever did.

In the *Lyrical Ballads* and the *Excursion*, Wordsworth's poetry underscores the contrast between the kinds of language available to the speakers of his poems and thus shows how the "reality" of "the real language of men" is dislocated through poetic verse. In moving in and out of the consciousness of his speakers, Wordsworth achieves something akin to what critics of the novel have called free indirect discourse. This unmarked appropriation of thought and language implies judgment alongside sympathy, calling attention to itself as a form of linguistic representation, achieving the kind of artistic self-reference that Luhmann describes.

While the linguistic self-reference of Wordsworth's poetry focused mainly on illuminating the variations of language among social classes, Coleridge attended more to the languages of the disciplines themselves. He wrote several poems about the intersections of science, religion, and literature, including ones that represented conversations or confrontations among their languages. This relationship is perhaps captured most succinctly in his short, humorous poem "Verses Trivocular." While not generally considered central to the Coleridgean canon, this poem should not therefore be dismissed. Indeed, it beautifully captures in miniature much of Coleridge's poetic theory:

> Of one scrap of science I've evidence ocular.
> A heart of one chamber they call unilocular,
> And in a sharp frost, or when snow-flakes fall floccular,
> Your wise man of old wrapp'd himself in a Roquelaure,
> Which was called a Wrap-rascal when folks would be jocular.
> And shell-fish, the small, Periwinkle and Cockle are,
> So with them will I finish these verses trivocular.

"Trivocular" is, of course, a nonce word, invented to capture the etymological play among words belonging to very different vocabularies, while at the same time showing the particular capacity of poetry to manipulate and invent language. The "evidence ocular" of the first line invokes a scientific context in which empirical data reigns supreme, but the inversion of adjective and noun here calls attention to the poetic norm in which reversal of word order for the sake of emphasis or rhyme is permissible in a way it would not be in ordinary speech, or even in scientific discourse. "Unilocular," or having a single loculus or chamber, had currency in the eighteenth century in technical writings about medicine and natural history. "Floccular" similarly has a scientific referent, introduced into English through chemistry and physics; it signified a resemblance to "a small quantity of loosely aggregated matter resembling a flock of wool, held in suspension in, or precipitated from, a fluid."[57] In other words, "floccular" referred to wispy constellations of solid particles visible in a liquid suspension that resembled sheep's wool. "Flocculi" turn up, for example, in the description of a solution in Irish chemist Richard Kirwan's *Geological Essays* of 1799. Coleridge reminds us of the metaphor implicit in the technical term; understanding the third line of the poem requires understanding how the metaphor could be communicated to describe softly falling snow – snow that appeared as if suspended in a liquid – that would contrast with the sharp, stark solidity of icy frost. These two terms, "unilocular" and "floccular," are wrenched from their original linguistic contexts and made to take on new descriptive functions, while at the same time jarring the reader into realizing that they belong to other discourses. The words call attention to themselves and their origins, while at the same time, Coleridge shows that any word can be made poetic (or the subject of poetry) through metaphoric appropriation and syntactic placement.

Like "unilocular" and "floccular," the following rhyme "Roquelaure" (a knee-length coat) was also a word introduced into English in the eighteenth century and also had its origin in another language, in this case French. The terms of art from a number of different discourses (not all disciplinary) brought together within this "jocular" rhyme illustrate the ability of the poet to hold discordant languages in a suspended equilibrium through rhythm and rhyme. He then deflates his own term of art, by identifying the colloquial term "wrap-rascal," another eighteenth-century coinage, as referring to the same garment. The potential for replacing a high term with a low one interrogates the need for technical language at the same time that it suggests a preference for the technical term. Coleridge drives home the relationship between the linguistically sophisticated and the colloquial in line six, which culminates in a grouping that wrenches mundane linguistic content ("Periwinkle and Cockle are small shellfish") into a syntactic pattern only possible in poetry ("And shell-fish, the small, Periwinkle and Cockle are"). While the content of this line has to do with the binomial patterns or templates used in Linnaean classification, the effect of the line is to call attention to the idea of pattern and linguistic pairing itself.

In the final line, Coleridge returns us to his own neologism "trivocular" to end the poem. In so doing, he shows us how words can take on meanings within a poetic context, meanings which refuse to be singularly denotative. On one level, "trivocular" calls attention to the fact that Coleridge has used the meme "ocular" exactly three times previously in the poem (ocular, unilocular, jocular), and that he has also found three homophonic pronunciations with different spellings (Roquelaure, floccular, Cockle are). "Trivocular" also joins the idea that one must repeatedly vocalize, or make "vocular," these words in order to hear the relationship among them. It also suggests the potential triviality of the whole "ocular" endeavor: "trivia" + "ocular." While the poem specifies that it should be read with a sense of humor or play, it also shows how a common language can be made out of pieces taken from many different sources, and how poetry refuses to commit itself to any single one of them, forcing them to communicate with one another within the bounds of the poem.

Despite their differences on the origin of such a communal language, both Wordsworth and Coleridge share a similar ideal of poetry as a repository of a purified English tongue that would both be intelligible to all and catch the reader's imagination in a way that the "smooth market-coin" of modern urban language did not. The alternative they offered, however, became more the province of the specialist than they had imagined – poetry and its study took its place as one of the many coterie fields of knowledge depicted in the *Encyclopédie*'s diagram, much as Bacon had predicted.

We can likewise see the seeds of the eventual growth of the literary field towards autonomy from other forms of writing in the romantics' double recognition that poetry needed to be set apart from ordinary, conversational speech while at the same time refusing the specialized language of an intellectual discipline. The autonomy of the field was predicated on a political statement about the autonomy of poetic language. The dissatisfaction Wordsworth and Coleridge frequently expressed with both the learned scientist and the vulgar reader tended to detach poetry both from the learned world and from the popular one.

By choosing not to define the poet as a producer of new knowledge – or of new language – poetry did not fit the new eighteenth-century model of the intellectual disciplines arranged around individual objects of study. And while the romantics rejected the "object of study" as the guiding premise of their discipline, preferring instead to take all knowledge, not a single object, into their purview, the object-based model tended to be the one embraced by the newly organized universities of the nineteenth and twentieth centuries.[58] The incompatibility of the poet's career with this model is perhaps evinced most clearly in the development of the nineteenth-century university. It was not the writing of vernacular poetry but the study of it that held a place in the curriculum. The reading of "literature" was thus sliced apart from the composition of it in the evolution of English and American universities, which partitioned disciplines by the materials under consideration.

Then again, another way of reading the Encyclopedic chart would be to remark that it is not that less space has been devoted to the arts, but rather that the realm of imagination – given space equal to that of "memory" and "reason" – is divided up into fewer disciplines. The intellectual terrain of poetry is just as broad as that of history or philosophy, but the number of specialties that cover the field of poetry is much smaller. The result might be that in contrast to the increasingly specialized state of its competitor disciplines, the knowledge produced by poetry is less divided and more unified.

Coda: Common Sense and Common Language

Scene five of Bertolt Brecht's *Galileo* opens with a burst of laughter emerging from an assemblage of monks, scholars, and prelates in the Collegium Romanum. They exchange witticisms about Galileo's alleged proof that the earth revolves around the sun. A small group gather to pretend that the earth is indeed moving beneath their feet, forcing them to reel drunkenly about the stage:

A MONK: It's rolling fast, I'm dizzy. May I hold onto you, Professor? (*He sways dizzily and clings to one of the scholars for support.*)
THE SCHOLAR: Old Mother Earth's been at the bottle again. Whoa!
MONK: Hey! Hey! We're slipping off! Help!
SECOND SCHOLAR: Look! There's Venus! Hold me, lads. Whee!
SECOND MONK: Don't, don't hurl us off onto the moon. There are nasty sharp mountain peaks on the moon, brethren!
VARIOUSLY: Hold tight! Hold tight! Don't look down! Hold tight! It'll make you giddy![1]

Brecht's scene beautifully draws out the struggle that new knowledge confronts in overcoming the mind's enthrallment to received wisdom and to what Adam Smith has called "the natural prejudices of sense." Indeed, early in his career, Adam Smith commented on the reception of the Copernican system of astronomy, as supported by Galileo:

When it appeared in the world, it was almost universally disapproved of, by the learned as well as by the ignorant. The natural prejudices of sense, confirmed by education, prevailed too much with both, to allow them to give it a fair examination. A few disciples only, whom he himself had instructed in his doctrine, received it with esteem and admiration.

The kind of knowledge that goes by the name "common sense," a mixture of natural predilections and educational biases, often runs counter to what researchers find in their intellectual labors. As Smith has so succinctly put

it: habits of the imagination "suffer the greatest violence when obliged
to pursue" new ways of looking at the world. Unsettling, revolutionary
knowledge first spreads itself within a field of knowledge among like- or
open-minded scholars and students, trained in the methods that led to
the discovery, who subsequently develop the apparatus for convincing a
wider range of scholars and then ultimately a lay public – or an assem-
bly of churchmen prone to jeering – that the "natural prejudices of the
imagination" need to be "overturned." Calling practitioners of a discipline
"disciples," as Adam Smith often does, seems especially apt, regardless of
discipline. Once these disciple-initiates are inducted into the mysteries of
a new discovery, they take on the responsibility of explaining new ideas in
a manner that is palatable to what Smith has appropriately deemed "the
natural taste of mankind."

Yet, despite Galileo's or Copernicus's difficulties, Smith also intuits that
it is much easier for a natural scientist or a mathematician to convince
non-experts of the accuracy of his or her position because it is difficult –
often impossible – for a lay audience to test results couched in expert idioms, forged by disciplinary procedures, and dependent on specialized
apparatus. Indeed, according to Smith, Descartes had managed "for near
a century together" to deceive the French nation in believing his writings
on the "revolutions of heavenly bodies" because few had the mental, physical, and linguistic equipment to challenge him. In contrast, as many of his
compatriots had done, Smith suggests that anyone possessed of a reading
knowledge of English and a modicum of self-awareness might claim the
ability to judge the writings of a moral philosopher because said philosopher addressed objects to which all persons seemed to have access (their
own moral sentiments) in a language (English, French, German, etc.)
similarly available to everyman. Then as now, those who work on moral
or literary subjects open themselves up to ridicule precisely because they
often challenge the grounds of common sense while relying at least in part
on common language to relay their message, a position easily made subject
to parody.

However, as George Berkeley remarked in his 1710 *Principles of Human
Knowledge*, common sense and common language are perhaps too closely
linked for one to be used objectively to evaluate the other. As Berkeley
writes, "language is suited to the received opinions, which are not always
the truest … [I]t is impossible – even in the most rigid, philosophic reasonings – so far to alter the bent and genius of the tongue we speak as
never to give a handle for cavillers to pretend difficulties and inconsist-
ences." That is, the language of common life rarely lets go of perceptual or

otherwise traditional idioms, even when they are no longer believed to be fact. This is perhaps easier to see in the sciences than in the humanities. Berkeley provides one example drawn from astronomy: "They who ... are convinced of the truth of the Copernican system do nevertheless say 'the sun rises,' 'the sun sets,' ... and if they affected a contrary style in common talk it would without a doubt appear very ridiculous."[2] The naïve visual realism implicit in such statements as "the sun rises" runs counter to what scientists – and, by Berkeley's time, a general public as well – know to be true. When pressed, few would argue for the superiority of the English language's built-in representations of the relationship between the sun and the earth over those derived from Newtonian physics. But even though we latter-day Copernicans subscribe wholeheartedly to the heliocentric model of the universe, we still tell our friends that we drove up the coast to enjoy the gorgeous sunset, while knowing full well that it is the earth, not the sun, whose revolution causes the sun's nightly disappearance. We still use the common phrase, even when it no longer represents either expert knowledge or the *sensus communis*. More often than we acknowledge, there is a radical disconnect between the language we use in common conversation and what either experts or lay persons believe about the workaday world. If the very function of academic research regardless of discipline is, as Jonathan Culler has on occasion suggested, to dispute or at least to question commonly held views, then the tight alliance between common sense and common language needs to be broken or at least loosened.[3]

Physicist N. David Mermin has commented on the weakness of everyday languages for describing disciplinary technicalities: "Built into ordinary language – in its use of tenses, for example – are many implicit assumptions about the nature of temporal relations that we now know to be false." He describes the traps of everyday speech that make it difficult to communicate certain ideas in a straightforward manner. Physicists, however, have recourse to a non-vernacular language – mathematics – that has little overlap with the language of common life and thus is pliable in a way that ordinary language is not. In the twenty-first century, physicists are rarely confronted with the ridicule that Galileo faced for his counterintuitive writings because few non-physicists expect to be able to understand the technicalities. It has become second nature for non-scientists to trust the details to the scientists – the mathematics must work if the plane flies.[4] It is now primary to the idea of a science that it will have a technical terminology that departs from ordinary expression, even when it partly shares a vocabulary with that language.

However, philosophers who struggle to describe what a moral sense is, or how ideas are formed, or how markets perform in a recession, nonetheless continue to be held accountable for their language's contradiction of common sense as embodied by common language. The commitment to broadly intelligible language dies hard in the Anglo-American tradition, both within humanistic disciplines themselves and in the minds of a reading public. For example, if we revisit the writings of Gilbert Ryle, we notice that he writes that philosophers (alongside members of other humanistic disciplines as well as most professionals) "would all be well advised to try very hard to write in plain and blunt words." He follows this exortion with the caveat:

Hobbes who had [the] virtue of writing plainly and bluntly was a lesser philosopher than Kant who lacked it; and Plato's later dialogues, though harder to translate, have powers which his early dialogues are without. Nor is the simplicity of his diction in Mill's account of mathematics enough to make us prefer it to the account given by Frege whose diction is more esoteric.[5]

What is striking about Ryle's account is that he never stops to consider that there might be a connection between Kant's brilliance and his difficulty, or between Frege's insight and his occasional impenetrability. The moralistic strain that runs through Anglo-American humanities has trouble admitting that struggle towards new ideas may very well entail a difficulty in expression. The physicist's argument with which Chapter 1 ended – that the only true way to gain access to nature's beauty is through its language, mathematics – denies another well-known truth in science: namely, that there are often multiple ways to express the same problem and not all of them are mathematical.

The German tradition is friendlier to difficulty of expression in the humanities and social sciences, for reasons that go beyond the scope of this project. However, as we have seen, as much as public criticism has condemned the use of specialized languages, academics of all stripes have found them necessary to do their work. It is worth noting that claims to found a new science are often closely coupled with declarations of new vocabularies. For example, Frederic Engels's 1886 preface to the first English edition of Marx's *Capital* remarks: "There is ... one difficulty we could not spare the reader: the use of certain terms in a sense different from what they have, not only in common life, but in ordinary political economy." For Engels, "this was unavoidable" because:

Every new aspect of science involves a revolution in the technical terms of that science. This is best shown by chemistry, where the whole of the terminology is radically changed about once in twenty years, and where you will hardly find a single organic compound that has not gone through a whole series of different names. Political economy has generally been content to take, just as they were, the terms of commercial and industrial life, and to operate with them, entirely failing to see that by so doing it confined itself within the narrow circle of ideas expressed by those terms ... [A]ll industry, not agricultural or handicraft, is indiscriminately comprised in the term of manufacture, and thereby the distinction is obliterated between two great and essentially different periods of economic history: the period of manufacture proper, based on the division of manual labour, and the period of modern industry based on machinery.[6]

In other words, Marx is not writing entirely in the language of common life and this is a necessary part of defining the *science* of political economy. While Engels draws out an analogy between chemistry and political economy to make the case for the scientific nature of the latter, his case was nonetheless a harder one to prove than chemistry's precisely because Marx continued to use many of the same words employed in common life, in contradistinction to chemistry, which, by the time Engels was writing, had adopted a new, diagrammatic representational system that was drawing as much as it was language.

Almost fifty years ago, Northrop Frye suggested that literary criticism could be made into a science, and its practitioners in English literature departments could likewise be transformed into finely tuned empirical investigators. Similarly, in his recent essay on the science and culture wars, John Guillory wonders, "Whether it will be possible now to give up the conflict of the faculties in favor of a smaller but surer place [for literary scholarship] among the sciences is the question before us." (Guillory's implied answer is a muffled "yes.") Though neither proposes it directly, Guillory's or Frye's respective desires to have literary criticism, philosophy, and the like classed as "sciences" rather than "humanities" would seem to depend on a simultaneous assertion that their disciplinary productions depart from both common sense and the language of common life because at times they need to do so.

I end this study with the assertion that a discipline's claim to systematic generation of knowledge often depends on a transformation of language. Although this transformation requires justification, disciplines that have squarely asserted that they have both special procedures and special means of representation are generally awarded a higher status in the modern university and in public culture. Perhaps it is time for the humanistic disciplines to address how their methods accord them a special claim to a particular field of knowledge and how, at the same time, their methods of representing this knowledge in language are likewise distinctive.

Notes

CHAPTER I THE ECONOMIES OF KNOWLEDGE

1 In "What is Enlightenment?" Foucault almost begs for an escape from questions that demand that readers take a stance for or against enlightenment and urges the consideration instead of the Enlightenment as a historical period with an inescapable legacy, regardless of what our particular values are. Michel Foucault, "What Is Enlightenment?" in *Foucault Reader*, ed. Paul Rabinow (New York: Pantheon, 1984), 42–43.

As historians have often pointed out, England did not have an "enlightenment" in precisely the same way that France or even Germany did. However, scholars have also demonstrated that in English letters, the metaphor of illumination or enlightenment was often used to describe both the process of educating readers and the commitment to advancing the study of nature and of humankind. So, if the term "enlightenment" is not strictly accurate as a descriptor of a British historical period, the metaphor of enlightenment certainly thrived during the mid-eighteenth century in Great Britain. See Roy Porter, *Enlightenment: Britain and the Creation of the Modern World* (London: Penguin, 2000), xvii. Porter takes as his point of departure for identifying an enlightenment in eighteenth-century England a 1985 essay by historian J.G.A. Pocock in which Pocock argues that while England lacked a "*parti des philosophes*," an organized intelligentsia who broke with the ruling powers, it nonetheless had its own species of philosophical and cultural enlightenment, one that put England in the vanguard of scientific and humanistic modernity while leaving it politically and sometimes religiously conservative. J.G.A. Pocock, *Virtue, Commerce, and History: Essays on Political Thought and History, Chiefly in the Eighteenth Century* (Cambridge University Press, 1985).

2 See Adrian Johns, *The Nature of the Book: Print and Knowledge in the Making* (University of Chicago Press, 1998), 49–50, and James Stephens, *Francis Bacon and the Style of Science* (University of Chicago Press, 1975), 1.

3 Oliver Goldsmith, *Collected Works of Oliver Goldsmith*, ed. Arthur Friedman, 5 vols. (Oxford: Clarendon, 1966), 2.161.

4 Goldsmith seems to have felt some ambivalence on this point. In his periodical *The Bee*, Goldsmith laments that despite the encouragement a reading public

gives to those who repeat received opinions, "the writer who never deviates, who never hazards a new thought, or a new expression, though his friends may compliment him upon his sagacity, though criticism lifts her feeble voice in her praise, will seldom arrive at any degree of perfection." *Ibid.*, 428–29.

5 Porter, *Enlightenment: Britain and the Creation of the Modern World*, 11.

6 Michael Warner offers a trenchant critique of Eisenstein's print culture in which he argues that one must treat print culture as an effect, not simply a cause, of social, political, and cultural developments in the eighteenth century. Michael Warner, *The Letters of the Republic: Publication and the Print Sphere in Eighteenth-Century America* (Cambridge, MA and London: Harvard University Press, 1990), esp. 5–9.

7 Jürgen Habermas acknowledges that the ideal of the public sphere was often far from its reality, although many scholars writing after Habermas have overlooked his qualifications. However, as I discuss in this chapter, even the ideal was rather different from his depiction of it. Habermas, *The Structural Transformation of the Public Sphere: An Inquiry into a Category of Bourgeois Society,* trans. Thomas Burger and Frederick Lawrence (Cambridge, MA: MIT Press, 1991). For more on both the strengths and the limitations of Habermas's model, see "The Public and the Nation," *Eighteenth-Century Studies* 29, no. 1 (1995), the special issue of *Eighteenth-Century Studies* which considers how Habermas's model might be refined or expanded to take into account gender, class, and nation.

Harold Mah has recently called his fellow historians to account for their misreading of Habermas. Mah suggests that scholars have misunderstood Habermas's conception of the public sphere when they treat it as a hegemonic *space* into which individuals enter and then successfully "fuse into unity," becoming "a single, unified being, a mass subject." He argues that Habermas depicted the public sphere as a response to social fragmentation, only loosely held together by shared communicative goals and always confronting the possibility of collapse. Mah's point is well taken, although it is as much a refinement of Habermas's theory as a correction of misinterpretations of Habermas. Harold Mah, "Phantasies of the Public Sphere: Rethinking the Habermas of Historians," *Journal of Modern History* 72 (2000).

Reinhart Koselleck gives attention to the separation between the intellectual and the political realms that contributed to both the desire for and the ineffectiveness of public participation in state matters. Though he calls on English philosophies of the seventeenth century, Koselleck's *Critique and Crisis,* originally published in 1959, applies more acutely to the French case than to the English one, suggesting that local, nationally focused models may in certain respects be more effective in representing historical development than pan-European or trans-Atlantic ones. However, on a more general level, my study is deeply informed by Koselleck's attention to the manner in which the separation of learned writing from the realities of everyday life can have political consequences. Reinhart Koselleck, *Critique and Crisis: Enlightenment and the Pathogenesis of Modern Society* (Cambridge, MA: MIT Press, 1988).

8 These lines refer in part to Clifford Siskin, *The Work of Writing: Literature and Social Change in Britain, 1700–1830* (Baltimore: Johns Hopkins University Press, 1998), 20. While Siskin is right to point to the connection between changes in the representation of knowledge and the emergence of modern disciplinarity, his claim that the emergence of literature as a discipline focused on the "stylistic engagement of the reader" enabled the other disciplines to leave this task to authors of imaginative literature and literary critics and focus on their own specialization seems historically inaccurate, and, in any case, peculiarly unrelated to the evidence he provides. The chronology implicit in his argument runs against what we know about the development of the eighteenth-century disciplines – the emergence of physics as a discipline (and the public recognition that it had become so) certainly predated imaginative literature's taking on the function Siskin describes. And while Wordsworth did assert that poetry created a "common ground" on which all forms of knowledge could meet, more than anything else his assertion constitutes a belated attempt to specify for poetry a particular area of expertise that would stake its claim in relation to the already-specialized domains of knowledge with which it competed for attention. (See Siskin, *The Work of Writing: Literature and Social Change in Britain, 1700–1830*, 97–98.)

   Additionally, Siskin's declaration that the eighteenth and nineteenth centuries rejected a model in which "every kind" of knowledge "was a *branch* of philosophy" seems partly, but only partly, correct. Philosophy did ultimately cease to be the general category under which most intellectual disciplines could be adumbrated. However, the displacement of philosophy as the root of the intellectual tree did not entail a wholesale rejection of a disciplinary model in which fields of knowledge were considered as branching off from one another. Nineteenth-century editions of encyclopedias and thesauri testify that branching diagrams based on the metaphor of the tree of knowledge continued to be a way to describe the disciplinary division of knowledge, and they are still used today in modified form to represent the relations among university disciplines. What changed in the eighteenth century was what the branches were thought to represent. (See Siskin, *The Work of Writing: Literature and Social Change in Britain, 1700–1830*, 20.)

   For a succinct summary of the traditional divisions of the liberal arts and sciences, see Paul O. Kristeller's monumental article, "The Modern System of the Arts: A Study in the History of Aesthetics, Part I," *Journal of the History of Ideas* 12, no. 4 (1951), 506–8.

9 Jonathan Kramnick offers a lucid and useful analysis of the development of literary criticism as a profession in *Making the English Canon: Print-Capitalism and the Cultural Past, 1700–1770* (Cambridge University Press, 1998). However, in relating the general argument of this book to the wider arena of knowledge in his recent article on disciplinarity, he may slightly exaggerate the difference between the task of the humanist and that of other intellectuals in the eighteenth century by making too much of Locke's deferral to Newton's genius early in his *Essay*. Passages in Locke's *Essay*, and indeed much philosophy

from the first half of the eighteenth century, show that philosophers did not assume that their task was fundamentally different from that of the scientists. Kramnick's article nonetheless constitutes a powerful and succinct statement of the degree to which many humanistic disciplines struggled with the popular representation of their expertise. Jonathan Brody Kramnick, "Literary Criticism among the Disciplines," *Eighteenth-Century Studies* 35, no. 3 (2002): 346–47.

10 Though they often make arguments for the importance of not focusing on the written or printed word as the subject of their study, historians of science have, in recent years, collected a wealth of information about the interaction of natural philosophers with their audiences through print. See especially Steven Shapin and Simon Schaffer, *Leviathan and the Air-Pump: Hobbes, Boyle, and the Experimental Life* (Princeton University Press, 1985); Larry R. Stewart, *The Rise of Public Science: Rhetoric, Technology, and Natural Philosophy in Newtonian Britain* (New York: Cambridge University Press, 1992); and Jan Golinski, *Science as Public Culture: Chemistry and Enlightenment in Britain, 1760–1820* (Cambridge University Press, 1992).

11 See especially John Guillory, "The Sokal Affair and the History of Criticism," *Critical Inquiry* 28 (2002): 508. Whether such a reunion is possible remains for me an open question. If we adopt in part Kuhn's model of the sciences as fields in which "a firm research consensus" is a necessary prerequisite to a notion of progress in a discipline, it is not entirely clear whether or not such a thing would be possible in disciplines such as English, philosophy, theology, or even, at times, history. The parts of the humanities in Anglo-American universities that can indeed be transformed into human sciences have perhaps been underexplored, despite many attempts to do so. (See Kuhn, *The Structure of Scientific Revolutions*, 3rd edn. [Chicago: University of Chicago Press, 1996], 11–15.)

In a similar vein, although from a different point of view, Gayatri Spivak has recently offered a vision of how the discipline of comparative literature might "renovate" itself by allying itself with Area Studies, a field or fields generally ranked among the social sciences. Her call to action suggests that the global reach of Area Studies might reinvigorate a discipline that is collapsing because its foundation in European literature is, too, while simultaneously suggesting that the social sciences might also benefit from closer ties to the humanities. Gayatri Chakravorty Spivak, *Death of a Discipline* (New York: Columbia University Press, 2003).

12 Along these lines, it is perhaps worth revisiting at least one aspect of Koselleck's 1959 *Critique and Crisis*. Koselleck identifies an "intellectual stratum" in eighteenth-century societies whose moral and political philosophies took little notice of the exigencies of the political realm, increasingly moving into their own, private sphere without achieving their political goals.

13 Kramnick offers a new reading of this statement, arguing that it inaugurated a particularly eighteenth-century rhetorical position in which individuals who set themselves up as experts could simultaneously claim that "they were doing no particular labor – that they were merely reading and talking like the rest of the community" at the same time that "they were ushering in a new age of enlightened, public culture." Kramnick, "Literary Criticism among the Disciplines," 351.

14 See *Tatler* No. 89 (November 3, 1709). Steele, of course, was equally committed to exposing what he called the hypocrisy of the learned world, beginning from the premise that much that passed as learning was merely speculation or bickering rather than a contribution to the store of knowledge. See also *Tatler* No. 51 (August 6, 1709). Richard Steele, *The Tatler*, ed. A. Chalmers, 4 vols., *The British Essayists with Prefaces, Historical and Biographical* (Boston: 1856).

15 As Addison suggests in his political periodical *The Freeholder* (1715–16), the relationship between politics and the public was different from the relationship between the intellectual disciplines and the public in one respect: the public elected their government representatives. But many fewer individuals could vote than could hold opinions about political matters, and in shaping the climate of opinion, apart from an ability to intervene or participate more directly, the public took on similar roles in the political and literary realms.

16 For importantly related yet nonetheless differently inflected conceptions of disciplines from that advanced here, see in particular Thomas S. Kuhn, *The Structure of Scientific Revolutions*, 3rd edn. (University of Chicago Press, 1996) and Jacques Rancière, "Thinking Between Disciplines: An Aesthetics of Knowledge," trans. Jon Roffe, *Parrhesia* 1 (2006): 8.

17 Talcott Parsons, "Professions," in *International Encyclopedia of the Social Sciences*, ed. David Sills (New York: Macmillan-The Free Press, 1968), 536.

     In my focus on the publications of particular disciplines and their reception, my interests overlap in part with those of the Gulbenkian Commission on the Restructuring of the Social Sciences, led by Immanuel Wallerstein, which lists the following set of characteristics common to the social sciences' elevation to disciplinary status between 1850 and 1945:

1. The "institutionalization of training," which consisted of the establishment "in the principal universities first chairs, then departments offering courses leading to degrees in the discipline";
2. The "institutionalization of research: the creation of journals specialized in each of the disciplines: the construction of associations of scholars along disciplinary lines (first national, then international)";
3. And "the creation of library collections catalogued by the disciplines."

     This commission's goals differ from mine in large part because they were forward-looking rather than backward-looking, as adumbrated under their titular mission to restructure the social sciences.

18 Michel Foucault, *The Archaeology of Knowledge*, trans. A.M. Sheridan Smith (New York: Pantheon, 1972), 31–33; Ellen Messner-Davidow, David R.

Shumway, and David J. Sylvan, *Knowledges: Historical and Critical Studies in Disciplinarity* (Charlottesville: University of Virginia Press, 1993).

19   Biologists are not in full agreement about *the* definition of species, and it seems likely that there will never be a single definition that works both conceptually and practically for every kind of organism. The definition cited here comes from E.O. Wiley and R.L. Mayden, "The Evolutionary Species Concept," *Species Concepts and Phylogenetic Theory: A Debate*, eds. Q.D. Wheeler and R. Meier (New York: Columbia University Press, 1997). In "A Hierarchy of Species Concepts: The Denouement in the Saga of the Species Problem," Mayden surveys twenty-two definitions of species currently in play and pronounces this one the most general for conceptual (although not operational) purposes (*Species: The Units of Biodiversity*, eds. M.F. Claridge, A.H. Dawah, and M.R. Wilson [London: Chapman and Hall, 1997], 381–424). The second definition in the text comes from Bill McKelvey, "Organizational Systematics: Taxonomic Lessons from Biology," *Management Science* 24, no. 13 (1978), 1431.

20   This phrasing comes from David Sloan Wilson and Jin Yoshimura, "On the Coexistence of Specialists and Generalists," *American Naturalist* 144 (1994), 692. The topic is treated widely in the literature on biological evolution.

21   A useful general account of classificatory methods in biological systematics written for purposes of application to other fields is Bill McKelvey, *Organizational Systematics: Taxonomy, Evolution, Classification* (Los Angeles: UCLA Press, 1982). See esp. 42–49. McKelvey follows M. Beckner's *The Biological Way of Thought* in defining polythetic groups as "Groups whose members share most attributes in common; each attribute used to help define the group is held by many members but no attribute is held by all members" (459).

22   *Literary Language and its Public in Late Latin Antiquity and in the Middle Ages* (Princeton University Press, 1993), 18.

23   Immanuel Kant, *Conflict of the Faculties*, trans. Mary J. Gregor (Norwalk, CT: Abaris Books, 1979).

Andrew Abbott defines the modern professions according to their "knowledge system[s]" and their respective "degree[s] of abstraction." This definition theorizes professions as applications of academic systems of knowledge determined by real world needs for such conceptual structures and their practical functions. This definition of profession presupposes, in a more generous way than Kant, that disciplines of knowledge preexist or at least underpin the formation of a profession; it makes the professions rest on disciplinary bodies of knowledge. (*The System of the Professions: An Essay on the Division of Expert Labor* [University of Chicago Press, 1988].)

My own book aligns itself a bit more closely with Geoffrey Millerson's earlier account of the British professions in suggesting that the narrative lines – from either a theoretical or a historical point of view – that connect an initial "organization of personnel" to a formal profession do not necessarily run parallel. In other words, it may be difficult to identify one underlying characteristic, historical or theoretical, that defines the group of organizations we now call professions, and perhaps, by extension, disciplines. (*The Qualifying Associations* [London: Routledge, 1964].)

24 William Whewell, *History of the Inductive Sciences*, 3rd edn., *Cass Library of Science Classics 7* (London: Cass, 1967), 2.144, 221.

25 Percy Bysshe Shelley, *Shelley's Prose, or the Trumpet of a Prophecy*, ed. David Lee Clark (London: Fourth Estate, 1988), 294.

26 Adam Smith, "'Early Draft' of Part of *the Wealth of Nations*," in *Lectures on Jurisprudence*, ed. R.L. Meek, D.D. Raphael, and P.G. Stein (Oxford University Press, 1978), 574.

Smith expands on the division of intellectual labor in his *Lectures on Jurisprudence*, although he compressed his discussion of this topic significantly in the final version of *The Wealth of Nations*. Scholars have noted that Smith does not seem to have rejected or even revised his perspective on intellectual labor, but in preparing *The Wealth of Nations* for publication, he instead decided to emphasize the dependence of his theory of value on mechanical and manufacturing labor over and above all other kinds of work. (See Ronald L. Meek and Andrew S. Skinner, "The Development of Adam Smith's Ideas of the Division of Labour," *Economic Journal* 83, no. 332 [1973]: esp. 1102, 1105.) Following J.A. Schumpeter's classic *History of Economic Analysis*, several economic historians have observed that Smith's insistence on the division of labor as the primary and perhaps only source of economic progress was the chief innovation of the *Wealth of Nations*, and Smith was also in the vanguard among political economists in emphasizing the *productive* value of the work done by manufacturers and merchants alongside agricultural laborers. However, philosophers – like porters, MPs, and any professionals who did not create or sell a material product – continued to be classed as *unproductive* laborers in Smith's system, and the published version of the *Wealth of Nations* attends much more to productive than to unproductive work in the division of labor. (See Paul J. McNulty, "Adam Smith's Concept of Labor," *Journal of the History of Ideas* 34, no. 3 [1973]: 349–50; J.A. Schumpeter, *History of Economic Analysis* [New York: Oxford University Press, 1954], 187; J.G. West, "Adam Smith's Two Views on the Division of Labour," *Economica* 31, no. 121 [1964]: 24.)

As discussed later in this chapter, in the 1790s, Edinburgh professor Dugald Stewart would challenge Smith's emphasis on the degree to which the division of *productive* labor defined economic progress. Indeed, the aspect of *The Wealth of Nations* that Smith's contemporaries and immediate successors often found most interesting was its perceived defense of unregulated free trade; though, as other scholars have pointed out, Smith's advocacy of high wages, his interest in the intellectual and moral development of workers, and his insistence on fairness indicate that Smith himself had a much more complicated scenario in mind. (See M.G. Marshall, "Luxury, Economic Development, and Work Motivation: David Hume, Adam Smith, and J.R. Mcculloch," *History of Political Economy* 32, no. 3 [2000]: 636; M.G. Marshall, "Scottish Political Economy and the High Wage Economy: Hume, Smith, and Mcculloch," *Scottish Journal of Political Economy* 45, no. 3 [1998]; Richard F. Teichgraeber, III, "'Less Abused Than I Had Reason to Expect': The Reception of the Wealth of Nations in Britain, 1776–1790," *Historical Journal* 30, no. 2 [1987].)

27 Dugald Stewart, *Dissertation: Exhibiting the Progress of Metaphysical, Ethical, and Political Philosophy, since the Revival of Letters in Europe*, ed. William Hamilton, *The Collected Works of Dugald Stewart* (Edinburgh: Thomas Constable and Co., 1844), 12. Stewart instead advocated a new division of knowledge by object rather than by faculty, which would preserve many of the traditional divisions that Bacon or the *Encyclopédie* represented, but at the same time would not have need of the fictional constructs of the intellectual faculties and would instead rely on the objects at hand.

28 Francis Bacon's description of the system of human knowledge was given visual form alongside D'Alembert's *Discours Préliminere* to the *Encyclopédie*. While bearing strong influences of medieval and classical arrangements of the fields of knowledge, Bacon and the *Encyclopédie*'s system also reflect a struggle to represent newer beliefs about the relationship of fields of knowledge to one another. That their system was not universally held is testified to by Ephraim Chambers's 1728 English *Cyclopedia*, which offered its own binary-branching tree of knowledge. Chambers's tree appears rather different from the Bacon-*Encyclopédie* version, in that it uses Aristotelian rules for classification but not Aristotle's own system. Attempts to account for the relation of fields of knowledge continue throughout the eighteenth century and well into the next; Jeremy Bentham offers a competing (and, as is typical, unduly confusing) tree of knowledge in his educational treatise *Chrestomathia*, and Peter Mark Roget's still-familiar thesaurus attempts a similar diagram in order to classify groups of words. See Francis Bacon, *The Advancement of Learning*, ed. G.W. Kitchin (Philadelphia: Paul Dry Books, 2001); Ephraim Chambers, *Cyclopedia: Or, an Universal Dictionary of Arts and Sciences*, 2 vols. (London, 1728); Jeremy Bentham, *Chrestomathia*, ed. M.J. Smith and W.H. Burston, *Works of Jeremy Bentham* (New York: Clarendon, 1983); Peter Mark Roget, *Roget's Thesaurus of English Words and Phrases: Facsimile of the First Edition 1852* (London: Bloomsbury Books, 1992).

Paul O. Kristeller surveys a host of European depictions of the systems of arts and sciences, touching briefly on some of their differences with respect to the fine arts. See Paul Oskar Kristeller, "The Modern System of the Arts: A Study in the History of Aesthetics, Part 1," *Journal of the History of Ideas* 12, no. 4 (1951): 518–21. Anthony Grafton also gives a dazzling comparison of old versus new systems of knowledge in *Defenders of the Text, 1450–1800* (Cambridge, MA: Harvard University Press, 1991).

29 In 1728, Chambers wondered if "all [the] Inconveniences, and strain and stretch things" of the historical Aristotelian systems were in fact worthwhile. He writes, "I do not know whether it might not be more for the general

Interest of Learning, to have all the Inclosures and Partitions thrown down, and the whole laid in common again, under one undistinguishe'd Name. Our Inquiries, in such case, would not be confin'd to so narrow a Channel; but we should be led to explore, and pursue many a rich Mine and Vein, now doom'd to lie neglected, because out of the way." Chambers was not alone in such speculation, but though at times inconvenient, such divisions were also productive in directing the course of research, as Thomas Kuhn argues in *The Structure of Scientific Revolutions*.

30 Smith, "'Early Draft' of Part of *the Wealth of Nations*," 570.

31 "On the Character and Duty of an Academick" (The Johnsonians, 2000), 12–13, reprinted from *Hospitality: A Discourse Occasioned by Reading His Majesty's Letter* (London, 1793), 42–43.

32 In his 1893 *De la division du travail social*, Émile Durkheim adopts an organicist metaphor/model to characterize the need – moral and economic – for the division of labor. While, unlike Marx and Engels, Durkheim shares some of the philosophic optimism of his eighteenth-century predecessors, in the pre-Darwinian moment of Smith, Hume, and their contemporaries the balance of trade perhaps serves as well or better to identify the period's own commitment to both social and economic aspects of the division. Émile Durkheim, *The Division of Labor in Society*, trans. W.D. Halls (New York: Free Press, 1997).

33 David Hume, *Essays, Moral, Political, and Literary*, ed. Eugene F. Miller (Indianapolis: Liberty Classics, 1985), 270–71.

34 Adam Ferguson, *An Essay on the History of Civil Society, 1767*, ed. Duncan Forbes (Edinburgh University Press, 1966), 180.

35 Following the classical references of eighteenth-century writers, scholars have pointed out that one can indeed find classical precedents for discussions of the division of labor. Plato's *Dialogues* call attention to the division of labor between the carpenter and the shoemaker, and Plato notes elsewhere that "Quantity and quality are therefore more easily produced when a man specialises more appropriately on a single job for which he is naturally fitted." (Plato, *The Republic*, trans. H.D.P. Lee [Harmondsworth and Baltimore: Penguin, 1974]). While it is safe to say that the ancient world had trades and occupations, as Karl Marx pointed out, some form of social division of labor exists in even rudimentary societies; the difference lay in the fact that the modern world witnessed a division of labor which pervaded all aspects of life and came to define all social, intellectual, and economic relationships. See V. Foley, "The Division of Labour in Plato and Smith," *History of Political Economy* 6, no. 2 (1974); Karl Marx, *Capital: A Critique of Political Economy*, ed. Ernest Mandel, trans. Ben Fowkes, 3 vols. (New York: Vintage Books, 1977), 1.472; Ali Rattansi, *Marx and the Division of Labour* (London and Basingstoke: Macmillan Press, 1982), 3–4.

36 David Hume, *Essays, Moral, Political, and Literary*, ed. Eugene F. Miller (Indianapolis: Liberty Classics, 1985), 102. Ferguson, *An Essay on the History of Civil Society,* (1767), 179.

37 Hume, *Essays, Moral, Political, and Literary*, 271.

38   In his essays on the modern system of the arts, Paul O. Kristeller describes the eighteenth century as an age in which "critical writing" on the visual arts and music "for laymen" proliferated. As my succeeding chapters show, a parallel phenomenon occurred in the sciences. Paul Oskar Kristeller, "The Modern System of the Arts: A Study in the History of Aesthetics, Part 2," *Journal of the History of Ideas* 13, no. 1 (1951): 17. See also Kristeller, "The Modern System of the Arts: A Study in the History of Aesthetics, Part 1."

Michael McKeon briefly treats the conception of the division of labor in relation to the division of knowledge in *The Secret History of Domesticity: Public, Private, and the Division of Knowledge*, although he is more concerned with a distinction between public and domestic knowledge than with disciplinary versus popular, which do not make parallel cuts through eighteenth-century social history. (Baltimore: The Johns Hopkins University Press, 2005).

39   Adam Smith, *Lectures on Jurisprudence*, ed. R.L. Meek, D.D. Raphael, and P.G. Stein (Oxford University Press, 1978), 347. See also, Smith, "'Early Draft' of Part of *the Wealth of Nations*," 570.

40   John Stuart Mill would later pursue this idea in his *Principles of Political Economy* of 1848.

41   Dugald Stewart, *Lectures on Political Economy*, ed. William Hamilton, vols. 8 and 9, *The Collected Works of Dugald Stewart* (Edinburgh: 1855), 315.

42   Dugald Stewart, *Outlines of Moral Philosophy*, ed. Knud Haakonssen, 2nd edn., vol. 6, *Collected Works of Dugald Stewart* (Bristol: Thoemmes, 1994), 5. (Part 2, III.i.120)

43   There are, of course, many intellectual way stations between the Scottish philosophers of the eighteenth century and Marxian economics. The nineteenth-century theories of Schiller, Hamman, Hölderlin, Hegel, and their lesser-known contemporaries took up many of the negative effects of the division of intellectual labor on the whole individual. While the German situation differed from the British both in political organization and in the degree of state control of institutions, Hegel nonetheless could and did draw on the philosophy of the Scottish Enlightenment in writing his own philosophy of right. He borrowed the vocabulary of the division of labor and related core ideas from Smith and Ferguson, although Hegel gave a more prominent place than Smith had to how the division of labor bore on the social lives of individuals. The labor theories of the Scottish Enlightenment also saw further development in the British context, in the nineteenth-century writings of David Ricardo and in the mid-century Owenite communities. Marx himself knew all of these sources, as well as economic writings in French by Henri Storch and Frédéric Skarbek. On Hegel and his Scottish sources, see Raymond Plant, *Hegel* (Bloomington: Indiana University Press, 1973), 16–22. On modern, pre-Marxian theories of the division of labor more generally, see Rattansi, *Marx and the Division of Labour*, 15–41. On Marx's French sources, see Marx, *Capital: A Critique of Political Economy*, 471.

44   In describing his conception of hegemony, Antonio Gramsci writes, "If social classes do not exercise power directly but through political and cultural

intermediaries, then the role of these intermediaries – the intellectuals – in maintaining and reproducing a given economic and social order (in the exercise of hegemony), is of decisive importance ... The *division of labour* in class society separates manual from mental (intellectual) workers and largely reserves intellectual functions – which are functions of power – to specific social groups who reproduce themselves through the education system" (italics mine). Antonio Gramsci, *The Antonio Gramsci Reader: Selected Writings, 1916–1935*, ed. David Forgacs (New York University Press, 2000), 300.

45 *Ibid.*, 304.
46 See Peter Galison and Bruce Helvy, eds., *Big Science: The Growth of Large Scale Research* (Stanford University Press, 1992).
47 Charles Babbage, *On the Economy of Machinery and Manufactures*, 4th ed. (London: John Murray, 1846), chapter 20, sections 241–46.
48 Hannah Arendt, *The Human Condition*, 2nd edn. (University of Chicago Press, 1998), 92.
49 *Wealth of Nations*, I.331.
50 Arendt, *The Human Condition*, 90.
51 See John Barrell, *The Birth of Pandora and the Division of Knowledge* (London: Macmillan, 1992).
    Smith seems to have felt some ambivalence towards this distinction, lauding its virtues in the opening pages of the *Wealth of Nations* and regretting its negative consequences in the final book. For an attempt to bring these two views into concord, see West, "Adam Smith's Two Views on the Division of Labour."
52 See, for example, J.T. Desaguliers, *A Course of Experimental Philosophy*, 2nd edn., 2 vols. (London: W. Innys, T. Longman, T. Shewell and C. Hitch, and M. Senex, 1745), x. This advertising technique is discussed in more detail in Chapter 3.
53 Marx, too, had addressed the difference between producers and consumers in the context of material versus intellectual labor, in which the former produced goods and the latter used them.
54 Were this analysis to be taken forward into the twentieth century, we would need to add another kind of division of intellectual labor, the kind one finds in the modern sciences and social sciences in which a single research project can no longer be done by a single individual. This kind of division of labor – that of so-called "big science" – resembles more closely the capitalist division inside the factory that Marx describes, in which the ultimate product of the research group (a new method of analysis, a new drug, and so on) depends on the contributions of many members and in which no one person's contribution could generally stand on its own as a research product.
55 See Joseph M. Levine, "Strife in the Republic of Letters," in *Commercium Litterarium, 1600–1750: La Communication Dans La République Des Lettres: Conférences Des Colloqes Tenus à Paris 1992 Et à Nimègue 1993*, ed. Hans and Françoise Waquet Bots (Amsterdam: APA-Holland University Press, 1994).
56 The triple division I outline here shadows in certain respects that triparate system generated by one of Marx's sources, Frédéric Skarbek's *Théorie des richesses socials*. Skarbek concentrates on the divisions necessary to the production of material goods in a capitalist society; my study addresses how

intellectuals generate a parallel economy of knowledge, in which the principles are not usually directed toward financial gain. Frédéric Skarbek, *Théorie
des Richesses Sociales*, 2nd edn., 3 vols. (Paris: 1839), 84–85. Cited and translated in Marx, *Capital: A Critique of Political Economy*, 471.

57 My study, while a response to Habermas, is equally inspired by Bourdieu's
spatial projection of the fields of power operative on nineteenth-century
French literature.

58 See, for example, the work of Herbert Simon, *The Sciences of the Artificial*, 3rd
edn. (MIT Press, 1996).

59 Martine Groult points out that the four definitions of "discipline" given
explicitly in d'Alembert's *Encyclopédie* focus exclusively on the negative and
indeed nonscholarly aspects of "discipline," but that the work taken as a
whole yields up a more positive definition that resembles our modern sense
of a systematized intellectual discipline. ("Introduction," *L'Encyclopédie ou la
création des disciplines* [CNRS, 2003]: 4–5.)

60 Tony Becher, "The Significance of Disciplinary Differences," *Studies in
Higher Education* 19.2 (1994): 153.

61 Steve Fuller, "Disciplinary Boundaries: A Critical Synthesis," *4S Review* 3.1
(1985): 5, 12.

62 See especially George Stigler, "The Division of Labor is Limited by the Extent
of the Market," *Journal of Political Economy* 59.3 (1951): 185–93.

63 *American Economic Review*, 35.4 (September 1945): 519–30.

64 These works include Dominque Foray's *The Economics of Knowledge*, David
Warsh's *Knowledge and the Wealth of Nations*, Ernst Helmstädter's collec-
tion *The Economics of Knowledge Sharing*, Aldo Geuna's *The Economics of
Knowledge Production*, Loet Leydesdorff's *The Knowledge-Based Economy*,
Brian Arthur's several papers published as *Increasing Returns and Path
Dependency in the Economy*, and Dale Neef's *The Knowledge Economy*, among
others.

65 Foray, *The Economies of Knowledge*, 5. See also Olivier Favereau, "Theory of
Information: From Bounded Rationality to Interpretive Reason," in Pascal
Petit, ed., *Economics and Information* (Dordrecht: Kluwer, 2001), 125; and
Jacques Crémer, "Information in the Theory of Organization," in Petit, ed.,
Economics and Information, 132, 156.

66 See Paul M. Romer, "Two Strategies for Economic Development: Using Ideas and
Producing Ideas," *Proceedings of the World Bank Annual Conference on Development
Economics* 1992. Reproduced in David Klein, ed., *The Strategic Management of
Intellectual Capital* (Oxford: Butterworth-Heinemann, 1997), 211–38.

67 Jürgen Habermas, *The Philosophical Discourse of Modernity*, trans. Frederick
Lawrence (Cambridge, MA: MIT Press, 1987), 185.

68 Chambers, *Cyclopedia: Or, an Universal Dictionary of Arts and Sciences*, vi.

69 Hume, *Essays, Moral, Political, and Literary*, 535.

70 Dinitia Smith, "When Ideas Get Lost in Bad Writing; Attacks on Scholars
Include a Barbed Contest with 'Prizes,'" *New York Times*, February 27, 1999.
See also Butler's response, Judith Butler, "A 'Bad Writer' Bites Back," *New*

York Times, March 20, 1999. Marjorie Garber trenchantly describes this episode and unfolds its disciplinary implications in *Academic Instincts* (Princeton University Press, 2001).

71 James Gleick, "Science Viewpoint: The Human Face of Genius," *The Independent*, January 4, 1993.

72 Charles E. Caton, "Introduction," in *Philosophy and Ordinary Language*, ed. Charles E. Caton (Urbana: University of Illinois Press, 1963), v.

73 *Ibid.*, vi.

74 Gilbert Ryle, "Ordinary Language," in *Philosophy and Ordinary Language*, ed. Charles E. Caton, 108.

75 Caton, "Introduction," vii.
    Historian J.G.A. Pocock also discusses the languages of particular groups of writers writing on the same subject at particular historical moments. Pocock's groupings do not quite follow the same patterns as disciplines, but his observations about the languages belonging to these social and intellectual groups largely hold for my study as well:

    These languages will in strict fact have been sublanguages, idioms, and rhetorics, rather than languages in the ethnic sense, although in early modern history it is not uncommon to encounter polyglot texts that combine vernacular with Latin, Greek, and even Hebrew ... Those languages will vary in the degree of their autonomy and stability. From "idioms" they shade off in the direction of "styles."

    While my study generally finds itself in accord with Pocock's description, my fourth chapter suggests that the interconnection of "idiom" and "style" is perhaps more complex than he implies, which, admittedly, may be beside the point for Pocock insofar as he avers that "style" is not quite the historian's concern. He observes more than once that the historian's (or at least his) interest in language relates to what it is possible to say at a given moment in time. (*Virtue, Commerce, and History: Essays on Political Thought and History, Chiefly in the Eighteenth Century* [Cambridge University Press, 1985], 7, 9; *Politics, Language, & Time: Essays on Political Thought and History* [University of Chicago Press, 1960], 6.)

76 J.L. Austin, "The Meaning of a Word," in *Philosophy and Ordinary Language*, ed. Charles E. Caton, 14.

77 Richard Feynman, *The Character of Physical Law* (Cambridge, MA and London: MIT Press, 1965), 40, 55.

78 This inference may be fallacious and still describe rather well the school of philosophy advanced by Thomas Reid in the eighteenth century and simultaneously offer a reasonable characterization of Ryle's own school.

79 Ryle, "Ordinary Language," 122.

CHAPTER 2 THE LEARNED AND CONVERSABLE WORLDS

1 Those who wrote about language, rhetoric, and style in the eighteenth century rarely made distinctions between writing and speaking, or between written and spoken eloquence. The guiding fiction of much stylistic theory of

the long eighteenth century, which bled over into philosophies of language, was that polite conversation formed the model for the prose essay as well as philosophic and novelistic dialogue. Adam Potkay discusses this fiction of conversation in his work on David Hume's philosophy; see Adam Potkay, *The Fate of Eloquence in the Age of Hume* (Ithaca: Cornell University Press, 1994).

2 In the "Preface" to his *Dictionary of the English Language,* Johnson expresses his distress with the present state of the English language, recapitulating, with perhaps a greater degree of alarm, statements about the imprecision of "wild exuberance" of the English language that had been made by John Locke, Jonathan Swift, and certain critics of modern prose style. See Jonathan Swift, *A Proposal for Correcting, Improving and Ascertaining the English Tongue, 1712,* English Linguistics, 1500–1800, no. 213 (Menston, UK: Scolar Press, 1969), and Samuel Johnson, "Preface," in *Dictionary of the English Language* (Harlow, Essex: Longman, 1990).

3 For a fuller treatment of Latin's rise and fall as the dominant language in which books were written and printed, see Lucien and Henri-Jean Martin Febvre, *The Coming of the Book: The Impact of Printing, 1450–1800,* ed. Geoffrey Nowell-Smith and David Wootton, trans. David Gerard (London and New York: Verso, 1976), 248–61; Benedict Anderson, *Imagined Communities: Reflections on the Origin and Spread of Nationalism* (New York and London: Verso, 1991), 12–19, 34, 38–46; Marc Bloch, *Feudal Society: The Growth of Ties of Dependence,* trans. L.A. Manyon, vol. 1 (University of Chicago Press, 1961), 77; Erich Auerbach, *Literary Language and Its Public in Late Latin Antiquity and in the Middle Ages* (Princeton University Press, 1993), 247–77; Nicholas Ostler, *Ad Infinitum: A Biography of Latin* (New York: Walker & Co., 2008); George A. Kennedy, *Classical Rhetoric and Its Christian and Secular Tradition from Ancient to Modern Times,* 2nd edn. (Chapel Hill: UNC Press, 1999), 207, 249; and Andrew Fleming West, *Alcuin and the Rise of the Christian Schools* (New York: C. Scribner's Sons, 1901), 1–27, 100–102.

4 See, for example, Richard Foster Jones, *The Triumph of the English Language: A Survey of Opinions Concerning the Vernacular from the Introduction of Printing to the Restoration* (Stanford University Press, 1953), 32–33.

5 Much of this research has to do with endangered languages and language revitalization. For a useful overview, see Lenore A. Grenoble and Lindsay J. Whaley, *Saving Languages: An Introduction to Language Revitalization* (Cambridge University Press, 2006), esp. 8–13.

6 Richard Foster Jones, *The Triumph of the English Language,* 51.

7 While Hume's statement of this learned/conversable opposition is perhaps the most elegant of the eighteenth-century formulations, it certainly was not the first. His essay on the learned and conversable worlds drew on a letter to "Mr. Spectator" that appeared in October 1711: "It is a lamentable Circumstance, that Wisdom, or, as you call it, Philosophy, should furnish Ideas only for the Learned; and that a Man must be a Philosopher to know how to pass away his Time agreeably." And this *Spectator* article derived from Shaftesbury's representation of the "learned" and "fashionable" worlds in his treatise "The Moralists."

8   Douglas Lane Patey points to the ways in which Swift exposes modern philosophy's hypocrisy in attacking earlier systems for their penchant for taking resort in mystifying language. Douglas Lane Patey, "Swift's Satire on 'Science' and the Structure of Gulliver's Travels," *ELH* 48, no. 4 (1991). See also Brian McCrea, *Addison and Steele Are Dead: The English Department, Its Canon, and the Professionalization of Literary Criticism* (Cranbury, NJ: Associated University Presses, 1990), esp. 36.

9   Tobias Smollett, *The Adventures of Peregrine Pickle*, 2 vols. (London: Hutchinson & Co., 1904), 311.

10 Goldsmith, *Collected Works of Oliver Goldsmith*, 2.85.

11 *Ibid.*

12 Raymond Williams, *Writing in Society* (London: Verso, 1983), 121.

13 Addison writes, "By the Learned World I here mean at large, all those who are any way concerned in Works of Literature, whether in the Writing, Printing or Repeating Part." Addison and Steele, *The Spectator* 4.168.

14 Goldsmith, *Collected Works of Oliver Goldsmith*, 2.406.

15 For an exposition and analysis of this topic, see Robert Markley, "Sentimentality as Performance: Shaftesbury, Sterne, and the Theatrics of Virtue," in *The New Eighteenth Century: Theory, Politics, English Literature*, ed. Felicity Nussbaum and Laura Brown (New York and London: Methuen, 1987).

16 The great transgression of Richardson's *Pamela* against the mores of polite literature was that it represented a servant girl's ability to enter into a battle of conversational wit that could allow her entry into a more exalted realm; other novels continued to distinguish between the "conversable beings" of the middling and higher orders and the scarcely communicative masses of servants and social climbers, whose dialogue makes an appearance for satiric contrast with the sharp repartee of the other characters. For example, Chapter 15 of Sir Walter Scott's *Rob Roy* distinguishes between the conversable occupants of Osbaldistone Hall and the other denizens who go unmentioned.

17 Nancy Streuver, "The Conversable World: Eighteenth-Century Transformations of the Relation of Rhetoric and Truth," in *Rhetoric and the Pursuit of Truth: Language Change in the Seventeenth and Eighteenth Centuries*, ed. Thomas F. Wright (Los Angeles: William Andrews Clark Memorial Library–UCLA, 1985), 100.

18 See especially Addison's *Freeholder* No. 32, April 9, 1712.

19 David Hume, *Essays, Moral, Political, and Literary*, 535.

20 John Locke, "Some Thoughts Concerning Reading and Study for a Gentleman," in *The Works of John Locke*, ed. J.A. St. John (London, 1854), 499.

21 John Locke, *An Essay Concerning Human Understanding*, ed. Peter H. Nidditch (Oxford: Clarendon, 1975), II.32.8.

22 Hugh Blair, *Lectures on Rhetoric and Belles Lettres*, 434, 36.

23 The italics are Locke's. Locke, *An Essay Concerning Human Understanding*, 479. (III.9.8).

24 *Ibid.*, 476 (III.9.3).
25 The idea that learned discourse would need in all fields to take on a language of its own planted deeper roots in Germany and other European states in which academic production was earlier institutionalized than it was in England or America.
26 Joseph Addison, *The Freeholder*, ed. James Leheny (Oxford: Clarendon, 1979), 217. Popularizations and translations both figure prominently, side by side, in the learned review journals of the period. See Chapter 3 for more details.
27 Goldsmith, *Collected Works of Oliver Goldsmith*, 3.258.
28 Kramnick, "Literary Criticism among the Disciplines," 348.
29 Samuel Taylor Coleridge, *Biographia Literaria*, ed. James Engell and W. Jackson Bate, *Collected Works of Samuel Taylor Coleridge* (Princeton University Press, 1983), 170–71.
30 *Anthropology from a Pragmatic Point of View*, ed. Robert B. Louden (Cambridge University Press, 2006), 27.
31 *Tatler* No. 130 (September 10, 1710).
32 Richard Kirwan, "Of Chymical and Mineralogical Nomenclature," *Transactions of the Royal Irish Academy* 8 (1802), 59.
33 John Guillory discusses the twentieth century's version of the sciences/ humanities struggle in, "The Sokal Affair and the History of Criticism," where he finds that the implied politics of this debate hamstrings humanists and keeps them from enjoying a more favorable profile in the public domain.

CHAPTER 3 PHYSICS AND ITS AUDIENCES

1 While drawing on the joint historiography of science and enlightenment, this chapter responds most directly to Larry Stewart's *The Rise of Public Science*. Stewart downplays the role of the learned world in the spread of Newtonian physics, focusing mainly on its popular spread from the university to the coffeehouse world, among merchants, and in provincial corners of England. This chapter swings the emphasis back towards the learned world, to call attention to how Newtonian philosophy moved between the two and how its popularizers often underscored this distinction, protecting the specialized knowledge to establish their unique authority as dispensers of knowledge while promoting their abilities to teach its more accessible forms.
2 J.B. Shank makes a similar point about the broad application of the Newton brand in France to things that were not present in Newton's work (*The Newton Wars and the Beginning of the French Enlightenment* [University of Chicago Press, 2008], 30).
   On sixteenth- and seventeenth-century mechanics, including the simple machines, see Domenico Bertoloni Meli, *Thinking with Objects: The Transformation of Mechanics in the Seventeenth Century* (Baltimore: Johns

Hopkins University Press, 2006), esp. 18–40. For an example of how simple machines were used in popularizations of Newton, see 'sGravesande's *Mathematical Elements of Natural Philosophy.*

3 The argument made here about the manufacturing of public trust and public faith in seventeenth-century science differs from the process historians have pointed to in looking at Boyle and his fellow Royal Society experimental scientists. Accounts of Boyle's experimental science concentrated on how what could be seen was equated with what could be known. However, in the case of Newton, what *could not be seen* was as important as what could. Newtonian physics became a discipline precisely because it laid claim to an ability to generate specialized knowledge that could not be seen or fully comprehended by outsiders. (See especially Steven Shapin, *A Social History of Truth* [University of Chicago Press, 1994] and Shapin and Schaffer, *Leviathan and the Air-Pump.*

And, of course, Mario Biagioli's groundbreaking, interdisciplinary *Galileo, Courtier: The Practice of Science in the Culture of Absolutism* shows another process by which scientific discoveries could be credited by a social world, namely, through patronage networks. (University of Chicago Press, 1993.)

Perhaps the scholarly work closest to my own model is, not coincidentally, another study of Newton. In "Butter for Parsnips: Authorship, Audience, and the Incomprehensibility of the *Principia*," Rob Iliffe discusses Newton's reception "in terms of a mutual relationship between master and disciples," which "constituted a sort of concentric ring of competence extending inward from those who were held to understand nothing, to the center point inhabited – perhaps – by the author himself." His account of Newton and mine are complementary in that both address the relationship between rhetoric and audience in the presentation of Newtonian authority. (In *Scientific Authorship: Credit and Intellectual Property in Science,* eds. Mario Biagioli and Peter Galison [New York and London: Routlege, 2003], 33–65.)

4 The translation of Newtonian physics into visual and vernacular representations led to the eventual, partial intermixture between the doing and the knowing of physics, concomitant with physics' move from the learned into the conversable world through popularizations. The difference between the natural philosopher and the member of the reading public became their respective positions along the spectrum between learned and conversable. This continuum ranged from those who could contribute new knowledge to the field to those who could partially understand it or (in rare cases) possibly reproduce it afterwards.

5 See Geoffrey Holmes, *Augustan England: Professions, State and Society, 1680–1730* (Boston: George Allen & Unwin, 1982), esp. 19–28.

6 Stewart, *The Rise of Public Science: Rhetoric, Technology, and Natural Philosophy in Newtonian Britain,* xxix, 102.

7 From a letter from Craig to William Wotton, quoted in Stewart, 102.

8 Attempts to list the readers of the *Principia* and to account for their sophistication have frequently been made. See, for example, Paolo Casini, "Newton's

Principia and the Philosophers of the Enlightenment," *Notes and Records of the Royal Society of London* 42 (1988), Niccolò Guicciardini, *Reading the Principia: The Debate on Newton's Mathematical Methods for Natural Philosophy from 1687 to 1736* (Cambridge University Press, 1999), and A. Rupert Hall, "Newton in France: A New View," *History of Science* 13 (1975).

9 Henry Pemberton, Newton's literary executor, found it necessary to defend Newton against this joke; see the "Preface" to Henry Pemberton, *A View of Sir Isaac Newton's Philosophy* (Dublin: 1758).

    We might recall here the famous retort of Arthur Eddington – the scientist who achieved the first demonstration of Einstein's theory of relativity – when asked if it were true that only three people understood relativity. He hesitated briefly, then said, "I am trying to think who the third person is."

10 From the draft of a letter to Pierre des Maizeaux. In *The Mathematical Papers of Isaac Newton*, ed. D.T. Whiteside, 8 vols. (Cambridge and London: Cambridge University Press, 1967–1981), 8.523.

11 Isaac Newton, *The Principia: Mathematical Principles of Natural Philosophy*, eds. I. Bernard Cohen and Anne Miller Whitman (Berkeley: University of California Press, 1999), 793. Andrew Motte first translated and published Newton's *System of the World* in 1729. Cohen, Whitman, and Alexandre Koyré assemble and comment on the difference in Newton's several versions of book three in Isaac Newton, *Isaac Newton's "Philosophae Naturalis Principia Mathematica": The Third Edition (1726) with Variant Readings*, ed. Alexandre Koyré, I. Bernard Cohen, and Anne Whitman, 2 vols. (Cambridge University Press, 1972).

12 While Newton did not represent his work in popular form himself, through letters to Locke and Richard Bentley he did contribute to his popular reception. Newton wrote to Locke to offer a simplified version of the *Principia*, and he corresponded with Bentley on the relation of his work to natural religion.

    See H.W. Turnbull, ed., *The Correspondence of Isaac Newton*, 7 vols. (Cambridge University Press for the Royal Society, 1959–77).

13 While she urges us not to overstate the religious and political influences of Newtonianism, Margaret Jacob does point out that "[a]t its earliest popularization and explication, Newton's science was enlisted, with the consent of the master himself, in the attempt to justify and to explain in Christian terms the post-1688–89 order [in England]." Newtonian science reached much of England and France through the Boyle lectures, sermons that harnessed natural philosophy for the justification of a Christian order in the universe. Margaret Jacob, "Newtonianism and the Origins of Enlightenment: A Reassessment," *Eighteenth-Century Studies* 11, no. 1 (1977): 2.

14 Turnbull, ed., *The Correspondence of Isaac Newton* 2:437.

15 Newton himself was well aware of Halley's financial responsibility, which may have had some positive influence on his ultimate decision to include the contents of book three, although in altered form. When he thought he would not publish book three, Newton wrote to Halley that he considered changing the *Principia*'s title to represent more accurately its reduced content, but

he had thought better of it because, "Twill help ye sale of ye book w[hi]ch I ought not to diminish now tis yours." Turnbull, ed., *The Correspondence of Isaac Newton*, 2.434, 37.

16   Richard S. Westfall, *Never at Rest: A Biography of Isaac Newton* (Cambridge University Press, 1980), 247.

17   *Ibid.*, 459. Westfall argues that the substance of the book did not change substantially between revisions; however, I think it is more difficult to separate style and substance than Westfall would have us believe. And the presentation of the material did change substantially from a long, rather narrative format to a work that looked much more like the first two books, organized by lists of rules, theorems, and scholia.

     A. Rupert Hall comments that Newton's planned revisions had everything to do with his frustration with Hooke. See A. Rupert Hall, "Newton and His Editors," *Notes and Records of the Royal Society of London* 29, no. 1 (1974), 38.

18   See Jan Golinski, *Science as Public Culture: Chemistry and Enlightenment in Britain, 1760–1820* (Cambridge University Press, 1992), 1–5. Though I admire Golinski's book, I take issue with the founding premise of his introduction, namely that the current, commonplace assumption about scientific knowledge is that it is open, accessible shared knowledge. Or, if this were the conception in 1992, it no longer seems to be a widely held belief. In this age of very public battles over the patenting of genes and pharmaceuticals, over exclusive rights to cloning technologies or stem-cell lines, the general sense seems to be that science is as competitive and closed as any other highly specialized and often secretive business.

19   See especially Thomas Sprat's *History of the Royal Society*. As Jan Golinski has noted, "Science, at its point of origin, is not public at all." *Ibid.*, 2.

20   Isaac Newton, "Newton's System of the World," in *The Mathematical Principles of Natural Philosophy*, ed. W. Davis (London, 1803), 1.

21   *Ibid.*, 3.

22   I. Bernard Cohen comments on the impact of Newton's insistence on the mathematical properties of forces, rather than on a description of their causes, on his *Principia* in "Newton's Method and Newton's Style," in *Newton: Texts, Backgrounds, Commentaries*, ed. I. Bernard Cohen and Richard S. Westfall (New York: Norton, 1995), 131.

     At least one of Newton's early audience members celebrated the limited audience that the *Principia* could reach. Scottish mathematician David Gregory wrote to Newton, "tho your book is of so transcendent fineness and use that few will understand it, yet this will not I hope hinder you from discovering more hereafter to those few who cannot but be infinitely thankful to you on that account." Though Gregory perhaps estimates correctly the size of Newton's learned audience, he seems to have misjudged the number of persons who ultimately found it of great use and practical application. (Turnbull, ed., *The Correspondence of Isaac Newton*, 2.484.)

23   For more on this secrecy, see A. Rupert Hall, *Philosophers at War: The Quarrel between Newton and Leibniz* (Cambridge University Press, 1980), 8–9.

24 Guicciardini gives a wonderfully detailed and mathematically savvy account of the *Principia*'s life among the learned in the first fifty years of its existence, including the particular difficulties they would have faced in reading it. Guicciardini, *Reading the Principia: The Debate on Newton's Mathematical Methods for Natural Philosophy from 1687 to 1736* (Cambridge University Press, 1999).

25 William Whewell, *History of the Inductive Sciences*, 3rd edn., *Cass Library of Science Classics 7* (London: Cass, 1967), 128.

26 Newton, *The Principia: Mathematical Principles of Natural Philosophy*, 382. Peter Dear discusses the constructivist hypothesis – the belief that any mathematical formulation *could* be constructed – as foundational in Newton's justification of his proceeding by a mathematical rather than an experimental method. Peter Robert Dear, *Discipline & Experience: The Mathematical Way in the Scientific Revolution, Science and Its Conceptual Foundations* (University of Chicago Press, 1995), 8, 211.

27 To see an early example of how mathematicians tried to avoid the question of the correspondence between their variables or their analytical processes and the physical world, see William Emerson's explanation in *The Doctrine of Fluxions*. In it, he dismisses the whole problem as one of metaphysics while encouraging his audience to focus on the bigger picture. William Emerson, *The Doctrine of Fluxions* (London, 1743), vi.

28 Vol. 4, Book II (Edinburgh, 1787), 189, 190.

29 Birch, *History*, 4.484. In his 1837 *History of the Inductive Sciences*, William Whewell also mentions that by 1709–10, "the first edition of the *Principia* was become rare, and fetched a great price." Whewell also notes in his second edition that he had in 1846 printed his own edition of the *Principia* in Latin, to which he appends Newton's list for recommended reading prior to tackling the *Principia*. Whewell, *History of the Inductive Sciences*, 2.149, 50.

30 Hall, "Newton and his Editors," 42. The number of copies of the first edition is unknown; speculations have ranged from 250 copies to 300–400 copies. See Henry P. Macomber, "A Census of the Owners of Copies of the 1687 First Edition of Newton's 'Principia,'" *The Papers of the Bibliographical Society of America* 47, no. 3 (1953), 269, and A. N. L. Munby, "The Distribution of the First Edition of Newton's *Principia*," *Notes and Records of the Royal Society of London* 10 (1952), 37, cited in I. Bernard Cohen, *An Introduction to Newton's "Principia"* (Cambridge, MA: Harvard University Press, 1978). A letter from Cotes, the editor of the second edition of the *Principia*, to Newton suggests that there were 750 copies of the second edition, and a letter from Bentley suggests that at least 200 of them were sent to France and Holland. The third edition had 1250 copies, printed on a range of qualities of paper. See Cohen, *An Introduction to Newton's "Principia,"* 246, 84.

31 William James 'sGravesande, *Mathematical Elements of Natural Philosophy, Confirm'd by Experiments; or, an Introduction to Sir Isaac Newton's Philosophy*, trans. J.T. Desaguliers, 4th edn., 2 vols. (London: J. Senex, W. Innys, and J. Osborn and T. Longman, 1731), i.

This desire to admire and even own copies of a famous, erudite book that one cannot possibly read deserves remark. We can see a similar phenomenon much more recently in the sale of Stephen Hawking's *A Brief History of Time*, a work, although said to be for a wide audience, that was, for most, hardly readable beyond the first few pages. *A Brief History* nonetheless became a runaway bestseller. Hawking notes in the preface to the tenth-anniversary edition that he has "sold more books on physics than Madonna has on sex." Like Hawking, Newton benefited from good publicity. (Stephen Hawking, *A Brief History of Time: Updated and Expanded Tenth Anniversary Edition* [New York: Bantam Books, 1998], vii.)

32 Thomas Birch, "Isaac Newton," in *A General Dictionary* (London, 1738).

33 Whewell, *History of the Inductive Sciences*, 2.144.

34 I am heavily indebted, as are all modern scholars of Newton, to I. Bernard Cohen's work on Newton; see especially Cohen, *An Introduction to Newton's "Principia,"* 145–48.

35 For more on the private correspondence of the Newtonians, see the beautiful edition of Newton's correspondence edited by H.W. Turnbull. This well-documented edition includes letters that were not sent to or from Newton, but have relevance to Newton's work. Niccolò Guicciardini comments on many of these letters in his *Reading the Principia*, remarking on how this correspondence took place away from the public eye. Turnbull, ed., *The Correspondence of Isaac Newton*; Guicciardini, *Reading the Principia: The Debate on Newton's Mathematical Methods for Natural Philosophy from 1687 to 1736*, esp. 6.

36 Turnbull, ed., *The Correspondence of Isaac Newton*, 2.483; *Phil. Trans.* 119 (1695–97), 445–57.

37 J.T. Desaguliers, *A Course of Experimental Philosophy*, 2nd edn., 2 vols. (London: W. Innys, T. Longman, T. Shewell and C. Hitch, and M. Senex, 1745), x. At the time of writing his *Course*, Desaguliers estimated the number of Newtonian lecturers in England and elsewhere in the world at ten to twelve persons.

38 'sGravesande, *Mathematical Elements of Natural Philosophy, Confirm'd by Experiments; or, an Introduction to Sir Isaac Newton's Philosophy*, iii.

39 Newton's advice in book three for those "proficient in mathematics" who would like a shortcut through the *Principia* reads as follows:

[S]ince in books 1 and 2 a great number of propositions occur which might be too time-consuming even for readers who are proficient in mathematics, I am unwilling to advise anyone to study every one of these propositions. It will be sufficient to read with care the Definitions, the Laws of Motion, and the first three sections of book 1, and then turn to this book 3 on the system of the world, consulting at will the other propositions of books 1 and 2 which are referred to here.

Newton, *The Principia: Mathematical Principles of Natural Philosophy*, 793.

40 I. Bernard Cohen has an elegant discussion of these misalignments between mathematical theory and experimental observation in I. Bernard Cohen, *The Newtonian Revolution* (Cambridge University Press, 1980), 150–54.

41 Desaguliers, *A Course of Experimental Philosophy*, viii.

42 Other scholars have suggested that the division between the mathematical and experimental is not as clear as Shapiro would make it.

43 Stewart, *The Rise of Public Science: Rhetoric, Technology, and Natural Philosophy in Newtonian Britain*, 123–24.

44 In their work on the reception of Newtonianism in England, Betty Jo Teeter Dobbs and Margaret Jacob discuss Desaguliers's use of Newtonian philosophy as theoretical justification for his work in mechanics; however, I would lay even more emphasis on the fact that the use of Newton was justification (introduced after the fact) rather than the necessary source of Desaguiliers' innovations. *Newton and the Culture of Newtonianism* (Atlantic Highlands, New Jersey: Humanities Press, 1995).

45 The institution of "applied physics" as a subdiscipline of physics did not take shape until rather late in modern history, around 1920. Prior to the twentieth century, applications of physics fell under the domain of engineering and were not necessarily (or even usually) derived from advances in theoretical physics. By contrast, engineering was from its origins in the eighteenth century considered an applied field bound up with advances in mechanical technologies. The academic study of engineering in England came much later, in the nineteenth century. See the still influential A.M. Carr-Saunders and P.A. Wilson, *The Professions* (Oxford: Clarendon, 1933), esp. 156–58, 75–76.

46 See, for example, 'sGravesande's explanation of how mechanical demonstration may eventually help its readers to get closer to mathematical understanding. 'sGravesande also gives evidence for the existence of the mechanical devices he describes by noting the name and address of the artisan who made them for him.

   'sGravesande, *Mathematical Elements of Natural Philosophy, Confirm'd by Experiments; or, an Introduction to Sir Isaac Newton's Philosophy*, xvii–xviii.

47 Desaguliers, *A Course of Experimental Philosophy*, xi.

48 *Ibid.*, ix.

49 *Ibid.*, xi.

50 Pemberton, *A View of Sir Isaac Newton's Philosophy*, 1–2. Pemberton first published *A View* in 1728, the year after Newton's death and two years after the third edition of the *Principia* was published under his editorial guidance.

51 *Ibid.*, 2.

52 *Ibid.*

53 Larry Stewart has also remarked on the "broadening base of public knowledge of natural philosophy and the degree of sophistication a lecturer might impart." He dates this broadened base perhaps earlier than I would, however, since I have argued that the lecturers relied on this divide between themselves and their audiences much longer than Stewart has suggested. (See Stewart, *The Rise of Public Science: Rhetoric, Technology, and Natural Philosophy in Newtonian Britain*, 141.)

54 On the popularizers' echoes of Newton's claims that an unprepared audience has no right to complain, see, for example, Emerson, *The Doctrine of Fluxions*, vi.

55 Geoffrey Holmes, *Augustan England: Professions, State and Society*, 1680–1730 (Boston: George Allen & Unwin, 1982), 28.

56 See George Gordon, *Remarks Upon the Newtonian Philosophy*, 2nd edn. (London, 1719), 6.

57 "Preface" to John Conrad Francis de Hatzfeld, *The Case of the Learned Represented* (London, 1724).

58 This is common to many prefaces written by Newton's expositors. For a particularly wonderful example of this, see William Emerson, *A Short Comment on Sir I. Newton's Principia Containing Notes Upon Some Difficult Places of That Excellent Book* (London, 1770), iii.

59 "Preface" to Hatzfeld, *The Case of the Learned Represented*.

60 Gordon, *Remarks Upon the Newtonian Philosophy*, xii.

61 *Ibid.*, viii.

62 *Ibid.*, ix.

63 *Ibid.*, xlv.

64 *Ibid.*, vii.

65 *Ibid.*, viii.

66 This observation comes from Whewell, *History of the Inductive Sciences*, ii.150 – 51.

67 See A. Rupert Hall, *All Was Light: An Introduction to Newton's Opticks* (Oxford: Clarendon, 1993), esp. 183, 94.

68 Ephraim Chambers, *Cyclopedia: Or, an Universal Dictionary of Arts and Sciences*, vol. 4. Larry Stewart points out Chambers' definition in Stewart, *The Rise of Public Science*, 107.

69 Humphry Ditton, *The General Laws of Nature and Motion with Their Application to Mechanicks ... Being a Part of the Great Mr. Newton's Principles ... Accomodated to the Use of the Younger Mathematicians* (London, 1709), A7r.

70 *Ibid.*, A7v–A8r.

71 John Keill, *An Introduction to Natural Philosophy: Or, Philosophical Lectures Read in the University of Oxford, Anno. Dom. 1700*, 5th edn. (London, 1758), 1.

72 Alan Shapiro argues convincingly that the change from mathematical to experimental emphasis may not have arisen from a deliberate decision to shift the nature of his work in the direction of experimentalism, but rather because Newton's "goal of developing a mathematical science of color had become stymied." That is, he could not formulate mathematical laws for all he sought to explain. Alan E. Shapiro, "Experiment and Mathematics in Newton's Theory of Color," in *Newton: Texts, Backgrounds, Commentaries*, ed. I. Bernard Cohen and Richard S. Westfall (New York: Norton, 1995), 200–201. A. Rupert Hall and Marie Boas Hall have made a similar argument about Newton's attempts to find a theory of matter underlying the optics, for which he realized he had never found "enough experimental evidence to provide a firm basis for a definitive theory." (See "Newton and the Theory of Matter," in *The "Annus Mirabilis" of Sir Isaac Newton*, ed. Robert M. Palter [Cambridge, MA: MIT Press, 1970].)

73 Cohen, "Newton's Method and Newton's Style," 127.

74 Simon Schaffer traces the difficulty other natural philosophers had in repro-
    ducing Newton's experiments, and the information that Newton omits in
    order to idealize his process. This idealization, I would add, makes natural
    science look more like mathematics. It was through Desaguliers's revised
    experiments that they finally became replicable and more available for public
    view. See Simon Schaffer, "Glass Works," in *The Uses of Experiment: Studies in
    the Natural Sciences*, ed. David Gooding, Trevor Pinch, and Simon Schaffer
    (Cambridge University Press, 1989).

75 Emerson, *A Short Comment on Sir I. Newton's Principia Containing Notes
    Upon Some Difficult Places of That Excellent Book*, 130.

76 Margaret Bryan devised a board game to familiarize young people with
    astronomy. I have not been able to track down the date of the game's first
    issue, but its second edition is dated 1825. Sadly, the game lacks substantial
    intellectual content as well as being more than a little dull. Margaret Bryan,
    Science in Sport, or the Pleasures of Astronomy; a New Instructive Pastime
    (London: ca. 1825).

77 Eliza Haywood, *The Female Spectator*, 3rd edn., 4 vols. (London, 1750), 117.

78 *Ibid.*, 119.

79 *Ibid.*, 129–30.

80 *Ibid.*, 129.

81 *Ibid.*, 130.

82 See Ann B. Shteir, "Botanical Dialogues: Maria Jacson and Women's Popular
    Science Writing in England," *Eighteenth-Century Studies* 23, no. 3 (1990). See
    also G.S. Rousseau, "Science Books and Their Readers in the Eighteenth
    Century," in *Books and Their Readers in Eighteenth-Century England*, ed.
    Isabel Rivers (New York: St. Martin's Press, 1982).

83 Carter (1717–1806) was a largely self-educated scholar of ancient and modern
    languages, who published several poems and translations and wrote two arti-
    cles for Samuel Johnson's *Rambler*.

84 The work's context in Italy differed from that in England. Eighteenth-
    century Italy did not allow its natural philosophers the same publishing
    freedoms that English writers enjoyed after the lapse of the Licensing Act
    in 1695. In Italy, texts were subject to church censorship, and since 1616 the
    teaching of the Copernican, heliocentric system of the world as proven fact
    had been prohibited. Scientists, from Galileo forward, were allowed some
    leeway if they were willing to state that they considered the Copernican
    system as a scientific hypothesis, rather than as an established fact. Thus,
    in publishing the first Italian popularization of Newton's *Principia*, a work
    that insisted on a sun-centered system, Algarotti ran the risk of censorship
    and perhaps worse. Algarotti's text was placed on Italy's *Index Librorum
    Prohibitorum* until Algarotti affirmed to the Church that he recognized "the
    validity of the anti-Copernican decree of 1616." Only then could he reissue
    it. The innocent cast – scientifically speaking – of Algarotti's Newtonian

romance assumes a new hue when viewed in its original Italian setting. It also indicates why Algarotti devoted most of his book to the considerably less controversial *Opticks*, which does not touch directly on theological matters, rather than the *Principia*, which displaces the earth from the center of God's system. Galileo had himself presented some of his work in dialogue fashion, a method established since classical times for presenting a controversial opinion without affirming it directly. David Hume would do the same in the mid-eighteenth century in England to present controversial philosophical views on natural religion. However, Algarotti offers a spin on the conventions of philosophical dialogue in that his characters do not debate the pros and cons of the Newtonian system. The interlocutors' mutual pro-Newtonian position is never cloaked in ambiguity. The chief disguise of Algarotti's text is its interest in the coy flirtation of its interlocutors. Algarotti's characters engage in witty dialogue in order to expound upon Newton's system's interest to a modern, fashionably well-read person. (See Paolo Casini, *Newton E La Conscienza Europea, Società Editrice Il Mulino* [Bologna: Il Mulino, 1983], 226; Hall, *All Was Light: An Introduction to Newton's Opticks*, 231.)

85   The English edition was reissued later the same year. (Francesco Algarotti, *Sir Isaac Newton's Philosophy Explain'd for the Use of the Ladies. In Six Dialogues on Light and Colours*, trans. Elizabeth Carter, 2 vols. [London, 1739].) Other editions were published in 1742, 1765 (Glasgow), and 1772 under slightly modified titles. French translations of Algarotti's Italian work were also published in Paris and Amsterdam.

86   The Italian quotation in Algarotti's original came from Torquato Tasso's *Gerusalemme liberata*. In her English edition, Elizabeth Carter uses Edward Fairfax's English heroic verse translation, titled *Godfrey of Boulogne, Or The Recouerie of Ierusalem* (1st edn, 1600).

87   The mental theater Algarotti describes also resonates with the mental closet that John Locke imagines in his *Essay Concerning Human Understanding*:

> For, methinks, the understanding is not much unlike a closet wholly shut from light, with only some little openings left, to let in external visible resemblances, or ideas of things without: would the pictures coming into such a dark room but stay there, and lie so orderly as to be found upon occasion, it would very much resemble the understanding of a man, in reference to all objects of sight, and the ideas of them.

More striking is the correspondence to a passage in the first book of David Hume's *Treatise of Human Nature,* published in the same year as the English edition of Algarotti:

> The mind is a kind of theatre, where several perceptions successively make their appearance; pass, re-pass, glide away, and mingle in an infinite variety of positions and situations.

David Hume, *A Treatise of Human Nature*, ed. L.A. Selby-Bigge and P.H. Nidditch, 2nd edn. (Oxford: Clarendon, 1978), 253.

88 Algarotti, *Sir Isaac Newton's Philosophy Explain'd for the Use of the Ladies. In Six Dialogues on Light and Colours*, 2.222.
89 Benjamin Martin, *The General Magazine of Arts and Sciences, Philosophical, Philological, Mathematical, and Mechanical*, 5 vols. (London, 1759), vol. 1 ("The Young Gentleman and Lady's Philosophy ... By Way of Dialogue"), 3. Martin was a prolific writer who published a range of works on the arts and sciences and on mathematical instruments.
90 *Ibid.*, 1.1. Interestingly, Euphrosyne is the same name that Eliza Haywood uses for her female student in *The Female Spectator*.
91 *Ibid.*, 1.
92 *Ibid.*, 3.
93 *Guardian*, No. 24.
94 Keill, *An Introduction to Natural Philosophy: Or, Philosophical Lectures Read in the University of Oxford, Anno. Dom. 1700*, Lecture 1.
95 See, for example, Barbara J. Guzzetti *et al.*, "Influence of Text Structure on Learning Counterintuitive Physics Concepts," *Journal of Research in Science Teaching* 34, no. 7 (1997).
96 Adam Smith, "History of Astronomy," in I.S. Ross, ed., *Essays on Philosophical Subjects* (Oxford University Press, 1980), 76.
97 Tom Telescope, *The Newtonian System of Philosophy Adapted to the Capacities of Young Gentlemen and Ladies* (London, 1770), 3.
98 *Ibid.*, 51.
99 *Ibid.*, 6.
100 *Ibid.*, 21.
101 Emerson, *A Short Comment on Sir I. Newton's Principia*, 119.
102 Margaret Bryan, *A Compendious System of Astronomy in a Course of Familiar Lectures* (London, 1797), 103–4.
103 The most influential work in this vein is Larry Stewart's *The Rise of Public Science*.
104 *The Intelligibility of Nature: How Science Makes Sense of the World* (University of Chicago Press, 2006), 3.

CHAPTER 4 PHILOSOPHY'S PLACE BETWEEN
SCIENCE AND LITERATURE

1 David Hume, *The History of England: From the Invasion of Julius Caesar to the Revolution in 1688*, 6 vols. (Indianapolis: Liberty Classics, 1983), 6.542.
2 Emphasis mine. David Hume, "My Own Life," in *The Cambridge Companion to Hume*, ed. David Fate Norton (Cambridge University Press, 1993), 356.
3 Chambers, *Cyclopedia: Or, an Universal Dictionary of Arts and Sciences*, I.ii.
4 These definitions come from Ephraim Chambers; however, the later French *Encyclopédie* features similar divisions in its own map of human knowledge. Gary Hatfield discusses how the Aristotelian tradition of placing "the study

of the soul, including the rational soul and intellect, under the rubric of physics or natural philosophy" was alive and well in the eighteenth century; hence, metaphysics, moral philosophy, and psychology could all be considered forms of natural philosophy. Gary Hatfield, "Remaking the Science of Mind: Psychology as Natural Science," in *Inventing Human Science: Eighteenth-Century Domains*, ed. Roy Porter, Christopher Fox, and Robert Wokler (Berkeley, Los Angeles, London: University of California Press, 1995), 184.

5 Hume was not the first to make such an attempt. Philosophers of all stripes took up Newton's principles, using them to describe a new empirical method that could (in theory) be transferred to other fields. One of the earliest putative applications of Newton was Locke's *Essay Concerning Human Understanding* (1689/90). The Newtonian lecturer J.T. Desaguliers asserted: "The great Mr. Locke was the first who became a *Newtonian Philosopher* without the Help of Geometry." Locke imagined his own work as proceeding on empirical principles much the way that Newton did, without, of course, Newton's mathematics. Locke was taken by the explanatory power of the *Principia* coupled with its prominent rejection of previous systems based on hypotheses that could not be verified using experimental evidence. Locke's interest in Newtonianism primarily took the form of a strong advocacy of empiricism, not especially assiduously carried out in the *Essay* itself. Hume's engagement with Newton's writings was more pervasive.

6 Throughout the *Treatise*, Hume founds his arguments on analogies between the natural world and the moral world, assuming that both have similar structures:

[W]hen we consider how aptly *natural* and *moral* evidence cement together, and form only one chain of argument betwixt them, we shall make no scruple to allow, that they are of the same nature, and deriv'd from the same principles.

Hume again draws the parallel between mathematical and moral reasoning in his 1745 defense of the *Treatise* against William Wishart's "A specimen of the principles concerning religion and morality, said to be maintain'd in a book lately publish'd, intitled, A treatise of human nature." In this short pamphlet, Hume writes that "Moral Certainty may reach as high a Degree of Assurance as Mathematical," explaining that we can reach similar levels of conviction about the respective accuracy of each. Hume thus ascribes to mental phenomena the same consistency and determinism that Newton had assigned to physical events. He looked for correlates for the clockwork mechanisms of Newton's universe in the operation of human understanding. For example, Hume appropriates the principle of attraction (the core innovation of Newtonian physics) to suggest that ideas are likewise connected by "a kind of Attraction, which in the mental world will be found to have as extraordinary effects as in the natural, and to shew itself in as many and as various forms." Hume exploits physics analogies throughout the *Treatise*. For example, he compares the mechanics of levers to the way moral goods operate, and he later argues that our association between ideas of goodness and metaphors of height and between depravity and metaphors of lowness depends on our imaginative perception of the earth's gravity as exerting a downward force on all objects. (David Hume, *A Treatise of Human Nature*, ed. L.A. Selby-Bigge and P.H. Nidditch, 2nd edn. [Oxford: Clarendon, 1978], 406.)

Margaret Schabas and Michael Barfoot discuss Hume's use of metaphors drawn from natural philosophy, which inform Hume's moral, epistemological, and economic theories. As Schabas describes, students of Hume have long realized that Hume's theory of human behavior entails human predictability: future actions must be determinable based on past actions; Hume found in physics the model for how to describe the predictability of action. Norman Kemp Smith's classic study of Hume's philosophy gives some attention to Hume's attempts to derive a "statics and dynamics of the mind" on the basis of analogy, including the points at which it comes into conflict with the parts of his philosophy derived from Francis Hutcheson. J. de Salas, who also quotes Hume's eulogy to Newton, follows Nicholas Capaldi's and J. Noxon's work in examining the core principles that Hume derived from Newton; de Salas argues that "Hume ... does not distinguish between the attitude of the scientist to experience and that of the man in the street; he believes rather that the former is a manifestation of human nature itself which is present in the latter." Roger Smith argues that "'enlightenment' meant precisely an evolution of metaphysics into empirical science" for Hume and his contemporaries. Lionel Gossman has shown that Hume probably understood at least some higher mathematics, and Barfoot has demonstrated that Hume studied natural philosophy as a student at the University of Edinburgh. See Michael Barfoot, "Hume and the Culture of Science in the Early Eighteenth Century," in *Studies in the Philosophy of the Scottish Enlightenment*, ed. M.A. Stewart (Oxford University Press, 1990); Lionel Gossman, "Two Unpublished Essays on Mathematics in the Hume Papers," *Journal of the History of Ideas* 21 (1960); Margaret Schabas, "David Hume on Experimental Natural Philosophy, Money, and Fluids," *History of Political Economy* 33, no. 3 (2001); Roger Smith, "The Language of Human Nature," in *Inventing Human Science: Eighteenth-Century Domains*, ed. Roy Porter, Christopher Fox, and Robert Wokler (Berkeley, Los Angeles, and London: University of California Press, 1995), 90; Norman Kemp Smith, *The Philosophy of David Hume: A Critical Study of Its Origins and Central Doctrines* (London: Macmillan and Co., 1941), 73–76. See also Nicholas Capaldi, *David Hume: The Newtonian Philosopher* (Boston: Twayne, 1975); J. de Salas, "Hume and Newton: The Philosophical Discussion of a Scientific Paradigm," in *David Hume: Critical Assessments*, ed. Stanley Tweyman (London and New York: Routledge, 1995), 314; J. Noxon, *Hume's Philosophical Development: A Study of His Methods* (Oxford University Press, 1973), 84.

7 Some additional biographical data about their respective careers deserves brief mention. Unlike Newton, Hume did not work within an institutional structure that provided him with ready-made exponents. Other moral philosophers who worked within the Scottish university system had more success in this regard, as suggested later in the chapter where I discuss Thomas Reid. Newton's

relative freedom to seem obscure stemmed from his having others to advance his cause on his behalf. Hume enjoyed no such benefits. Hume also lacked the institutional support Newton had in the Royal Society and the University of Cambridge. Religious controversies over Hume's writings made him unwelcome on the faculties of Edinburgh and Glasgow. Nor did Hume have a hereditary independent living. Once he decided not to pursue a career in law, he had no guarantee of financial support or professional attention. Instead, he held various administrative posts and assorted other jobs while pursuing his writing. Without a university position and students to lecture, if Hume wanted to make a career as a moral philosopher, to be known meant to be read. Hume had a clear sense of this worldly truth from the beginning of his career.

8 Hume also poured some of the *Treatise*'s material that did not fit into either of the *Enquiries* into his essay "Of the Passions" (1757), later called "Dissertation on the Passions." John Sitter describes this shift in Hume's career as a "conversion experience" that mirrors a deeper, psychological change in the writer (*Literary Loneliness in Mid-Eighteenth-Century England* [Ithaca and London: Cornell University Press, 1982], esp. 37, 46).

   Hume was not the first English philosopher to make a shift from technical to popular forms. Shaftesbury made a similar move from his technical *Inquiry Concerning Virtue* (pub. 1699) to his more sociably framed *Characteristics*. (See Anthony Ashley [3rd Earl of Shaftesbury] Cooper, *Characteristicks of Men, Manners, Opinions, Times*, 3 vols. [Indianapolis: Liberty Fund, 2001]; Lawrence E. Klein, *Shaftesbury and the Culture of Politeness: Moral Discourse and Cultural Politics in Early Eighteenth-Century England* [Cambridge University Press, 1994], 49.) The case of Hume reveals a bit more than that of Shaftesbury because Hume's change in style was remarked and debated in the British press, in a way that Shaftesbury's was not.

9 It has been noted that "common sense" is a technical term in the usage of the common sense philosophers. This seems to me not quite an accurate characterization of their use of the term – it only seems technical to more recent readers who have lost part of the eighteenth-century signification of "common sense," discussed later in the chapter.

10 The examples here are legion. Ernest Mossner's biography of Hume takes into account many of the responses Hume received from his contemporaries. However, he puts them in service of his own, remarkable sympathy to Hume, downplaying the strength of their criticism and of their influence. (Ernest Campbell Mossner, *The Life of David Hume* [Edinburgh: Nelson, 1954].) While making reference to Hume's reviews, Norman Kemp Smith's carefully balanced account of Hume's decision to alter his philosophical style after the *Treatise* nonetheless focuses intently on Hume's own "readiness ... to adopt an attitude of criticism towards his own teaching." (Smith, *The Philosophy of David Hume: A Critical Study of Its Origins and Central Doctrines*, 519–36, esp. 524.) Jerome Christensen's *Practicing Enlightenment* is a particularly interesting case because he argues that Hume's career "exploited, facilitated, and

epitomized the operations of the commercial society which it persuasively represented," but Christensen nonetheless says little about writings other than Hume's own. Acknowledging this deliberate limitation, Christensen notes that his goal was to understand Hume's self-fashioning as a man of letters. (Jerome Christensen, *Practicing Enlightenment: Hume and the Formation of a Literary Career* [Madison: University of Wisconsin Press, 1987], 4.) M.A. Box's *The Suasive Art of David Hume* begins with a very useful chapter on the "climate of opinion" in which Hume wrote, but much as Christensen has done (though Box tries explicitly to distance himself from Christensen), he has selected material primarily to serve as prefatory background to discuss Hume on his own terms by discerning his motives and intentions. (M. A. Box, *The Suasive Art of David Hume* [Princeton: Princeton University Press, 1990], 34–52.)

Part of the scholarly focus on Hume was served by the nineteenth-century editions of his letters, which tend to include only the letters Hume himself wrote without the responses to them. While the decision to print his letters in isolation says, of course, as much about the availability of such letters as anything else, it had important consequences for Hume scholarship. We could contrast these editions with the major twentieth-century edition of Newton's letters, which compiles letters to, from, and about Newton.

The possibility of taking into account Hume's larger reception history has become much easier recently with the publication of James Fieser's series *Early Responses to Hume*. I am heavily indebted to Fieser's work, without which this chapter would have been much more difficult to write. (See James Fieser, *Early Responses to Hume's Metaphysical and Epistemological Writings*, 2 vols. [Bristol, England: Thoemmes, 2000]; James Fieser, *Early Responses to Hume's Moral, Literary and Political Writings*, 2 vols. [Bristol, England: Thoemmes, 1999]; James Fieser, *Early Responses to Hume's Writings on Religion*, 2 vols. [Bristol, England: Thoemmes, 2001]. At this writing, additional volumes are forthcoming.)

11   Antonia Forster, "Review Journals and the Reading Public," in *Books and Their Readers in Eighteenth-Century England: New Essays*, ed. Isabel Rivers (London and New York: Leicester University Press, 2001), 172. Forster is not alone in her bias; for example, in writing his introduction to the *Critical Review*, James Basker attributes to the *Critical* innovations already well in place in earlier journals, such as reporting on books from abroad and trying to keep track of scientific developments. The actual difference between the earlier journals and the *Monthly* and *Critical* seems to me to be that these journals managed to pitch themselves better to a broad audience and succeeded in gaining that audience. In these efforts, they defeated not only these earlier journals, but also many journals started simultaneously with the *Monthly* and *Critical*. James G. Basker, "Introduction," in *The Critical Review, or Annals of Literature, 1756–1763* (London: Pickering & Chatto, 2002).

12   Frank Donoghue, *The Fame Machine: Book Reviewing and Eighteenth-Century Literary Careers* (Stanford University Press, 1996).

13 For more on this journal, see William Thomas Lowndes, *The Bibliographer's Manual*, ed. Henry G. Bohn, 6 vols. (London: Bell & Sons, 1890.) See also the useful journal summaries in vol. 1 of Alvin Sullivan, ed., *British Literary Magazines*, 4 vols. (Westport, CT: Greenwood Press, 1983).

14 1735; 330.

15 July 1736, article 41; "Preface," Jan 1735.

16 1739, 105–6.

17 107. Boswell's book is prone to disappoint most readers – even the "poor Clergyman" and the "young Gentleman" to whom he addresses it – because attaining its recommendations would seem to require a lifetime of study. He asks his readers to master the learned languages, logic, ethics, physics, metaphysics, geography, chronology, history, classical learning, and natural philosophy (110). Boswell also appends suggestions for further reading in painting, architecture, and heraldry, although the *Works of the Learned* points out that, for Boswell, these "arts are properly of mechanical Consideration, and do not, strictly speaking, come within the Compass of *Learning*" (109). These, for him, fall into the category of the conversable: necessary attainments for the complete gentleman who respects "the Humour and Taste of the World," unnecessary to the scholar (110). Boswell comes down firmly in favor of a university education as the only avenue to true learning, quarreling with the popular notion "some are fond of advancing" that one can omit a formal study of logic and metaphysics from an education and instead acquire a learned aura through "good Conversation, by Reading, by Imitation" and by the self-directed study of mathematics. For him – though not always for this journal's authors – learnedness comes through long study and training. Boswell's message is at odds somewhat with the journal's, as Boswell tends to frustrate efforts to take shortcuts to knowledge.

18 I discuss this letter later in the chapter. Ernest Mossner "discovered" this review in the early 1950s; see Ernest Campbell Mossner, "The First Answer to Hume's Treatise: An Unnoticed Letter of 1740," *Journal of the History of Ideas* 12, no. 2 (1951).

19 Indeed, while many Hume scholars have pointed out the *Common Sense* commentary on Hume, none have previously made the connection between that "anonymous" review and *The Works of the Learned* review of Strutt's work, which identifies the author; nor have they pointed out that this author is favored by *The Works of the Learned* in a way that Hume is not.

20 1735, 337.

21 Immanuel Kant, *Prolegomena to Any Future Metaphysics*, ed. Lewis White Beck (Indianapolis: Bobbs-Merrill, 1950), 8.

22 The Aristotelian works described as being for a more general public are now generally referred to as the "lost dialogues." On the lost dialogues see, for example, Anton-Hermann Chroust, "Eudemus or On the Soul: A Lost Dialogue of Aristotle on the Immortality of the Soul," *Mnemosyne*, 4th series, 19.1 (1966), 17–18.

23 The advertisement was added upon the *Treatise's* completion in 1740.
    Since the *Treatise's* publication, Hume's direct addresses to his audience have prompted uncharitable readers to regard Hume as a panderer,

concerned more with fame and praise than with truth. Hume's twentieth-century biographer, Ernest Mossner, has countered this longstanding drift in Hume criticism by responding that Hume imagined his audience as limited to the learned members of the public, seeking from them confirmation that he had indeed made an important contribution to the store of philosophical knowledge. Both Mossner's and his predecessors' assessments, however, require reading Hume with one eye deliberately closed. Each slants Hume's own inconsistent descriptions of his relationship to his audience in the direction of its own particular critical sympathies. Indeed, the *Treatise*'s vacillation on who its audience is indicates that Hume had not settled the question for himself. It is precisely his indecision which makes his case of interest.

24 Hume, *A Treatise of Human Nature*, xiii, 138–39.

25 Hume prepared an abstract of his own work to send to *The History of the Works of the Learned*, in the hopes that it would draw attention to his *Treatise*. Before he could send it, however, this journal printed its famously excoriating review of the *Treatise*. The *Works of the Learned* review was the second published commentary on the *Treatise* in Britain; the first came in the form of a letter to the editor of *Common Sense: Or the Englishman's Journal* on July 5, 1740. The author did not sign his name, but noted that he was the author of *An Essay Towards Demonstrating the Immateriality and Free-Agency of the Soul*, a publication whose very title indicates its passionate opposition to Hume's account of agency. The author of this pamphlet is generally identified as Samuel Strutt. Predictably, Strutt soundly condemned Hume and his book. Hume had attracted the attention of four Continental journals as well. The German *Göttingische Zeitungen von gelehrten Sachen* published brief unflattering remarks on the *Treatise* in its January 7, 1740 issue. The *Bibliothèque Raisonnée des ouvrages des savans de l'Europe*, a French journal (printed in Amsterdam to avoid strict French censorship) dedicated to reviewing new books, included two separate reviews of the *Treatise*. In its April–June 1740 installment, the *Bibliothèque* discussed books one and two; a year later, it addressed book three. The reservations that the *Bibliothèque* expresses towards the *Treatise* are gentler versions of the criticisms advanced in the other reviews. The short-lived French monthly *Nouvelle Bibliothèque* also considered the *Treatise* in its July and September 1740 issues. This review does not evaluate the *Treatise*'s philosophical merits, instead preferring to summarize Hume through loose translation while expressing occasional doubts about the *Treatise*'s efficacy in fulfilling its stated goals.

For more of an overview of commentary on Hume's writing, see James Fieser, "The Eighteenth-Century British Reviews of Hume's Writings," *Journal of the History of Ideas* 57, no. 4 (1996): 646–47.

26 James Boswell reports an ancedote about Henry Home, Lord Kames, who, upon being asked to read the treatise, replied: "I'll do any thing to oblige you. But you must sit by and try to beat your Book into my head." Kames would later write about his own response to the *Treatise* in less amused terms. James Boswell, *Private Papers of James Boswell from Malahide Castle*, 18 vols.

[Mount Vernon, NY: W.E. Rudge, privately printed, 1928–34], xv.273–74. Quoted in Mossner, *The Life of David Hume*, 118.

27   Anonymous, "Review of *A Treatise of Human Nature*," in *Early Responses to Hume's Metaphysical and Epistemological Writings*, ed. James Fieser (Bristol, England: Thoemmes Press, 2000), 39.

28   *Ibid.*, 50.

29   Hume, *A Treatise of Human Nature*, xiv.

30   See especially *Ibid.*, 286–72.

31   Ernest Mossner credits William Warburton with this anonymous review, primarily based on its extreme irony. Mossner, *The Life of David Hume*, 123, 618–19.

32   This is not to say that this reviewer anticipated twentieth-century deconstructionism in using Hume's tools to take apart Hume's philosophy but rather to argue that Hume and his audiences were both acutely aware of how his method could be dismantled. That is, in designating the limitations of human knowledge, Hume admitted the limitations of his own knowledge. But to suggest that his own discovery about the limitations of reason could be the only secure knowledge left standing at the end of his own devastating, skeptical critique has seemed to many of his readers impossibly brash and self-confident. Reviewers allied their complaints about his skepticism with their critiques of Hume's brazen self-assurance, or what one writer terms his "egoisms": his critique left no one else any other ground to stand on.

33   Hume, *A Treatise of Human Nature*, 264.

34   Anonymous, "Review of *A Treatise of Human Nature*," 38.

35   Goldsmith, *Collected Works of Oliver Goldsmith*, vol. 2, 189, 90.

36   Anonymous, "Review of *A Treatise of Human Nature*," 48.

37   John Valdimir Price has written a very rich and thoughtful essay to explore what philosophical books were and who read them in the eighteenth century, based mainly on the audiences described within philosophical books themselves. John Valdimir Price, "The Reading of Philosophical Literature," in *Books and Their Readers in Eighteenth-Century England*, ed. Isabel Rivers (New York: St. Martin's Press, 1982).

38   Anonymous, "Review of *Treatise*, Book Iii," in *Early Responses to Hume's Moral, Literary, and Political Writings*, ed. James Fieser (Bristol, England: Thoemmes Press, 1999), 2.

39   No evidence exists one way or the other as to Hume's knowledge of his brief German review. (See Mossner, *The Life of David Hume*.)

40   *Idler* No. 70.

41   Hume, *A Treatise of Human Nature*, 455.

42   *Ibid.*, 251.

43   Anonymous, "Letter to the Editor," in *Early Responses*, 89.

44   *Ibid.*, 91.

45   *Ibid.*, 2.

46 This quotation comes, of course, from Samuel Johnson's famed remarks about the vulnerability of young unfurnished minds to their reading. In this instance, Johnson is more concerned with novel reading rather than philosophy books. William Godwin would later approach the same subject from a more liberal vantage in his essay "Of Choice in Reading":

> Books will perhaps be found, in a less degree than is commonly imagined, the corrupters of the morals of mankind. They form an effective subsidiary to events and the contagion of vicious society; but, taken by themselves, they rarely produce vice and profligacy where virtue existed before. Every thing depends upon the spirit in which they are read ... The power of books in generating virtue, is probably much greater than in generating vice.

47 The first definition is from Reid, which the OED lists under "common sense"; the latter two definitions also come from the OED. For Reid, "common sense" was not a term of art, although it may seem so to us now because the currently popular signification of the term ("good sound practical sense") is narrower than the eighteenth-century sense of the term. John Haldane argues otherwise in his article on Thomas Reid's use of the term; however, I find in Haldane's definition a refinement of meanings already present in eighteenth-century England. John Haldane, "Thomas Reid: Life and Work," *American Catholic Philosophical Quarterly* 74, no. 3 (2000): 319. As Nicholas Wolterstorff has shown, "it is not clear" in all cases which sense of common sense Reid meant at any given time; the term seems to move among definitions from "judgment" or "reason" to "certain belief-forming faculties shared in common" to "shared beliefs or judgments." Nicholas Wolterstorff, "Reid on Common Sense, with Wittgenstein's Assistance," *American Catholic Philosophical Quarterly* 74, no. 3 (2000): 492.

48 Thomas Reid, "An Inquiry into the Human Mind on the Principles of Common Sense," in *Thomas Reid's Inquiry and Essays*, ed. Ronald E. Beanblossom and Keith Lehrer (Indianapolis: Hackett, 1983), 11.

49 Fieser, *Early Responses to Hume's Metaphysical and Epistemological Writings*, I.171.

50 *Ibid.*, 146.

51 Samuel Taylor Coleridge, *Biographia Literaria*, ed. James Engell and W. Jackson Bate, *Collected Works of Samuel Taylor Coleridge* (Princeton University Press, 1983), 157.

52 Reid, "An Inquiry into the Human Mind on the Principles of Common Sense," 15.

53 Robert Markley discusses how the eighteenth century's "selective misreading" of Shaftesbury's philosophy transformed it from a statement of aristocratic political authority to instruction for how the middle classes might learn to exhibit aristocratic good breeding. Robert Markley, *Fallen Languages: Crises of Representation in Newtonian England, 1660–1740* (Ithaca: Cornell University Press, 1993).

54 Thomas Reid, *Essays on the Intellectual Powers of Man*, ed. Keith Lehrer and Arnold Beanblossom (Indianapolis: Bobbs-Merrill, 1975), 10.

55 Hume, "My Own Life," 352–53.
56 *Ibid.*
57 Donald Bond, *The Spectator* (London: Clarendon Press, 1965), xviii–xx.
    For a history of the genre in England from the seventeenth century forward, see Hugh Walker, *The English Essay and Essayists* (New York: E.P. Dutton & Co., 1923). Chapter 5 treats the genesis of the periodical essay through the work of Daniel Defoe, Addison, and Steele; Chapter 6 addresses their imitators, including David Hume.
58 *Spectator* No. 476.
59 Their casual, conversational pose belied how elegantly formed and how precisely balanced their sentences typically were. Indeed, the *Spectator* papers have often been taken as a model for English prose style. Hugh Blair's *Lectures on Rhetoric and Belles Lettres*, for example, take Addison's *Spectator* papers on "The Pleasures of the Imagination" as the model for perspicuous prose in English.
60 Longer works during this period were often, of course, also called "Essays," perhaps most notably a range of philosophical writings. In the *Essay Concerning Human Understanding*'s "Epistle to the Reader" Locke writes that his essay had arisen out of a conversation among "five or six Friends meeting at my Chamber," and was written in a "discontinued way" over the succeeding months "by incoherent parcels ... after long intervals of neglect," and "as my Humour or Occasions permitted" (7). Hence, Locke's titling the work an *Essay* indicates its often unsystematic structure and abrogates responsibility for any thoroughgoing, structural logic. The title also makes gestures towards an audience: an essay is not for "Men of large Thoughts and quick Apprehensions" or "Masters of Knowledge" but rather for the humbler domain of "Men of my own size" (8). Locke does write in a more casual style than many of his seventeenth-century predecessors in systematic philosophy, if only because he writes in English, like Francis Bacon in his essays, rather than in Latin, as in Bacon's *De Augmentis Scientiarum* (*Advancement of Knowledge*). However, though it shared stylistic traits with Bacon's essays and Addison and Steele's, Locke's kind of essay – a many-hundred-page meditation on human understanding – was generically taken as at least slightly more difficult work for readers than those of Addison and Steele. Indeed, Addison and Steele saw much of the project of their *Spectator* as communicating Locke's philosophy in a popular form.
61 For a fuller discussion of elegant writing in this period, see Potkay, *The Fate of Eloquence in the Age of Hume*.
62 Fieser, *Early Responses to Hume's Metaphysical and Epistemological Writings*, xxii.
63 Sir Leslie Stephen, *History of English Thought in the Eighteenth Century*, ed. Crane Brinton, 2 vols. (New York: Harbinger, 1962), ii.73. Stephen seems to have liked the first *Enquiry* despite, or because of, Hume's reconfiguring it.

64 David Hume, *An Enquiry Concerning Human Understanding*, ed. Tom L. Beauchamp (Oxford University Press, 1999), 107.

65 *Ibid.*, 124.

66 William Rose, "Review of *Enquiry Concerning the Principles of Morals*," in *Early Responses to Hume's Moral, Literary, and Political Writings*, ed. James Fieser (Bristol, England: Thoemmes Press, 1999), 11–12.

67 In a talk at Stanford University, editor and author William Germano distinguished a scholarly book from a trade book with this remark: "A good definition of a trade book is a book that has one idea that is repeated over and over again." This definition would seem to hold equally well in regard to eighteenth-century popular books, although the publishing categories of "trade" and "scholarly" had not yet come into being.

68 Fieser, 44.

69 *Rambler* 14 (May 5, 1750).

70 Thomas Sprat, *History of the Royal Society* (St. Louis: Washington University Press, 1958).

71 Brian Vickers, "The Royal Society and English Prose Style: A Reassessment," in *Rhetoric and the Pursuit of Truth: Language Change in the Seventeenth and Eighteenth Centuries*, ed. Thomas F. Wright (Los Angeles: William Andrews Clark Memorial Library–UCLA, 1985), 23.

72 To take one famous example of how well Addison's version of Locke made it into the general, learned attitude towards language: in the Preface to his dictionary Johnson writes, *"words are the daughters of earth, and . . . things are the sons of heaven.* Language is only the instrument of science, and words are but the signs of ideas: I wish, however, that the instrument might be less apt to decay, and that signs might be permanent, like the thing which they denote."

73 George Berkeley, *Philosophical Commentaries*, ed. A.A. Luce and T.E. Jessop, vol. 1, *The Works of George Berkeley, Bishop of Cloyne* (London: Thomas Newlson and Sons Ltd., 1948), 22.

74 See especially 1.5–8, 2.6 from his 1764/1785 *An Inquiry into the Human Mind, on the Principles of Common Sense*.

75 See, for example, J.L. Austin's remarks on the ordinary language conceptions that underlie scientist models of the world in his *Philosophical Papers* (ed. J.O. Urmson and G.J. Warnock [London: Oxford University Press, 1961 (1970)], 185).

76 Even the vernacular language of scientific disciplines looks very different from parlance outside the discipline: a mathematician's statement "that's intuitively obvious" or "that's trivial" means that an observation does not have to be proven explicitly in mathematical terms, not because it has any bearing on what is obvious about the world but rather because others inside the discipline would know how to find the solution without having it worked out for them.

77 Anonymous, "Review of *Treatise*, Book III," 10.

78 Hume, "My Own Life," 352.

79 Reid is not entirely consistent on this point; in his later *Essays on the Intellectual Powers of Man*, he proposes that "the best and purest writers in the language" be used as a standard, though perhaps this just raises the bar a little without changing the problem. It still begs the question as to how innovation in philosophy is possible. Thomas Reid, "Essays on the Intellectual Powers of Man," in *Thomas Reid's Inquiry and Essays*, ed. Ronald E. Beanblossom and Keith Lehrer (Indianapolis: Hackett, 1983), 150.

80 *Ibid.*, 146, 44.

81 Reid, "An Inquiry into the Human Mind on the Principles of Common Sense," 15.

82 Reid, *Essays on the Intellectual Powers of Man*, 143. Defenders of Reid have suggested that his position is one of unflinching honesty, a willingness to admit (and then assert dogmatically) that at base, "the common dicta of mankind ... are unfounded" because a "reasoned theory of them" is not possible, and thus we must fall back on what everyone knows. See John Veitch, "Philosophy in the Scottish Universities," *Mind* 2, no. 6 (1877), 221–22. However, much of what is called Reid's moral uprightness, his unwillingness to deceive and desire to speak plainly, seems an evasion of investigation as much as anything else. Certain expositors of Reid embrace this idea, arguing that "The philosophy of common sense is to make itself unnecessary ... It is not valuable as a search after truth; it has made no positive discoveries and will make none ... Its philosophical value is polemical." (See S.A. Grave, *The Scottish Philosophy of Common Sense* (Oxford: Clarendon, 1960), esp. 130–31.)

83 Kant, *Prolegomena to Any Future Metaphysics*, 7.

84 *Ibid.*, 10.

85 Dugald Stewart, *Introduction to the Elements of the Philosophy of the Human Mind*, ed. Knud Haakonssen, 11 vols., vol. 2–4, *Collected Works of Dugald Stewart* (Bristol: Thoemmes, 1994), 3.101, 106.

86 Dugald Stewart, *Outlines of Moral Philosophy*, ed. Knud Haakonssen, 11 vols., vol. 6, *Collected Works of Dugald Stewart* (Bristol: Thoemmes, 1994): 361, 77.

87 On this topic, see also Robin Valenza and John Bender, "Hume's Learned and Conversable Worlds" in *Just Being Difficult*, ed. Jonathan Culler (Stanford University Press, 2003).

88 Dugald Stewart, *Dissertation: Exhibiting the Progress of Metaphysical, Ethical, and Political Philosophy, since the Revival of Letters in Europe* in *The Collected Works of Dugald Stewart*, ed. William Hamilton (Edinburgh: Thomas Constable and Co., 1844), 20.

89 Thomas Henry Huxley, *Hume* (London and New York: Macmillan, 1902), 11. Quoted in Smith, *The Philosophy of David Hume: A Critical Study of Its Origins and Central Doctrines*, 519–20. Smith also cites similar assessments by John Stuart Mill in the *Westminster Review* (1824, 2.346) and others.

90 In *A History of the Modern Fact*, Mary Poovey discusses Hume's use of the essay:

Hume's attempt to accord the essay prestige equivalent – or even superior – to that of moral and natural philosophy was not successful, of course ... the systematic and general knowledge projects associated with philosophy continued to gain authority in the second half of the eighteenth century.

The "systematic and general knowledge" projects to which she refers apply to aspects of Hume's writings that eventually came under the domain of social sciences, rather than the humanities. In other words, the fields that Hume tried to encompass split apart. (Mary Poovey, *A History of the Modern Fact: Problems of Knowledge in the Sciences of Wealth and Society* (University of Chicago Press, 1998).

John Haldane discusses the continued appeal of Reid's "stylistic rigour" in the nineteenth century in Britain and North America. Haldane, "Thomas Reid: Life and Work," 323.

CHAPTER 5 POETRY AMONG THE
INTELLECTUAL DISCIPLINES

1 M.H. Abrams has argued that science had come to replace history as the "opposite" of poetry because emphasis had shifted from the difference between the description of actual events (history) and portrayals of idealized events (poetry) to the difference between regarding aspects of the world "as they *seem* to exist to the *senses*, and to the passions ... in the spirit of genuine imagination" (poetry) and treating things with "the unemotional and objective description characteristic of physical science" (science). Abrams's point is well taken, but as I argue in this chapter, the difference between the *beaux arts* and the philosophic disciplines also ran deeper than their respective associations with the imagination and reason. M.H. Abrams, *The Mirror and the Lamp: Romantic Theory and the Critical Tradition* (New York: Oxford University Press, 1953), 298–99.
2 See, for example, D'Alembert's essay on the "Éléments des Sciences" in the *Encyclopédie.*
3 Paul Monroe, *Source Book of the History of Education for the Greek and Roman Period* (Barcelona and Singapore: Athena University Press, 2003), 347.
4 On the "debar[ring]" of branches of learning from the university curriculum in the middle ages, see Jacques Verger, "Patterns," in *A History of the University in Europe*, vol. 1, ed. H. de Ridder-Symoens (Cambridge University Press, 1992), 42.
5 William Wordsworth, *The Prose Works of William Wordsworth*, ed. W.J.B. Owen and Jane Worthington Smyster, 3 vols. (Oxford: Clarendon Press, 1974), I.129.
6 *Ibid.,* I.324, 25.
7 Sidney writes in his "Defence" that in contrast with poetry, each of the other branches of learning "hath ... the workes of nature for its principle object, without which they could not consist, and on which they so depend, as they become actors and players, as it were, of what Nature will have set forth." In other words, all of the other disciplines in the tree of knowledge depend on

nature to give them their direction; according to Sidney, because the poet's mind is not constrained to a single object or field of study, his ability to discover knowledge is superior to that of the philosopher or historian. (Sidney, *Sir Philip Sidney: Selected Prose and Poetry*, 107.) R.S. Crane has observed that "What is common [to sixteenth-century views of the humanities] – and to the many variant statements of one or another of them set forth in the Renaissance – is the disposition to think of poetry as a form of learning, the essential characteristics and values of which may be determined by bringing it into comparison with other recognized arts and sciences. It is from this point of view that Sidney approaches the question of poetry in his *Defence*; only, instead of subordinating poetry to some other art, he wishes to show that all others must be subordinated to it. Poetry is not a subordinate art, but the supreme form of human learning." (Ronald Salmon Crane, *The Idea of the Humanities, and Other Essays Critical and Historical*, 2 vols. [University of Chicago Press, 1967], I.47.)

8 *The Excursion* VIII.200–202. Unless otherwise noted, quotations of Wordsworth's poetry are cited from William Wordsworth, *The Poetical Works of William Wordsworth*, ed. E. de Selincourt and Helen Darbishire, 2nd edn., 5 vols. (Oxford: Clarendon Press, 1956–65). Ian Wylie has argued that Coleridge's poetic productivity in the late 1790s in fact stems from his attempts to grapple with his reading of Newton's works and popularizations of them. Ian Wylie, *Young Coleridge and the Philosophers of Nature* (Oxford: Clarendon, 1989), 17.

9 Samuel Taylor Coleridge, *Biographia Literaria*, ed. James Engell and W. Jackson Bate, *Collected Works of Samuel Taylor Coleridge* (Princeton University Press, 1983), 9.

10 Bentham, *The Rationale of Reward* (London, 1830), 207.

11 Wordsworth, *The Poetical Works of William Wordsworth*, 2.125.

12 Adam Ferguson, *An Essay on the History of Civil Society, 1767*, ed. Duncan Forbes (Edinburgh University Press, 1966), 179.

13 Coleridge, *Biographia Literaria*, Ch. 11.

14 Raymond Williams, *Culture and Society, 1780–1850* (New York: Anchor Books, 1958), esp. 39 and 47.

15 Smith, *The Wealth of Nations*, 28–29.

16 Coleridge includes this motto in *Biographia Literaria*, 20. Sentiments related to this aphorism have appeared often in writings on art since classical antiquity, but Coleridge is generally credited with expressing it in this particularly succinct, enduring form. See William Ringler, "*Poeta Nascitur Non Fit*: Some Notes on the History of an Aphorism," *Journal of the History of Ideas* 2.4 (1941), 497.

17 Maureen McLane has noted that, "Wordsworth's 'Poet,' allied with a generalized human pleasure-project, is implicitly an enemy of both professionalization and of specialization." In her reading, Wordsworth's close alliance between "human" and "poet" marks his resistance to specialization. (Maureen N. McLane, *Romanticism and the Human Sciences: Poetry,*

Population, and the Discourse of the Species (Cambridge University Press, 2000), 6.

18 Thomas Pfau goes so far as to argue that Wordsworth made the task of soul-creation into a middle-class profession, aimed at readers of the same class. Pfau chooses to disregard Wordsworth's stated antipathy to the develop-ment of poetry in order to argue that Wordsworth's poetry itself is nothing short of a series of "retelling[s]" of "the story of the poet's vocational com-mitment to the imaginative recovery of an otherwise unattainable, precapi-talist past." In other words, Wordsworth's explicit refusal to class the poet as a professional underpinned his program of defining the role of the poet for his own age. Thomas Pfau, *Wordsworth's Profession: Form, Class, and the Logic of Early Romantic Cultural Production* (Stanford University Press, 1997), 10.

19 Coleridge derides "the natural, but not therefore the less partial and unjust distinction, made by the public itself between *literary*, and all other prop-erty," asking "should we pass by all higher objects and motives ... is the character and property of the individual, who labours for our intellectual pleasures, less entitled to a share of our fellow feeling, than that of the wine-merchant or milliner?" Coleridge, *Biographia Literaria*, 43.

20 Wordsworth, *The Prose Works of William Wordsworth*, 3.83. Critic Peter Murphy has remarked that Wordsworth nonetheless wanted popularity, but on his own terms. Murphy, *Poetry as an Occupation and an Art in Britain, 1760–1839, Cambridge Studies in Romanticism 3* (Cambridge University Press, 1993), 183.

21 Wordsworth, *The Prose Works of William Wordsworth*, 3.62.

22 For a discussion of Wordsworth's own economic circumstances in relation to his early refusal "to publish except for 'some pecuniary recompense,'" see Mark Schoenfeld, *The Professional Wordsworth: Law, Labor, and the Poet's Contract* (Athens, Georgia: University of Georgia Press, 1996).

23 Wordsworth, *The Prose Works of William Wordsworth*, 3.64.

24 Northrop Frye, *Anatomy of Criticism: Four Essays* (Princeton University Press, 1957), 4; Jerome McGann, *The Romantic Ideology: A Critical Investigation* (Chicago and London: University of Chicago Press, 1983), 1.

25 Italics mine. This catalog highlights but does not exhaust Wordsworth's vari-ation on this theme.

26 Coleridge, *Biographia Literaria*, 18.

27 For a discussion of this process of accretive definition, see Donald W. Livingston, *Hume's Philosophy of Common Life* (University of Chicago Press, 1984), and Robin Valenza, "Editing the Self: David Hume's Narrative Theory," *The Eighteenth Century: Theory and Interpretation* 43 (Summer 2002).

28 In *The Mirror and the Lamp*, M.H. Abrams strives throughout to identify an object at the center of nineteenth-century poetry, and usually identifies the poet himself as that object. This, in part, is his solution to the difference between eighteenth- and nineteenth-century poetry: eighteenth-century

poets were content with the task of mirroring what was already known; nineteenth-century poets concerned themselves with projecting knowledge about themselves. But while these writers often make themselves subjects of the poem, they do not function analogously to the objects at the core of the natural or the human sciences.

29 Ludwig Wittgenstein, *Zettel*, ed. G.E.M. Anscombe and G.H. von Wright, trans. G.E.M. Anscombe (Berkeley and Los Angeles: Basil Blackwell, 1967), 29.

30 Niklas Luhmann, *Art as a Social System*, trans. Eva M. Knodt (Stanford University Press, 2000), 136, 146.

31 Thomas Gray, *The Works of Thomas Gray in Prose and Verse*, ed. Edmund Gosse, 4 vols. (London: Macmillan and Co., 1884), 2.108.

32 On Johnson's dictionary and its use of literature, see Robin Valenza, "How Literature Becomes Knowledge: A Case Study," *ELH* 76.1 (2009).

33 Pope's characterization of Homer's diction looks strikingly like Wordsworth's description of the true language of poetry in his prefaces; indeed, Pope and the romantics were largely in agreement in their appreciation of Homer's language. Where they differed was on Pope's translation of it. Thus Pope's use of the term "poetical diction" became negatively valenced because it was associated with Pope's version of Homer, not Homer's poetry itself. Alexander Pope, *The Prose Works of Alexander Pope, the Earlier Works, 1711–1720*, ed. Norman Ault (Oxford: Basil Blackwell, 1936), 233.

   F.W. Bateson gives a concise review of the term "poetic diction" and some of its early uses in *English Poetry and The English Language*, 3rd edn. (Oxford: Clarendon, 1973), 60:

   The special vocabulary of poetic diction can be paralleled in the numerous technical terms of science, philosophy, and politics that were coined in the eighteenth century. The motives that led the chemists to create a word like "phlogiston" (first used in 1733) were ultimately identical with those that induced Thomson and the rest to call fishes a "finny tribe."

34 Coleridge, *Biographia Literaria*, 39.

35 *Ibid.*, 18, 40.

36 *Ibid.*, 40. Wordsworth expressed his objections to Pope's style in his third "Essay on Epitaphs," in which he derided Pope's epitaphs for being absent of feeling and "little better than a tissue of false thoughts, languid and vague expression, unmeaning antithesis, and laborious attempts at discrimination." Wordsworth, *The Prose Works of William Wordsworth*, II.80.

37 This sentiment had, of course, been expressed in more elegant phrasing in Sidney's "Defence": "verse" is "an ornament and no cause to Poetrie, since there have bene many most excellent Poets that never versified, and now swarme many versifiers that need never answere to the name of Poets." And it will reappear in Wordsworth's prefaces.

38 Oliver Goldsmith, *The Works of Oliver Goldsmith*, ed. Peter Cunningham, 12 vols. (New York: Harper, 1900), 6.70, 71.

39 J. Paul Hunter has argued that, by its very nature, any poetry in "[r]hymed verse, and especially verse that is rhymed concentratedly and without the predictable interruption of intervening clusters of sounds, tends to employ a smaller vocabulary than unrhymed verse or prose. The reason for the tendency is, if not transparent, at least translucent. Such poetry must find a certain number of like-sounding terms, and also must arrange them into a more or less expected metrical pattern, a procedure that almost automatically eliminates many words because of their pronunciations." To follow on Hunter's argument, we might observe that writers such as Goldsmith developed a theory of poetry that fit the practice, making a virtue of the necessity of choosing from a limited pool of words. J. Paul Hunter, "Sleeping Beauties: Are Historical Aesthetics Worth Recovering?" *Eighteenth-Century Studies* 34, no. 1 (2000): 11.

40 Wordsworth, *The Prose Works of William Wordsworth*, ed. Alexander B. Grosart, 3 vols. (New York: AMC, 1967), II.87.

41 Addison and Steele, *The Spectator*, 2.389. Addison regards much of the rest of Milton's writing as perfectly in keeping with an "easy Language as may be understood by ordinary Readers," but though universally intelligible, this category for Addison nonetheless remains apart from language that would be used in common conversation.

42 As Brian Vickers has noted, "[I]t should be evident that none of the scientists connected with the Society actually wrote like an artisan, a countryman, or a merchant." Brian Vickers, "The Royal Society and English Prose Style: A Reassessment," in *Rhetoric and the Pursuit of Truth: Language Change in the Seventeenth and Eighteenth Centuries*, ed. Thomas F. Wright (Los Angeles: William Andrews Clark Memorial Library–UCLA, 1985), 17. Addison never claimed to write in such a style himself; his Latin and Greek mottoes would have given the lie to any such profession. See Addison and Richard Steele, *The Spectator*, ed. Gregory Smith, 4 vols. (London: Dent, 1979), 1.118.

43 For a classic account of these terms, see Jerome S. Bruner, Jacqueline J. Goodnow, and George A. Austin, *A Study of Thinking* (New York: John Wiley & Sons, 1956), 11.

44 One could regard both Wordsworth's theories, and those of the eighteenth-century poets, as derived along different lines from Locke's *Essay Concerning Human Understanding*. The eighteenth-century poets embraced the Lockean divorce between word and thing; as Samuel Johnson wrote, "Language is only the instrument of science, and words are but the signs of ideas." Wordsworth holds faster to the sensationalist or associationalist approach to language derived from Locke. He looks to language to embody an experience of the world, but at the same time, he suggests that language users are always caught up in the habitual thought-patterns embedded in language itself. Hans Aarsleff discusses Wordsworth's debt to Locke in Hans Aarsleff, *From Locke to Saussure: Essays on the Study of Language and Intellectual History* (Minneapolis: University of Minnesota Press, 1982).

45 Wordsworth, *The Prose Works of William Wordsworth*, II.135.

46 Gray, *The Works of Thomas Gray in Prose and Verse*, 2.109.

47 In *Biographia Literaria*, Coleridge writes of poetic diction since the Renaissance:

> Yet when the torch of ancient learning was re-kindled, so cheering were its beams, that our eldest poets, cut off by Christianity from all *accredited* machinery, and deprived of all *acknowledged* guardians and symbols of the great objects of nature, were naturally induced to adopt, as a *poetic* language, those fabulous personages, those forms of the supernatural in nature, which had given them such dear delight in the poems of their great masters. (75–76)

48 Terry Eagleton discusses the "linguistic revolution" of the twentieth century that moved from expressive or representational theories of language to productive ones, a turn in literary criticism that draws heavily on philosophy of language and linguistics. However, at the same time, we might also recognize that these disciplines grew out of romantic literary theories in Germany and England, and this is why romantic literature is so malleable to these critical tools. Terry Eagleton, *Literary Theory: An Introduction* (Minneapolis: University of Minnesota Press, 1983), 60.

49 As Mr. Spectator had remarked almost a century earlier, "a Man seldom sets up for a Poet, without attacking the Reputation of all his Brothers in the Art." Coleridge's *Biographia Literaria* suggests as much in its response to the "Preface to the Lyrical Ballads." In other words, Wordsworth's attack on Gray was seen even in its own time as an attempt to establish an independent reputation. Bond, *The Spectator*, 2.252 (No. 253).

50 Coleridge, *Biographia Literaria*, 64.

51 *Ibid.*, 122–23.

52 *Ibid.*, 30–31.

53 *Ibid.*, 56.

54 *Ibid.*, Ch. 16.

55 Wordsworth, *The Prose Works of William Wordsworth*, II.67, 68, 60.

56 *Ibid.*, 68.

57 This definition comes from the second edition of the OED.

58 John Guillory gives attention to some of the modern consequences of this structural divide in "The Sokal Affair and the History of Criticism," *Critical Inquiry* 28.2 (2002 Winter): 470–508.

CODA: COMMON SENSE AND COMMON LANGUAGE

1 Bertolt Brecht, *Galileo*, ed. Eric Bentley, trans. Charles Laughton (New York: Grove, 1966), 71.

2 George Berkeley, *Principles of Human Knowledge and Three Dialogues between Hylas and Philonous*, ed. G.J. Warnock (Glasgow: Collins, 1962), 89, 90.

3 See, for example, Jonathan Culler, *Literary Theory: A Very Short Introduction* (New York: Oxford University Press, 1997), 4.

4 As Peter Dear notes in his recent book, it is not at all clear that engineering feats are proof of scientific theories at all; "the history of science shows time and again [that] it is sometimes unclear that the world even contains the natural objects referred to by the theory supposedly being 'applied'" *The Intelligibility of Nature; How Science Makes Sense of the World* (University of Chicago Press, 2006), 3.

5 Ryle, "Ordinary Language," 122.

6 Frederick Engels, "Editor's Note to the First American Edition," in Karl Marx, *Capital*, ed. Frederick Engels, trans. Samuel Moore and Edward Aveling (Chicago: Charles H. Kerr & Co., 1921), 29.

Works Cited

Aarsleff, Hans. *From Locke to Saussure: Essays on the Study of Language and Intellectual History.* Minneapolis: University of Minnesota Press, 1982.

Abbott, Andrew. *The System of Professions: An Essay on the Division of Expert Labor.* University of Chicago Press, 1988.

Abrams, M. H. *The Mirror and the Lamp: Romantic Theory and the Critical Tradition.* New York: Oxford University Press, 1953.

Addison, Joseph. *The Freeholder,* ed. James Leheny. Oxford: Clarendon, 1979.

Addison, Joseph, and Richard Steele. *The Spectator,* ed. Gregory Smith. 4 vols. London: Dent, 1979.

Algarotti, Francesco. *Sir Isaac Newton's Philosophy Explain'd for the Use of the Ladies. In Six Dialogues on Light and Colours,* trans. Elizabeth Carter. 2 vols. London, 1739.

Amory, Thomas. *The Life and Opinions of John Buncle, Esq.* London: Routledge, 1904.

Memoirs of Several Ladies of Great Britain. London, 1755.

Anderson, Benedict. *Imagined Communities: Reflections on the Origin and Spread of Nationalism.* London and New York: Verso, 1991.

Arendt, Hannah. *The Human Condition.* 2nd edn. University of Chicago Press, 1998.

Arrow, Kenneth J. *The Economics of Information.* Cambridge, MA: Belknap Press, 1984.

Arthur, W. Brian. *Increasing Returns and Path Dependence in the Economy.* Ann Arbor: University of Michigan Press, 1994.

Auerbach, Erich. *Literary Language and Its Public in Late Latin Antiquity and in the Middle Ages.* Princeton University Press, 1993.

Austin, J. L. "The Meaning of a Word." In Charles E. Caton, ed., *Philosophy and Ordinary Language,* 1–21. Urbana: University of Illinois Press, 1963.

Babbage, Charles. *On the Economy of Machinery and Manufactures.* 4th edn. London: John Murray, 1846.

Bacon, Francis. *The Advancement of Learning,* ed. G. W. Kitchin. Philadelphia: Paul Dry Books, 2001.

Baker, Ernest A. "Introduction." In *The Life of John Buncle, Esq.* New York: Dutton, 1904.

Barfoot, Michael. "Hume and the Culture of Science in the Early Eighteenth Century." In M.A. Stewart, ed., *Studies in the Philosophy of the Scottish Enlightenment*. Oxford University Press, 1990.

Barrell, John. *The Birth of Pandora and the Division of Knowledge*. London: Macmillan, 1992.

Basker, James G. "Introduction." In *The Critical Review, or Annals of Literature, 1756–1763*, ix–xliv. London: Pickering & Chatto, 2002.

Bateson, Frederick Wilse. *English Poetry and the English Language*. 3rd edn. Oxford: Clarendon, 1973.

Becher, Tony. *Academic Tribes and Territories: Intellectual Enquiry and the Cultures of Disciplines*. 2nd edn. Buckingham: Open University, 2001.

"The Significance of Disciplinary Differences," *Studies in Higher Education*. 19.2 (1994), 151–61.

Beckner, Morton. *The Biological Way of Thought*. Berkeley: University of California Press, 1968.

Bentham, Jeremy. *Chrestomathia*, ed. M.J. Smith and W.H. Burston, *Works of Jeremy Bentham*. New York: Clarendon, 1983.

The Rationale of Reward. London, 1830.

Berkeley, George. *Philosophical Commentaries*, ed. A.A. Luce and T.E. Jessop, Vol. 1, *The Works of George Berkeley, Bishop of Cloyne*. London: Thomas Newlson and Sons Ltd., 1948.

Principles of Human Knowledge and Three Dialogues between Hylas and Philonous, ed. G.J. Warnock. Glasgow: Collins, 1962.

Biagioli, Mario. *Galileo, Courtier: The Practice of Science in the Culture of Absolutism*. University of Chicago Press, 1993.

Birch, Thomas. *The History of the Royal Society of London*. London, 1756–57.

"Isaac Newton." In *A General Dictionary*, 776–802. London, 1738.

Blair, Hugh, Linda Ferreira-Buckley and S. Michael Halloran, eds. *Lectures on Rhetoric and Belles Lettres*, Carbondale: Southern Illinois University Press, 2005.

Bloch, Marc. *Feudal Society: The Growth of Ties of Dependence*, trans. L.A. Manyon. Vol. 1. University of Chicago Press, 1961.

Bond, Donald. *The Spectator*. London: Clarendon Press, 1965.

Boswell, James. *Private Papers of James Boswell from Malahide Castle*. 18 vols. Mount Vernon, NY: W.E. Rudge, privately printed, 1928–34.

Boswell, John. *A Method of Study: Or, A Useful Library*. 2 vols. London, 1739.

Box, M.A. *The Suasive Art of David Hume*. Princeton University Press, 1990.

Brecht, Bertolt. *Galileo*, trans. Charles Laughton, ed. Eric Bentley. New York: Grove, 1966.

Bruner, Jerome S., Jacqueline J. Goodnow, and George A. Austin. *A Study of Thinking*. New York: John Wiley & Sons, 1956.

Bryan, Margaret. *A Compendious System of Astronomy in a Course of Familiar Lectures*. London, 1797.

Science in Sport, or the Pleasures of Astronomy; a New Instructive Pastime. London, ca. 1825.

Burnet, James (Lord Monboddo). *Of the Origin and Progress of Language*. 6 vols. London, 1773–92.

Capaldi, Nicholas. *David Hume: The Newtonian Philosopher*. Boston: Twayne, 1975.

Carr-Saunders, A. M., and P. A. Wilson. *The Professions*. Oxford: Clarendon, 1933.

Casini, Paolo. *Newton E La Conscienza Europea, Società Editrice Il Mulino*. Bologna: Il Mulino, 1983.

"Newton's *Principia* and the Philosophers of the Enlightenment." *Notes and Records of the Royal Society of London* 42 (1988): 35–52.

Caton, Charles E. "Introduction." In Charles E. Caton, ed., *Philosophy and Ordinary Language*. Urbana: University of Illinois Press, 1963.

Chambers, Ephraim. *Cyclopedia: Or, an Universal Dictionary of Arts and Sciences*. 2 vols. London, 1728.

Christensen, Jerome. *Practicing Enlightenment: Hume and the Formation of a Literary Career*. Madison: University of Wisconsin Press, 1987.

Chroust, Anton-Hermann. "Eudemus or On the Soul: A Lost Dialogue of Aristotle on the Immortality of the Soul." *Mnemosyne*, 4th series, 19.1 (1966): 17–30.

Cohen, I. Bernard. *An Introduction to Newton's "Principia."* Cambridge, MA: Harvard University Press, 1978.

"Newton's Method and Newton's Style." In I. Bernard Cohen and Richard S. Westfall, eds., *Newton: Texts, Backgrounds, Commentaries*. New York: Norton, 1995.

The Newtonian Revolution. Cambridge University Press, 1980.

Coleridge, Samuel Taylor. *Biographia Literaria*. In James Engell and W. Jackson Bate, eds., *Collected Works of Samuel Taylor Coleridge*. Princeton University Press, 1983.

Cooper, Anthony Ashley (3rd Earl of Shaftesbury). *Characteristicks of Men, Manners, Opinions, Times*. 3 vols. Indianapolis: Liberty Fund, 2001.

Crane, Ronald Salmon. *The Idea of the Humanities, and Other Essays Critical and Historical*. 2 vols. University of Chicago Press, 1967.

Crémer, Jacques. "Information in the Theory of Organization." In Pascal Petit, ed., *Economics and Information*. Dordrecht: Kluwer, 2001.

Culler, Jonathan. *Literary Theory: A Very Short Introduction*. New York: Oxford University Press, 1997.

d'Alembert, Jean Le Rond. *Preliminary Discourse of the Encyclopedia of Diderot*, trans. Richard N. Schwab. Indianapolis and New York: Bobbs-Merrill, 1963.

Daston, Lorraine and Katharine Park. *Wonders and the Order of Nature, 1150–1750*. New York: Zone Books, 1998.

Davie, Donald. *Purity of Diction in English Verse*. New York: Schocken Books, 1967.

de Ridder-Symoens, H, ed. *A History of the University in Europe*, vol. 1. Cambridge University Press, 1992.

de Salas, J. "Hume and Newton: The Philosophical Discussion of a Scientific Paradigm." In Stanley Tweyman, ed., *David Hume: Critical Assessments*, 311–26. London and New York: Routledge, 1995.

Dear, Peter Robert. *Discipline & Experience: The Mathematical Way in the Scientific Revolution, Science and Its Conceptual Foundations.* University of Chicago Press, 1995.

 The Intelligibility of Nature: How Science Makes Sense of the World. University of Chicago Press, 2006.

Desaguliers, J.T. *A Course of Experimental Philosophy.* 2nd edn. 2 vols. London: W. Innys, T. Longman, T. Shewell and C. Hitch, and M. Senex, 1745.

Ditton, Humphry. *The General Laws of Nature and Motion with Their Application to Mechanicks ... Being a Part of the Great Mr. Newton's Principles ... Accommodated to the Use of the Younger Mathematicians.* London, 1709.

Dobbs, Betty Jo Teeter, and Margaret C. Jacob. *Newton and the Culture of Newtonianism.* Atlantic Highlands, New Jersey: Humanities Press, 1995.

Donoghue, Frank. *The Fame Machine: Book Reviewing and Eighteenth-Century Literary Careers.* Stanford University Press, 1996.

Durkheim, Émile. *The Division of Labor in Society,* trans. W. D. Halls. New York: Free Press, 1997.

Eagleton, Terry. *Literary Theory: An Introduction.* Minneapolis: University of Minnesota Press, 1983.

Emerson, William. *The Doctrine of Fluxions.* London, 1743.

 A Short Comment on Sir I. Newton's Principia Containing Notes Upon Some Difficult Places of That Excellent Book. London, 1770.

Engels, Frederick. "Editor's Note to the First American Edition." In Karl Marx, *Capital,* ed. Frederick Engels, trans. Samuel Moore and Edward Aveling. Chicago: Charles H. Kerr & Co., 1921, 27–32.

Favereau, Oliver. "Theory of Information: From Bounded Rationality to Interpretive Reason," In Pascal Petit, ed., *Economics and Information.* Dordrecht: Kluwer, 2001.

Febvre, Lucien and Henri-Jean Martin. *The Coming of the Book: The Impact of Printing, 1450–1800,* trans. David Gerard, ed. Geoffrey Nowell-Smith and David Wootton. London and New York: Verso, 1976.

Ferguson, Adam. *An Essay on the History of Civil Society, 1767,* ed. Duncan Forbes. Edinburgh University Press, 1966.

Feynman, Richard. *The Character of Physical Law.* Cambridge, MA and London: MIT Press, 1965.

Fieser, James. *Early Responses to Hume's Metaphysical and Epistemological Writings.* 2 vols. Bristol, England: Thoemmes, 2000.

 Early Responses to Hume's Moral, Literary and Political Writings. 2 vols. Bristol, England: Thoemmes, 1999.

 Early Responses to Hume's Writings on Religion. 2 vols. Bristol, England: Thoemmes, 2001.

 "The Eighteenth-Century British Reviews of Hume's Writings." *Journal of the History of Ideas* 57, no. 4 (1996): 645–57.

Foley, V. "The Division of Labour in Plato and Smith." *History of Political Economy* 6, no. 2 (1974): 220–42.

Foray, Dominique. *Economics of Knowledge.* Cambridge, MA: MIT Press, 2004.

Forster, Antonia. "Review Journals and the Reading Public." In Isabel Rivers, ed., *Books and Their Readers in Eighteenth-Century England: New Essays*. London and New York: Leicester University Press, 2001, pp. 171–90.

Foucault, Michel. *The Archaeology of Knowledge*, trans. A. M. Sheridan Smith. New York: Pantheon, 1972.

The Order of Things: An Archaeology of the Human Sciences. New York: Vintage Books, 1994.

"What Is Enlightenment?" In *Foucault Reader*, ed. Paul Rabinow. New York: Pantheon, 1984.

Frye, Northrop. *Anatomy of Criticism: Four Essays*. Princeton University Press, 1957.

Fuller, Steve. "Disciplinary Boundaries: A Critical Synthesis" *4S Review* 3.1 (1985), 2–15.

Galison, Peter and Bruce Helvy, eds. *Big Science: The Growth of Large Scale Research*. Stanford University Press, 1992.

Garber, Marjorie. *Academic Instincts*. Princeton University Press, 2001.

Geuna, Aldo. *The Economics of Knowledge Production: Funding and the Structure of University Research*. Cheltenham, Glos.: Edward Elgar, 1999.

Giddens, Anthony. *The Consequences of Modernity*. Stanford University Press, 1990.

Gleick, James. "Science Viewpoint: The Human Face of Genius." *The Independent*, 4 January 1993.

Goldsmith, Oliver. *Collected Works of Oliver Goldsmith*, ed. Arthur Friedman. 5 vols. Oxford: Clarendon, 1966.

The Works of Oliver Goldsmith, ed. Peter Cunningham. 12 vols. New York: Harper, 1900.

Golinski, Jan. *Science as Public Culture: Chemistry and Enlightenment in Britain, 1760–1820*. Cambridge University Press, 1992.

Gordon, George. *Remarks Upon the Newtonian Philosophy*. 2nd edn. London, 1719.

Gossman, Lionel. "Two Unpublished Essays on Mathematics in the Hume Papers." *Journal of the History of Ideas* 21 (1960): 442–49.

Grafton, Anthony. *Defenders of the Text, 1450–1800*. Cambridge, MA: Harvard University Press, 1991.

Gramsci, Antonio. *The Antonio Gramsci Reader: Selected Writings, 1916–1935*, ed. David Forgacs. New York University Press, 2000.

Grave, S. A. *The Scottish Philosophy of Common Sense*. Oxford: Clarendon, 1960.

Gray, Thomas. *The Works of Thomas Gray in Prose and Verse*, ed. Edmund Gosse. 4 vols. London: Macmillan and Co., 1884.

Grenoble, Lenore A. and Lindsay J. Whaley. *Saving Languages: An Introduction to Language Revitalization*. Cambridge University Press, 2006.

Groult, Martine. "Introduction." *L'Encyclopédie ou la création des disciplines*. Paris, France: CNRS Editions, 2003.

Guicciardini, Niccolò. *Reading the Principia: The Debate on Newton's Mathematical Methods for Natural Philosophy from 1687 to 1736*. Cambridge University Press, 1999.

Guillory, John. "The Sokal Affair and the History of Criticism." *Critical Inquiry* 28 (2002): 470–508.

Guzzetti, Barbara J., Wayne O. Williams, Stephanie A. Skeels, and Shwu Ming Wu. "Influence of Text Structure on Learning Counterintuitive Physics Concepts." *Journal of Research in Science Teaching* 34, no. 7 (1997): 701–19.

Habermas, Jürgen. *The Structural Transformation of the Public Sphere: An Inquiry into a Category of Bourgeois Society*, trans. Thomas Burger and Frederick Lawrence. Cambridge, MA: MIT Press, 1991.

    The Philosophical Discourse of Modernity, trans. Frederic Lawrence. Cambridge, MA: MIT Press, 1987.

Haldane, John. "Thomas Reid: Life and Work." *American Catholic Philosophical Quarterly* 74, no. 3 (2000): 317–44.

Hall, A. Rupert. *All Was Light: An Introduction to Newton's Opticks*. Oxford: Clarendon, 1993.

    "Newton and His Editors." *Notes and Records of the Royal Society of London* 29, no. 1 (1974): 29–52.

    "Newton in France: A New View." *History of Science* 13 (1975): 233–50.

    Philosophers at War: The Quarrel between Newton and Leibniz. Cambridge University Press, 1980.

Hall, A. Rupert, and Marie Boas Hall. "Newton and the Theory of Matter." In Robert M. Palter, ed., *The "Annus Mirabilis" of Sir Isaac Newton*. Cambridge, MA: MIT Press, 1970, pp. 54–67.

Hatfield, Gary. "Remaking the Science of Mind: Psychology as Natural Science." In Roy Porter, Christopher Fox, and Robert Wokler, eds., *Inventing Human Science: Eighteenth-Century Domains*. Berkeley, Los Angeles, London: University of California Press, 1995, pp. 184–231.

Hatzfeld, John Conrad Francis de. *The Case of the Learned Represented*. London, 1724.

Hawking, Stephen. *A Brief History of Time: Updated and Expanded Tenth Anniversary Edition*. New York: Bantam Books, 1998.

Haywood, Eliza. *The Female Spectator*. 3rd edn. 4 vols. London, 1750.

Helmstädter, Ernst, ed. *The Economics of Knowledge Sharing: A New Institutional Approach*. Cheltenham, Glos.: Edward Elgar, 2003.

Holmes, Geoffrey. *Augustan England: Professions, State and Society, 1680–1730*. Boston: George Allen & Unwin, 1982.

Hume, David. *An Enquiry Concerning Human Understanding*, ed. Tom L. Beauchamp. Oxford University Press, 1999.

    Essays, Moral, Political, and Literary, ed. Eugene F. Miller. Indianapolis: Liberty Classics, 1985.

    The History of England. 6 vols. Indianapolis: Liberty Classics, 1983.

    "My Own Life." In David Fate Norton, ed., *The Cambridge Companion to Hume*. Cambridge University Press, 1993.

    A Treatise of Human Nature, ed. L. A. Selby-Bigge and P. H. Nidditch. 2nd edn. Oxford: Clarendon, 1978.

Hunter, J. Paul. "Sleeping Beauties: Are Historical Aesthetics Worth Recovering?" *Eighteenth-Century Studies* 34, no. 1 (2000): 1–20.

Huxley, Thomas Henry. *Hume*. London and New York: Macmillan, 1902.

Iliffe, Rob. "Butter for Parsnips: Authorship, Audience, and the Incomprehensibility of the *Principia*." In Mario Biagioli and Peter Galison, eds., *Scientific Authorship: Credit and Intellectual Property in Science*. New York and London: Routledge, 2003, pp. 33–65.

Jacob, Margaret. "Newtonianism and the Origins of Enlightenment: A Reassessment." *Eighteenth-Century Studies* 11, no. 1 (1977): 1–25.

Johns, Adrian. *The Nature of the Book: Print and Knowledge in the Making*. University of Chicago Press, 1998.

Johnson, Samuel. "On the Character and Duty of an Academick." The Johnsonians, 2000. Reprinted from *Hospitality: A Discourse Occasioned by Reading His Majesty's Letter*. London, 1793, 42–43.

"Preface." In *Dictionary of the English Language*. Harlow, Essex: Longman, 1990.

The Works of Samuel Johnson. 18 vols. New Haven: Yale University Press, 1958–2005.

Jones, Richard Foster, *The Triumph of the English Language: A Survey of Opinions Concerning the Vernacular from the Introduction of Printing to the Restoration*. Stanford University Press, 1953.

Jones, William Powell. "Newton Further Demands the Muse." *Studies in English Literature 1500–1900* 3 (1963): 287–306.

The Rhetoric of Science: A Study of Scientific Ideas and Imagery in Eighteenth-Century English Poetry. Berkeley: University of California Press, 1966.

Kant, Immanuel. *Anthropology from a Pragmatic Point of View*, ed. Robert B. Louden. Cambridge University Press, 2006.

Conflict of the Faculties, trans. Mary J. Gregor. Norwalk, CT: Abaris Books, 1979.

Prolegomena to Any Future Metaphysics, ed. Lewis White Beck. Indianapolis: Bobbs-Merrill, 1950.

Keill, John. *An Introduction to Natural Philosophy: Or, Philosophical Lectures Read in the University of Oxford, Anno. Dom. 1700*. 5th edn. London, 1758.

Kennedy, George A. *Classical Rhetoric and its Christian and Secular Tradition from Ancient to Modern Times*. 2nd edn. Chapel Hill: UNC Press, 1999.

Kirwan, Richard. "Of Chymical and Mineralogical Nomenclature." *Transactions of the Royal Irish Academy* 8 (1802): 53–76.

Klein, Lawrence E. *Shaftesbury and the Culture of Politeness: Moral Discourse and Cultural Politics in Early Eighteenth-Century England*. Cambridge University Press, 1994.

Knorr Cetina, Karin. *Epistemic Cultures: How the Sciences Make Knowledge*. Cambridge, MA and London: Harvard University Press, 1999.

Koselleck, Reinhart. *Critique and Crisis: Enlightenment and the Pathogenesis of Modern Society*. Cambridge, MA: MIT Press, 1988.

Kramnick, Jonathan Brody. "Literary Criticism among the Disciplines." *Eighteenth-Century Studies* 35, no. 3 (2002): 343–60.

Making the English Canon: Print-Capitalism and the Cultural Past, 1700–1770. Cambridge University Press, 1998.

Kristeller, Paul Oskar. "The Modern System of the Arts: A Study in the History of Aesthetics, Part 1." *Journal of the History of Ideas* 12, no. 4 (1951): 496–527.

"The Modern System of the Arts: A Study in the History of Aesthetics, Part 2." *Journal of the History of Ideas* 13, no. 1 (1951): 17–46.

Kuhn, Thomas S. "Second Thoughts on Paradigms." In *The Structure of Scientific Theories*, ed. F. Suppe. Urbani: University of Illinois Press, 1974, pp. 459–82.

The Structure of Scientific Revolutions. 3rd edn. University of Chicago Press, 1996.

"Letter to the Editor." In James Fieser, ed., *Early Responses to Hume's Metaphysical and Epistemological Writings*, 64–84. Bristol, England: Thoemmes Press, 2000.

Levine, Joseph M. "Strife in the Republic of Letters." In *Commercium Litterarium, 1600–1750: La Communication Dans La République Des Lettres: Conférences Des Colloqes Tenus à Paris 1992 Et à Nimègue 1993*, ed. Hans and Françoise Waquet Bots, 301–19. Amsterdam: APA–Holland University Press, 1994.

Livingston, Donald W. *Hume's Philosophy of Common Life.* University of Chicago Press, 1984.

Locke, John. *An Essay Concerning Human Understanding*, ed. Peter H. Nidditch. Oxford: Clarendon, 1975.

"Some Thoughts Concerning Reading and Study for a Gentleman." In J. A. St. John, ed., *The Works of John Locke.* London, 1854, pp. 497–504.

Leydesdorff, Loet. *The Knowledge-Based Economy: Modeled, Measured, Simulated.* Boca Raton: Universal Publishers, 2006.

Lowndes, William Thomas. *The Bibliographer's Manual*, ed. Henry G. Bohn. 6 vols. London: Bell & Sons, 1890.

McClane, Maureen N. *Romanticism and the Human Sciences: Poetry, Population, and the Discourse of the Species.* Cambridge University Press, 2000.

McCrea, Brian. *Addison and Steele Are Dead: The English Department, Its Canon, and the Professionalization of Literary Criticism.* Cranbury, NJ: Associated University Presses, 1990.

McGann, Jerome. *The Romantic Ideology: A Critical Investigation.* Chicago and London: University of Chicago Press, 1983.

McKelvey, Bill. "Organizational Systematics: Taxonomic Lessons from Biology." *Management Science* 24, no. 13 (1978): 1428–40.

Organizational Systematics: Taxonomy, Evolution, Classification. Los Angeles: UCLA Press, 1982.

McKeon, Michael. *The Secret History of Domesticity: Public, Private, and the Division of Knowledge.* Baltimore: The Johns Hopkins University Press, 2005.

McNulty, Paul J. "Adam Smith's Concept of Labor." *Journal of the History of Ideas* 34, no. 3 (1973): 345–66.

Machlup, Fritz. *Knowledge, Its Creation, Distribution, and Economic Significance.* 3 vols. Princeton University Press, 1980–84.

The Production and Distribution of Knowledge in the United States. Princeton University Press, 1962.

Macomber, Henry P. "A Census of the Owners of Copies of the 1687 First Edition of Newton's 'Principia.'" *The Papers of the Bibliographical Society of America* 47, no. 3 (1953): 269–300.

Mah, Harold. "Phantasies of the Public Sphere: Rethinking the Habermas of Historians." *Journal of Modern History* 72 (2000): 153–82.

Markley, Robert. *Fallen Languages: Crises of Representation in Newtonian England, 1660–1740*. Ithaca: Cornell University Press, 1993.

"Sentimentality as Performance: Shaftesbury, Sterne, and the Theatrics of Virtue." In Felicity Nussbaum and Laura Brown, eds., *The New Eighteenth Century: Theory, Politics, English Literature*. New York and London: Methuen, 1987, pp. 210–30.

Marshall, M. G. "Luxury, Economic Development, and Work Motivation: David Hume, Adam Smith, and J.R. Mc Culloch." *History of Political Economy* 32, no. 3 (2000): 631–48.

"Scottish Political Economy and the High Wage Economy: Hume, Smith, and Mc Culloch." *Scottish Journal of Political Economy* 45, no. 3 (1998): 309–28.

Martin, Benjamin. *The General Magazine of Arts and Sciences, Philosophical, Philological, Mathematical, and Mechanical*. 5 vols. London, 1759, vol. 1 (*The Young Gentleman and Lady's Philosophy* ... By Way of Dialogue).

Marx, Karl. *Capital: A Critique of Political Economy*, trans. Ben Fowkes, ed. Ernest Mandel. 3 vols. New York: Vintage Books, 1977, vol. 1.

Mayden, R.L. "A Hierarchy of Species Concepts: The Denouement in the Saga of the Species Problem." In M.F. Claridge, A.H. Dawah, and M.R. Wilson, eds., *Species: The Units of Biodiversity*. London: Chapman and Hall, 1997, pp. 381–424.

Meek, Ronald L., and Andrew S. Skinner. "The Development of Adam Smith's Ideas of the Division of Labour." *Economic Journal* 83, no. 332 (1973): 1094–1116.

Meli, Domenico Bertoloni. *Thinking with Objects: The Transformation of Mechanics in the Seventeenth Century*. Baltimore: Johns Hopkins University Press, 2006.

Messner-Davidow, Ellen, David R. Shumway, and David J. Sylvan. *Knowledges: Historical and Critical Studies in Disciplinarity*. Charlottesville: University of Virginia Press, 1993.

Meyer, Gerald Dennis. *The Scientific Lady in England 1650–1760: An Account of Her Rise, with Emphasis on the Major Roles of the Telescope and Microscope*, ed. Leon Howard, J.J. Espey, Ada Nisbet and H.T. Swedenberg. *English Studies*. Berkeley and Los Angeles: University of California Press, 1955.

Mill, John Stuart. *Principles of Political Economy*. London, 1848.

Millerson, Geoffrey. *The Qualifying Associations*. London: Routledge, 1964.

Monroe, Paul. *Source Book of the History of Education for the Greek and Roman Period*. Barcelona and Singapore: Athena University Press, 2003.

Mossner, Ernest Campbell. "The First Answer to Hume's Treatise: An Unnoticed Letter of 1740." *Journal of the History of Ideas* 12, no. 2 (1951).

The Life of David Hume. Edinburgh: Nelson, 1954.

Munby, A.N.L. "The Distribution of the First Edition of Newton's *Principia*." *Notes and Records of the Royal Society of London* 10 (1952): 28–39.

Murphy, Peter T. *Poetry as an Occupation and an Art in Britain, 1760–1839, Cambridge Studies in Romanticism 3*. Cambridge University Press, 1993.

Neef, Dale, ed. *The Knowledge Economy*. Oxford: Butterworth-Heinemann, 1998.

Neef, Dale, *et al.*, eds. *The Economic Impact of Knowledge*. Oxford: Butterworth-Heinemann, 1998.

Newton, Isaac. *Isaac Newton's "Philosophae Naturalis Principia Mathematica": The Third Edition (1726) with Variant Readings*, ed. Alexandre Koyré, I. Bernard Cohen and Anne Whitman. 2 vols. Cambridge University Press, 1972.

The Mathematical Papers of Isaac Newton, ed. D. T. Whiteside. 8 vols. Cambridge and London: Cambridge University Press, 1967–81.

"Newton's System of the World." In *The Mathematical Principles of Natural Philosophy*, ed. W. Davis. London, 1803.

The Principia: Mathematical Principles of Natural Philosophy, ed. I. Bernard Cohen and Anne Miller Whitman. Berkeley: University of California Press, 1999.

Nicolson, Marjorie Hope. *Newton Demands the Muse: Newton's Opticks and the Eighteenth Century Poets, History of Ideas Series 2*. Princeton University Press, 1946.

Noxon, J. *Hume's Philosophical Development: A Study of His Methods*. Oxford University Press, 1973.

Ostler, Nicholas. *Ad Infinitum: A Biography of Latin*. New York: Walker & Co., 2008.

Parsons, Talcott. "Professions." In David Sills, ed., *International Encyclopedia of the Social Sciences*. New York: Macmillan–The Free Press, 1968.

Patey, Douglas Lane. "Swift's Satire on 'Science' and the Structure of Gulliver's Travels." *ELH* 48, no. 4 (1991): 809–39.

Pemberton, Henry. *A View of Sir Isaac Newton's Philosophy*. Dublin, 1758.

Pfau, Thomas. *Wordsworth's Profession: Form, Class, and the Logic of Early Romantic Cultural Production*. Stanford University Press, 1997.

Plant, Raymond. *Hegel*. Bloomington: Indiana University Press, 1973.

Plato. *The Republic*, trans. H. D. P. Lee. Harmondsworth and Baltimore: Penguin, 1974.

Pocock, J. G. A. *Politics, Language, & Time: Essays on Political Thought and History*. Chicago and London: University of Chicago Press, 1960.

Virtue, Commerce, and History: Essays on Political Thought and History, Chiefly in the Eighteenth Century. Cambridge University Press, 1985.

Poovey, Mary. *A History of the Modern Fact: Problems of Knowledge in the Sciences of Wealth and Society*. University of Chicago Press, 1998.

Pope, Alexander. *The Prose Works of Alexander Pope, the Earlier Works, 1711–1720*, ed. Norman Ault. Oxford: Basil Blackwell, 1936.

Porter, Roy. *Enlightenment: Britain and the Creation of the Modern World*. London: Penguin, 2000.

Potkay, Adam. *The Fate of Eloquence in the Age of Hume*. Ithaca: Cornell University Press, 1994.

Price, John Valdimir. "The Reading of Philosophical Literature." In Isabel Rivers, ed., *Books and Their Readers in Eighteenth-Century England*. New York: St. Martin's Press, 1982, pp. 165–96.

Rancière, Jacques. "Thinking Between Disciplines: An Aesthetics of Knowledge," trans. Jon Roffe. *Parrhesia* 1 (2006): 1–12.

"The Public and the Nation." *Eighteenth-Century Studies* 29, no. 1 (1995).

Rattansi, Ali. *Marx and the Division of Labour*. London and Basingstoke: Macmillan Press, 1982.

Reid, Thomas. *Essays on the Intellectual Powers of Man*, ed. Keith Lehrer and Arnold Beanblossom. Indianapolis: Bobbs-Merrill, 1975.

"Essays on the Intellectual Powers of Man." In Ronald E. Beanblossom and Keith Lehrer, eds., *Thomas Reid's Inquiry and Essays*. Indianapolis: Hackett, 1983, pp. 127–296.

"An Inquiry into the Human Mind on the Principles of Common Sense." In Ronald E. Beanblossom and Keith Lehrer, eds., *Thomas Reid's Inquiry and Essay*. Indianapolis: Hackett, 1983, pp. 1–126.

"Review of *a Treatise of Human Nature*." In James Fieser, ed., *Early Responses to Hume's Metaphysical and Epistemological Writings*, 1–40, 44–63. Bristol, England: Thoemmes Press, 2000.

"Review of *Treatise*, Book 3." In James Fieser, ed., *Early Responses to Hume's Moral, Literary, and Political Writings*, 1–10. Bristol, England: Thoemmes Press, 1999.

Ringler, William. "*Poeta Nascitur Non Fit*: Some Notes on the History of an Aphorism." *Journal of the History of Ideas* 2.4 (1941): 497–504.

Roget, Peter Mark. *Roget's Thesaurus of English Words and Phrases: Facsimile of the First Edition 1852*. London: Bloomsbury Books, 1992.

Romer, Paul M. "Two Strategies for Economic Development: Using Ideas and Producing Ideas," Proceedings of the World Bank Annual Conference on Development Economics. 1992. Reproduced in David Klein, ed., *The Strategic Management of Intellectual Capital*. Oxford: Butterworth-Heinemann, 1997, pp. 211–38.

Rose, William. "Review of *Enquiry Concerning the Principles of Morals*." In James Fieser, ed., *Early Responses to Hume's Moral, Literary, and Political Writings*. Bristol, England: Thoemmes Press, 1999, pp. 11–27.

Rousseau, G. S. "Science Books and Their Readers in the Eighteenth Century." In Isabel Rivers, ed., *Books and Their Readers in Eighteenth-Century England*. New York: St. Martin's Press, 1982, pp. 197–255.

Ryle, Gilbert. "Ordinary Language." In Charles E. Caton, ed., *Philosophy and Ordinary Language*. Urbana: University of Illinois Press, 1963, pp. 108–27.

Schabas, Margaret. "David Hume on Experimental Natural Philosophy, Money, and Fluids." *History of Political Economy* 33, no. 3 (2001): 411–35.

Schaffer, Simon. "Glass Works." In David Gooding, Trevor Pinch and Simon Schaffer, eds., *The Uses of Experiment: Studies in the Natural Sciences*. Cambridge University Press, 1989, pp. 67–104.

Schoenfeld, Mark. *The Professional Wordsworth: Law, Labor, and the Poet's Contract*. Athens, Georgia: University of Georgia Press, 1996.

Schumpeter, J. A. *History of Economic Analysis*. New York: Oxford University Press, 1954.

'sGravesande, William James. *Mathematical Elements of Natural Philosophy, Confirm'd by Experiments; or, an Introduction to Sir Isaac Newton's Philosophy*, trans. J. T. Desaguliers. 4th edn. 2 vols. London: J. Senex, W. Innys, and J. Osborn and T. Longman, 1731.

Shank, J. B. *The Newton Wars & the Beginning of the French Enlightenment*. Chicago and London: University of Chicago Press, 2008.

Shapin, Steven. *A Social History of Truth.* University of Chicago Press, 1994.

Shapin, Steven and Simon Schaffer. *Leviathan and the Air-Pump: Hobbes, Boyle, and the Experimental Life.* Princeton University Press, 1985.

Shapiro, Alan E. "Experiment and Mathematics in Newton's Theory of Color." In I. Bernard Cohen and Richard S. Westfall, eds., *Newton: Texts, Backgrounds, Commentaries.* New York: Norton, 1995, pp. 191–202.

Shelley, Percy Bysshe. *Shelley's Prose, or the Trumpet of a Prophecy,* ed. David Lee Clark. London: Fourth Estate, 1988.

Shteir, Ann B. "Botanical Dialogues: Maria Jacson and Women's Popular Science Writing in England." *Eighteenth-Century Studies* 23, no. 3 (1990): 301–17.

Sidney, Sir Philip. *Sir Philip Sidney: Selected Prose and Poetry,* ed. Robert Kimbrough. 2nd edn. Madison: University of Wisconsin Press, 1983.

Simon, Herbert. *The Sciences of the Artificial.* 3rd edn. Cambridge, MA: MIT Press, 1996.

Siskin, Clifford. *The Work of Writing: Literature and Social Change in Britain, 1700–1830.* Baltimore: Johns Hopkins University Press, 1998.

Sitter, John. *Literary Loneliness in Mid-Eighteenth-Century England.* Ithaca and London: Cornell University Press, 1982.

Skarbek, Frédéric. *Théorie Des Richesses Sociales.* 2nd edn. 3 vols. Paris, 1839.

Smith, Adam. "'Early Draft' of Part of *the Wealth of Nations.*" In R. L. Meek, D. D. Raphael and P. G. Stein, eds., *Lectures on Jurisprudence.* Oxford University Press, 1978, pp. 562–81.

  "History of Astronomy." In W. P. D. Wightman and J. C. Bryce, eds., *Essays on Philosophical Subjects.* Indianapolis: Liberty Fund, 1982, pp. 33–105.

  Lectures on Jurisprudence, ed. R. L. Meek, D. D. Raphael and P. G. Stein. Oxford University Press, 1978.

  The Wealth of Nations. 2 vols. Indianapolis, Indiana: Liberty Press, 1981.

Smith, Dinitia. "When Ideas Get Lost in Bad Writing; Attacks on Scholars Include a Barbed Contest with 'Prizes.'" *New York Times,* February 27, 1999.

Smith, Norman Kemp. *The Philosophy of David Hume: A Critical Study of Its Origins and Central Doctrines.* London: Macmillan and Co., 1941.

Smith, Roger. "The Language of Human Nature." In Christopher Fox, Roy Porter, and Robert Wokler, eds., *Inventing Human Science: Eighteenth-Century Domains.* Berkeley, Los Angeles, and London: University of California Press, 1995, pp. 88–111.

Smollett, Tobias. *The Adventures of Peregrine Pickle.* 2 vols. London: Hutchinson & Co., 1904.

Spivak, Gayatri Chakravorty. *Death of a Discipline.* New York: Columbia University Press, 2003.

Sprat, Thomas. *History of the Royal Society.* St. Louis: Washington University Press, 1958.

Steele, Richard. *The Tatler,* ed. A. Chalmers. 4 vols. *The British Essayists with Prefaces, Historical and Biographical.* Boston, 1856.

Stephen, Sir Leslie. *History of English Thought in the Eighteenth Century,* ed. Crane Brinton. 2 vols. New York: Harbinger, 1962.

Stephens, James. *Francis Bacon and the Style of Science.* University of Chicago Press, 1975.

Stewart, Dugald. *Dissertation: Exhibiting the Progress of Metaphysical, Ethical, and Political Philosophy, since the Revival of Letters in Europe,* ed. William Hamilton, *The Collected Works of Dugald Stewart.* Edinburgh: Thomas Constable and Co., 1844.

Introduction to the Elements of the Philosophy of the Human Mind, ed. Knud Haakonssen, 11 vols. *Collected Works of Dugald Stewart.* Bristol, England: Thoemmes, 1994, vols. 2–4.

Lectures on Political Economy, ed. William Hamilton. Vols. 8 and 9, *The Collected Works of Dugald Stewart.* Edinburgh, 1855.

Outlines of Moral Philosophy, ed. Knud Haakonssen. 2nd edn. Vol. 6, *Collected Works of Dugald Stewart.* Bristol, England: Thoemmes, 1994.

Stewart, Larry R. *The Rise of Public Science: Rhetoric, Technology, and Natural Philosophy in Newtonian Britain.* New York: Cambridge University Press, 1992.

Stigler, George. "The Division of Labor is Limited by the Extent of the Market." *Journal of Political Economy* 59.3 (1951): 185–93.

Streuver, Nancy. "The Conversable World: Eighteenth-Century Transformations of the Relation of Rhetoric and Truth." In Thomas F. Wright, ed., *Rhetoric and the Pursuit of Truth: Language Change in the Seventeenth and Eighteenth Centuries.* Los Angeles: William Andrews Clark Memorial Library–UCLA, 1985, pp. 77–119.

Sullivan, Alvin, ed. *British Literary Magazines.* 4 vols. Westport, CT: Greenwood Press, 1983.

Swift, Jonathan. *A Proposal for Correcting, Improving and Ascertaining the English Tongue, 1712. English Linguistics, 1500–1800. No. 213.* Menston, UK: Scolar Press, 1969.

Teichgraeber, Richard F., III. "'Less Abused Than I Had Reason to Expect': The Reception of the Wealth of Nations in Britain, 1776–1790." *Historical Journal* 30, no. 2 (1987): 337–66.

Telescope, Tom. *The Newtonian System of Philosophy Adapted to the Capacities of Young Gentlemen and Ladies.* London, 1770.

Turnbull, H. W., ed. *The Correspondence of Isaac Newton.* 7 vols. Cambridge University Press for the Royal Society, 1959–77.

Valenza, Robin. "Editing the Self: David Hume's Narrative Theory." *The Eighteenth Century: Theory and Interpretation* 43 (2002).

"How Literature Becomes Knowledge: A Case Study." *ELH* 76.1 (2009).

Valenza, Robin and John Bender. "Hume's Learned and Conversable Worlds." In Jonathan Culler, ed., *Just Being Difficult.* Stanford University Press, 2003.

Veitch, John. "Philosophy in the Scottish Universities." *Mind* 2, no. 6 (1877): 207–34.

Vickers, Brian. "The Royal Society and English Prose Style: A Reassessment." In Thomas F. Wright, ed., *Rhetoric and the Pursuit of Truth: Language Change in the Seventeenth and Eighteenth Centurie.* Los Angeles: William Andrews Clark Memorial Library-UCLA, 1985.

Walker, Hugh. *The English Essay and Essayists*. New York: E.P. Dutton & Co., 1923.

Wallerstein, Immanuel, *et al. Open the Social Sciences: Report of the Gulbenkian Commission on the Restructuring of the Social Sciences*. Stanford University Press, 1996.

Warner, Michael. *The Letters of the Republic: Publication and the Print Sphere in Eighteenth-Century America*. Cambridge, MA and London: Harvard University Press, 1990.

Warsh, David. *Knowledge and the Wealth of Nations: A Story of Economic Discovery*. New York: Norton, 2006.

West, Andrew Fleming. *Alcuin and the Rise of the Christian Schools*. New York: C. Scribner's Sons, 1901.

West, J. G. "Adam Smith's Two Views on the Division of Labour." *Economica* 31, no. 121 (1964): 23–32.

Westfall, Richard S. *Never at Rest: A Biography of Isaac Newton*. Cambridge University Press, 1980.

Whewell, William. *History of the Inductive Sciences*. 3rd edn. *Cass Library of Science Classics 7*. London: Cass, 1967.

Wiley, E. O. and R. L. Mayden. "The Evolutionary Species Concept." In Q. D. Wheeler and R. Meier, eds. *Species Concepts and Phylogenetic Theory: A Debate*. New York: Columbia University Press, 1997.

Williams, Raymond. *Culture and Society, 1780–1850*. New York: Anchor Books, 1958

   Writing in Society. London: Verso, 1983.

Wilson, David Sloan and Jin Yoshimura. "On the Coexistence of Specialists and Generalists." *American Naturalist* 144 (1994).

Wittgenstein, Ludwvig. *Zettel*, trans. G.E.M. Anscombe, ed. G. E. M. Anscombe and G. H. von Wright. Berkeley and Los Angeles: Basil Blackwell, 1967.

Wolterstorff, Nicholas. "Reid on Common Sense, with Wittgenstein's Assistance." *American Catholic Philosophical Quarterly* 74, no. 3 (2000): 491–518.

Wordsworth, William. *The Poetical Works of William Wordsworth*, ed. E. de Selincourt and Helen Darbishire. 2nd edn. 5 vols. Oxford: Clarendon Press, 1956–65.

   The Prose Works of William Wordsworth, ed. Alexander B. Grosart. 3 vols. New York: AMC, 1967.

   The Prose Works of William Wordsworth, ed. W. J. B. Owen and Jane Worthington Smyster. 3 vols. Oxford: Clarendon Press, 1974.

Wylie, Ian. *Young Coleridge and the Philosophers of Nature*. Oxford: Clarendon, 1989.

Index

Addison, Joseph, 1, 4–5, 34, 37, 44–6, 50, 98,
    119–20, 125, 163–4, 182, 192–3, 212–13, 219,
    222, 230
Addison, Joseph and Richard Steele: *Spectator,
    The* 1, 4, 26, 34, 44, 79–80, 85, 98, 119, 163,
    191–2, 201, 203, 212, 219–20, 222–3, 227
Alcuin, 38, 191, 235
Alembert, Jean le Rond d', 12, 50, 185, 189, 215,
    224
Alexandria, library of, 23
Algarotti, (Conte) Francesco, 80–6, 201–2
Anderson, Benedict, 2–3, 5, 7, 123–4, 127,
    191, 222
applications, 4, 55–60, 66, 68, 70, 90, 110–12,
    183, 199, 204
Arendt, Hannah, 17, 188, 222
Aristotle, 7, 103, 125, 157, 185, 203, 208
Arrow, Kenneth, 23, 222
arts, 6, 12, 14, 21–2, 30, 43, 56, 96, 139, 143–5,
    147, 149, 151, 172, 180, 185, 187, 203, 208,
    215–16
Austen, Jane, 44–5
Austin, J.L., 31, 190, 213, 219, 223

Babbage, Charles, 17
Bacon, Sir Francis, 1, 11, 15, 25, 35, 42, 104, 125,
    139, 143, 146, 157, 172, 178, 185, 212, 223,
    233; *Advancement of Learning*, 11, 25, 104,
    139, 146, 185, 223; *De Augmentis*, 104, 212
Becher, Tony, 21
belles lettres, 14, 42, 83, 145
Bibliothéque Raisonée, 106, 110
biology, 7–8
Blair, Hugh, 48, 102, 116, 192, 212
botany, 80, 139
Bourdieu, Pierre, 149, 189
Boyle, Robert, 7, 8, 61, 66, 181, 194, 195, 232
branding, 22, 33, 43, 55, 61, 67, 111, 193
Buffon, Comte de (Georges-Louis LeClerc), 8
Butler, Judith, 28, 29, 189

Carter, Elizabeth, 80–1, 201–2, 222
Chambers, Ephraim, 11, 27, 74, 94, 98, 185, 189,
    200, 203, 224
Charlemagne, 38
chemistry, 7, 8, 10, 19, 52, 80, 136, 139, 144, 146,
    170, 176–7, 181, 196, 226
coffee houses, 5
coffee-table book, 35
Coleridge, Samuel Taylor, 14, 35, 51, 118,
    144–72, 193, 211, 216–20, 224, 235;
    Biographia Literaria, 144, 147, 153, 168, 193,
    211, 216–18, 220, 224
colleges, invisible, 7
common sense, 4, 25, 35, 43, 57, 71, 77, 86–8, 95,
    105, 111, 114–18, 124, 127, 131–2, 136, 168,
    173, 174, 176–7, 206, 211, 214
communities, imagined, 2, 7
conversability, 2, 5, 14, 18, 34, 40–7, 51, 53, 56,
    58, 78, 94, 99, 107, 123, 168, 191–4, 208
conversation, 5–6, 14, 44–6, 50–1, 57, 59, 81,
    84, 86, 95, 104, 120, 155, 157, 169, 175, 191,
    212, 219
copyright, 15, 24
counterintuitive, 57, 87, 88, 89, 115, 146

Dante, 103, 166–8
Daston, Lorraine, 1, 5, 224
Davy, Humphry, 8, 144
Defoe, Daniel, 46, 212
Derrida, Jacques, 24–5
Desaguliers, J.T., 67–9, 73, 85, 188, 197–201,
    204, 225, 232
Descartes, René, 86, 102, 104, 174
Dewey Decimal system, 24
Diderot, Denis, 11, 139, 224
disciplinarity, 19–20, 24, 146, 180
disciplines, 2–35, 40, 41, 43, 49–53, 56, 61, 65,
    74, 90, 92, 94–5, 100, 103, 126–9, 133–57,
    165–6, 169, 172, 174–6, 177, 180–4, 189–90,
    194, 213, 215, 220, 226; definition of, 5

Dryden, John, 158, 160
Durkheim, Emile, 5, 16, 186, 225

economics, 5, 9, 11, 13–16, 18, 22, 24, 157, 177, 184–8, 205, 217
Eisenstein, Elizabeth, 2, 179
encyclopedias, 11, 17, 50, 98, 139, 143, 172, 185, 189, 200, 203, 224, 226
Engels, Friedrich, 16, 176–7, 186
enlightenment, 1, 2, 5, 10, 34, 54, 102, 116–17, 126, 130, 150, 164, 178, 193, 205
essay, 13, 23, 25, 31, 37, 40, 43, 46–7, 49, 78, 94, 107, 119–21, 125, 137, 161, 177–8, 191, 206, 210–15
Europe, 3, 8, 16, 19, 38, 50, 52, 55, 65, 70, 99, 103, 109, 137, 147, 185, 209, 233

Ferguson, Adam, 14, 147, 186–7, 213, 216, 225
Feynman, Richard, 5, 31, 33, 190, 225
findings, disciplinary, 6, 17, 22, 40, 53, 61, 74, 134–6
Foucault, Michel, 6, 8, 9, 20, 178, 182, 226
fragmentation, intellectual and disciplinary, 2, 34, 167, 179
France, 8, 17, 30, 38, 39, 46, 80, 98–101, 104, 119, 133, 142, 149, 158, 171, 174, 178–9, 187, 189, 193, 195, 197, 202–3, 209, 222, 226–7, 232
Frye, Northrop, 152, 177, 217, 226
Fuller, Steve, 21

Galt, John, 46
Germany, 2, 8, 16, 101, 106, 133, 146, 150, 157, 174, 176, 178, 187, 193, 209–10, 220
Goldsmith, Oliver, 1–2, 34, 43, 44, 50, 109, 161, 164, 178, 192–3, 210, 218–19, 226
Gramsci, Antonio, 16, 187, 226
Gray, Thomas, 158, 165, 218–20, 226
Gregory, David, 65, 73, 196, 219, 222
Guillory, John, 5, 177, 181, 193, 220, 227
Gulbenkian Commission, 5, 182, 235

Habermas, Jürgen, 2–3, 24–5, 34, 179, 189, 227, 229
Halley, Edmund, 60, 65–6, 73, 195
Hayek, Friedrich, 23
Haywood, Eliza, 79–80, 85, 201, 203, 227
history, literary, 25–6, 149
Homer, 160, 218
humanities, 3, 6, 22, 26, 28–9, 33, 35–6, 53, 56, 95, 96, 129, 134–5, 175–7, 181, 193, 215–16
Hume, David, 5, 8, 13–15, 35, 40–1, 45–7, 92–137, 145, 150, 155, 184, 186, 189, 191–2, 202–34; *Enquiries*, 21, 50, 94, 120–4, 127, 136, 212–13, 227, 232; *History of England*, 92,

203, 227; *Treatise of Human Nature*, 94–6, 100–22, 124, 127, 130, 132–4, 137, 202, 204–10, 214, 222, 227, 230
Huxley, T.H., 137, 214, 228

information, 2, 5, 11, 13–14, 19, 23–4, 26, 71, 74, 83, 97, 104, 118, 124, 157, 181, 201
institutions, 6, 20, 21, 40–1, 46, 56, 61, 93, 96, 100, 124, 133, 187, 199, 205
invisible hand, 22

jargon, 27, 32, 51, 52, 106, 123, 125, 130, 155, 163
Johns, Adrian, 2, 178, 180, 187, 193, 228, 230, 233
Johnson, Samuel, 12, 37, 41, 42, 44, 47–9, 111, 117, 123, 145, 191, 201, 211, 213, 219, 228; *Idler*, 37, 210; *Rambler*, 123, 201, 213

Kant, Immanuel, 5, 9, 51, 103, 132, 133, 155, 176, 183, 208, 214, 228; *Prolegomena to Any Future Metaphysics*, 103, 132, 208, 214, 228
knowledge, 1, 4, 5, 6, 8–19, 21–4, 27–8, 33–5, 39–40, 42–3, 45–6, 48, 52, 56–9, 61, 64–5, 68, 70–1, 75, 78–80, 84, 88–90, 94, 98, 99, 102, 111, 114–15, 127, 129, 130–5, 137, 139, 142–4, 150, 152, 157–8, 167, 172–5, 177, 180, 182–3, 185, 187, 189, 193–4, 196, 199, 203, 208, 209–210, 214–16, 218; stickiness of, 23
Knox, Vicesimus, 120
Koselleck, Reinhart, 2, 179, 181, 228
Kuhn, Thomas, 21, 181–2, 186, 229

labor, 10–11, 16, 17, 80, 177; division of, 11–13, 15–19, 22, 145, 167, 184, 186–8; intellectual, 11, 14, 16, 18, 20, 41, 43, 52, 139, 143, 145, 184, 187, 188
Lamarck, Jean-Baptiste, 8
language, 7, 8, 21, 23–40, 43, 47–53, 55, 58, 62–3, 66, 69, 71, 75, 83, 85, 94, 97–100, 102–4, 110, 113, 116, 122, 123, 124, 126–37, 144–7, 149, 152–77, 190–3, 201, 208, 213, 214, 218–20; common, 4, 34, 38, 144, 166, 168; common life, 27, 37, 43, 52, 111–12, 115, 116, 120, 127, 128, 131, 133–4, 136, 153, 154, 155, 174–7; disciplinary, 21, 28, 29, 33, 34, 129, 145, 152, 165; everyday, 29, 126, 132, 175; expert, 2, 13, 114, 127, 139, 161, 168; jargon, 27, 32, 51, 52, 106, 123, 125, 130, 155, 163; Latin, 30, 38–40, 50, 55, 58–9, 65, 69, 98, 101, 103–4, 151, 162, 167–8, 183, 190–1, 197, 212, 213, 219, 222, 231; ordinary, 28–31, 39, 127, 134, 175, 213; technical, 26, 29–32, 38, 42, 51, 53, 108, 128, 142, 158, 165, 171; terminology, 31, 39, 130, 163, 165, 175–6;

vernacular, 30, 31, 34, 38–40, 48, 50, 58, 69, 75, 103–4, 127, 129, 133–4, 136, 138, 155, 166, 168, 172, 190, 194, 213
Latin, 30, 38, 39, 40, 50, 55, 58, 59, 65, 69, 98, 101–4, 151, 162, 167–8, 183, 190–1, 197, 212, 213, 219, 222, 231
learned world, 5, 19, 41–4, 47, 53, 55, 57, 64, 65, 70–2, 74, 75, 77, 115, 118, 124–5, 145, 172, 182, 193
learning, 1, 11, 13, 15, 23, 26, 28, 34, 42, 44, 46, 47, 50, 70, 74, 78–80, 88, 98, 99, 102, 114, 123, 124, 139, 142–3, 148, 149, 150, 165, 182, 208, 215, 220
Leland, John, 117
libraries, 23, 44, 51, 85, 99, 182
lingua communis, 4, 34, 38, 144, 166, 168
Linnaeus, 8, 166, 171
literati, 37, 148
literature, 2–4, 7, 11, 16, 20, 24–35, 39–44, 46, 50, 51, 57, 59, 64–5, 82–3, 92, 95–111, 119, 121–3, 131, 133, 136–7, 144, 145, 148–50, 158, 166, 168, 170, 172, 174, 177–8, 180–3, 189, 192, 195, 198, 207, 217, 220
Locke, John, 4, 14, 35, 42, 44, 47, 49, 50, 65, 94, 105, 116, 125, 126, 128, 129, 130–1, 136, 156, 180, 191, 192, 195, 202, 204, 212–13, 219, 222, 229
Luhmann, Niklas, 157, 169, 218

Malchup, Fritz, 23
Martin, Benjamin, 78, 84, 86, 87, 191, 201, 203, 210, 225, 229, 231, 232
Marx, Karl, 5, 16, 23, 176–7, 186–9, 229, 232
Marx, Karl and Friedrich Engels: *German Ideology*, 16
mathematics, 10, 17, 31, 33, 35, 42, 48, 50, 54–5, 57–69, 71, 73, 75–6, 80, 82, 84, 89–91, 94, 98, 100, 104, 112, 114, 122, 127–9, 133–9, 158, 174–6, 196–205, 208, 213, 226, 233
McGann, Jerome, 152, 217, 230
Mill, John Stuart, 35, 176, 187, 214, 230

New York Times, 26, 28, 189, 233
Newton, Isaac, 4, 10, 35, 49, 54–96, 104, 105, 111–15, 127–9, 133–4, 137, 144, 150, 180, 193–205, 207, 216, 222–35; *Opticks*, 76, 77, 101, 200, 202, 227, 231; *Principia*, 35, 49, 50, 54, 58–77, 92, 94, 95, 112, 133–4, 194–204, 224–31; *System of the World*, 60, 195, 196, 231

Parsons, Talcott, 5, 6, 182, 231
patent, 17, 24
pedantry, 47, 50–2, 86

perspicuity, 47–52, 157, 161, 168
Philosophical Transactions of the Royal Society, 60, 65–6, 100
philosophy, 7, 15, 18, 25, 27, 30–5, 50, 58, 61, 70, 74–88, 93–139, 144, 146, 149, 156, 158, 164–6, 172, 177, 180–1, 187, 190–3, 199, 204–5, 210–12, 214, 218, 220; moral, 12, 19, 92–5, 117, 118, 121, 127–9, 133, 136–7, 139, 204; natural, 56, 75, 76, 78, 79, 81, 83–8, 100, 127, 135, 195, 199, 204–5, 208, 214
Philosophy and Literature, 28
physics, 4, 7, 19, 27, 29–33, 35, 53–5, 57–8, 60, 65–9, 71, 73, 77–8, 80, 81, 87, 89–96, 127–8, 134, 139, 146, 149, 156, 163, 170, 175–6, 180, 193–4, 198–9, 203–5, 208, 227
Pocock, J.G.A., 178, 190, 231
poetic diction, 146, 154, 158–60, 165–6, 218, 220
poetry, 7, 10, 27, 35, 39, 57, 83, 96, 116, 139, 142–50, 152–72, 180, 215–18
polythetic, 6, 183
Pope, Alexander, 54, 71, 116, 160–1, 164, 218, 231
popularization, 2, 4, 34, 47, 50, 52, 55–7, 67–8, 70–1, 73, 76–90, 93, 111, 150, 193, 195, 199, 201
prejudice, natural, 36, 89, 173, 174; popular, 105; prevailing, 106, 116
print culture, 2, 57, 96, 131, 144, 179
print sphere, 34, 38
professionalization, 9, 56, 129, 147, 149, 216
professions, 9, 14–16, 24–5, 28, 38, 53, 56, 65, 81, 115, 131, 139, 147–51, 156, 163, 166–7, 170, 180, 183, 206, 217, 219
propriety, 47–50, 52, 53, 122, 161, 163
public, lay, 36, 89, 174
public sphere, 3, 34, 134, 179

Rancière, Jacques, 182, 231
reader, common, 40, 69, 105, 107, 110; general, 10, 28, 35, 59, 92, 94, 95, 99, 102, 104–7, 109, 111, 113, 115
reading, 26
Reid, Thomas, 35, 94, 97, 114–19, 127, 131–3, 190, 205, 211, 214, 215, 227, 232, 235
Republic of Letters, 1, 11, 28, 34, 43, 98, 101
Royal Society, 43, 56, 60–1, 64–6, 73, 85, 100–1, 125, 128, 163, 194–7, 206, 213, 219, 223, 224, 227, 230, 233–4
Ryle, Gilbert, 30–1, 32, 176, 190, 221, 232

science, 1, 3, 4, 10, 14, 15, 18, 21, 25, 27–8, 33, 35, 37, 41, 51, 54, 57, 64, 67–8, 70, 76–91, 94–5, 97, 100, 101, 107, 117, 123, 127–8, 132–8, 142–4, 165–6, 169–70, 175–7, 181, 193–6, 200–1, 203, 205, 213, 215, 218–19, 221; big, 17, 188 *scientia scientarum*, 25

sense, common, 4, 25, 35, 43, 57, 71, 77, 86–8, 95, 105, 111, 114–19, 124, 127, 131–2, 136, 168, 173–4, 176–7, 206, 211, 214

Shaftesbury, 3rd Earl of (Anthony Ashley Cooper), 44, 118–19, 191–2, 206, 211, 224, 228–9

Shelley, Percy Bysshe, 148, 184, 233

Smith, Adam, 5, 10–19, 22–3, 36, 41, 87, 89, 147–9, 166, 173, 174, 182, 184–9, 203, 205–6, 214, 216, 219, 222–3, 226, 229, 230, 233, 235; *Lectures on Jurisprudence*, 15, 184, 187, 233; *Lectures on Rhetoric and Belles Lettres*, 48, 102, 192, 232–3; *Theory of Moral Sentiments*, 147; *Wealth of Nations*, 11, 16, 18, 146–8, 184, 186–9, 216, 233, 234, 235

Smith, Charlotte, 44

Smollett, Tobias, 8, 43, 99, 192, 233

Snow, C.P., 33

sociability, 2, 5, 14, 18, 34, 45–6, 51

sociology, 5, 6, 21

specialization, 3, 4, 6, 10, 13–14, 19, 20, 22, 40, 85, 91, 129, 146–7, 149, 163, 180, 216; intellectual, 3, 12, 14, 15, 17, 19, 142, 146

speciation, 6, 9, 11, 12, 15, 16, 90, 92, 161, 178, 183

spectator, impartial, 27

Sprat, Thomas, 125, 163, 196, 213, 233

Steele, Richard, 5, 34, 37–8, 45, 50, 86, 119–20, 182, 192, 212, 219, 222, 230, 233; *Tatler*, 5, 182, 193, 233

Stewart, Dugald, 11, 12, 15, 16, 17, 22, 35, 132–3, 135, 136, 181, 184–5, 187, 193–4, 199–200, 203, 205, 214, 223, 233–4

style, 26, 27, 29, 40, 46, 50, 59, 63, 71, 95, 99–103, 109, 119–25, 130, 165, 175, 180, 190–1, 196, 206, 212, 215, 218–19

Swift, Jonathan, 42, 51, 119, 124, 191–2, 231, 234; *Gulliver's Travels*, 43, 119, 192, 231

systematics, 6, 183

trademark, 21, 24, 67

tree of knowledge, 11, 139, 143, 169, 180, 185, 215

universities, 3, 6, 8–10, 19, 30, 38, 40–1, 56, 72, 84, 93, 112, 115, 125, 133, 137, 160, 172, 177, 180–2, 193, 205, 208, 213

versification, 161

vocations, 151

Wallerstein, Immanuel, 182, 235

Weber, Max, 2, 6

Whewell, William, 63–4, 74, 135, 184, 197, 198, 200, 235

Williams, Raymond, 44, 148, 192, 216, 227, 235

Wittgenstein, Ludwig, 29, 157, 211, 218, 235

Wordsworth, William, 35, 142, 143–220, 231–2, 235

Wordsworth, William and Samuel Taylor Coleridge: *Lyrical Ballads*, 142, 146, 152–3, 169, 220

Works of the Learned, 96–108, 111, 117, 208–9